D1216775

Public Servant

THE MEMOIRS OF SIR JOSEPH POPE

THE EAST BLOCK FROM THE MAIN ENTRANCE OF THE
PARLIAMENT BUILDINGS, OTTAWA, 1882

THE PARLIAMENT BUILDINGS,
OTTAWA, 1882

SIR JOSEPH POPE, 1920

Public Servant

THE MEMOIRS OF SIR JOSEPH POPE

EDITED

AND

COMPLETED

BY

MAURICE POPE

TORONTO / OXFORD UNIVERSITY PRESS / 1960

*The scenes on the
previous pages
are reproductions of
wood-engravings from*
PICTURESQUE CANADA,
edited by G. M. *Grant* (1882).

PRINTED IN ENGLAND BY
HAZELL WATSON AND VINEY LTD
AYLESBURY AND SLOUGH

PART ONE:

AUTOBIOGRAPHICAL

PART TWO:

BIOGRAPHICAL

Preface

In the opening lines of these Memoirs, Sir Joseph Pope clearly states the reasons which led him to set down a record of his life. But unfortunately his powers declined before he was able to complete this, the last literary task to which he had set his hand.

On my father's death in 1926 it was found that he had brought the manuscript down to the year 1907, that is to say to a time nearly twenty years before his relinquishment of office. In the opinion of several of his former friends of some prominence in public life, not least of whom was the late Mr. Mackenzie King, the Memoirs contained much that was of interest to students of Canadian political history, and they unanimously expressed the view that the unfinished work should be brought to completion. It was in these circumstances that the task devolved upon me.

The original manuscript was not in such shape as to be ready for the printer. Considerable editing was necessary in order to eliminate passages that were merely of private interest. But it may be said that while the autobiographical section of these Memoirs does not show all that was originally contained therein, it prints nothing that is not from Sir Joseph Pope's pen. Further, it should be said that my father, evidently realizing that it would not be given to him to complete his labours, had blocked out material to the end of his official career.

Amongst his papers was found a number of large envelopes into
which he had classified letters and memoranda dealing with important missions with which he had been connected. In addition, there
were some notes written in his own hand, to the effect that when the
events of this or that year were being studied, recourse was to be had
to certain tin boxes in his possession. It was also fortunate that during
the whole of this period my father kept a diary in which he recorded
important events and précis of confidential conversations. Some of
this material has not been included in this work. In some instances
this was unavoidable owing to the necessity of compressing the
Memoirs into one volume. It can however be stated with some degree
of assurance that the greater part of the material in the biographical
section treats of matters regarding which it was my father's wish that
mention should be made. As to the treatment it has received, the
writer is conscious of the disability under which he laboured, in that
during the entire period from 1907 to 1926 he lived elsewhere than
in Ottawa.

The work was completed and submitted to a publishing firm in the
spring of 1930. But in those days the book trade was depressed along
with the rest of the national economy. In 1939 the manuscript was
returned to me. Came the war, followed by a long term of duty
abroad, neither of which was conducive to publication. It was only
in retirement that it was found possible to see about getting the
Memoirs into print.

Recently some additions have been made to the concluding
chapters.

Thirty years is a long time and all those from whom I sought
advice in those days are no longer with us. I wish nevertheless to
record the fact that I am grateful to the memories of the late Mr.
Hugh Guthrie and the late Senator Rodolphe Lemieux for their
helpful counsel. Not less am I beholden to Mr. I. M. Owen of the
Oxford University Press (Canadian Branch) whose keen, expert, yet
kindly criticism has been instrumental in removing from the biographical section many of the blemishes it originally contained.

                                                          M. P.

OTTAWA,
May 1959

Part One: Autobiographical

1854 – 1880

Early Days in Charlottetown | Journey to Montreal | First Visit to Ottawa | Illness | Transfer to Halifax | General Elections of 1878 | Appointed Private Secretary to James C. Pope | My Father's Death

THERE is some doubt in my own mind whether the story of my life possesses sufficient variety and interest to warrant its recital in print; but so many of my friends apparently think otherwise that I have been persuaded, against my inclination, and almost against my will, to chronicle some of the experiences of a long, if not particularly thrilling career.

I was born in Charlottetown, Prince Edward Island, on the 16th of August 1854, the eldest son of my father, William Henry Pope, lawyer, politician, and subsequently county court judge, who died at the comparatively early age of fifty-four years, leaving my mother and six sisters in straitened circumstances.

My earliest recollection is of the visit of the Prince of Wales, afterwards King Edward VII, to Charlottetown, in the summer of 1860. I remember His Royal Highness distinctly as he drove up the main street of the town, a pale, delicate-looking lad. I recollect, too—though of course I was too young to attach any significance to the fact—that he sat on the left hand of the Lieutenant-Governor who, though only a simple esquire, as the Queen's representative occupied the seat of honour in the carriage. Many years later I had occasion to recall this circumstance.

This royal visit was a red-letter day in the annals of Charlottetown, which, settled almost exclusively by immigrants from the United Kingdom, formed in their isolation from the outside world a community thoroughly British in tone, animated by the most loyal and devoted sentiments to the Throne and Person of our beloved Sovereign and of affection for the dear land of England. One was not compelled to listen in those days to any rubbish about 'nationhood' and 'equality of status' and all that sort of thing. Nobody agitated for or even suggested or dreamed that we should possess a distinct flag, or a brand-new national anthem of our own. The Union Jack and 'God Save the Queen' satisfied our loftiest aspirations, and we should have regarded any attempt to change either as a species of apostasy calling for the severest condemnation. We were proud of our colonial connection, and asked for nothing more.

The second public event impressed upon my memory is the visit of the delegates from Canada, Nova Scotia, and New Brunswick to discuss the great question of Confederation of the British North American colonies, who assembled in Charlottetown on the 1st of September 1864. I remember my father taking me on board the Canadian steamer *Victoria* which conveyed the delegates to Prince Edward Island, and recall being introduced to Messrs. Cartier, Brown, McGee, and perhaps one or two more. I remember, too, meeting George Brown at my father's house and climbing up on his knee, and his giving me sixpence. Such was my first acquaintance with Canadian statesmen.

There was in my youth scarcely any intercourse between Prince Edward Island and the other British North American colonies, with which we had little in common excepting our allegiance to the same crown. Our trade was chiefly with the United Kingdom and, during the period of the Reciprocity Treaty (1854–66), with the New England States. Most people who could afford to do so sent their sons to be educated in England, which, in common parlance, was always spoken of as 'home', even by those who had never seen or expected to see the white cliffs of Albion. I am glad to know this remains a common practice in my old home to this day. In this atmosphere of love and loyalty to the Motherland, I was nurtured and brought up.

My father, who during my early boyhood was actively engaged in politics, sometimes took me with him to what was known as the Colonial Building, a fine specimen of the colonial style of architecture which stood and still stands in Queen's Square, and at that time contained under one roof the executive, legislative, and judicial offices of the colony. The House of Assembly was composed of thirty representatives, the leading members of which in breeding and education were, I consider, at least fully the equal of those occupying similar positions at the present day. The same observation is, I think, true of the bench and bar, and in fact of professional men generally. Society was more sharply defined then than now. Education may not have been so diffused as at present, but people who knew their business generally knew it thoroughly, and those in the humbler walks of life were content to remain, as the catechism says, 'in that state of life in which it had pleased God to call them'. One did not often meet a man who gloried in his lack of acquaintance with elementary good manners, and who justified boorish ignorance on the ground that 'this is a democratic country'.

Politics ran high in that little community, I suppose on the principle that the smaller the pit the fiercer the rats fight, and the debates were principally confined to local issues. Moreover, speeches, as I recall them, were more in the unconventional style in vogue in England than in the set orations with which our ears are familiar. Nevertheless, there was some pretty fair speaking in that old House.

During my childhood my father was a good deal away from home. We lived about a mile out of town in a house surrounded by grounds laid out with a good deal of taste by my father, who delighted in landscape gardening. In those days many conveniences, now looked upon almost as essentials, were either unknown or inaccessible to us. We had a manservant, who with his family occupied a cottage on the grounds, and two or three domestics. We also kept a horse and carriage, which in our situation was indispensable, but were without furnace, gas, electric light, running water, telephone, tram-cars, or motors, so that with a large family of young children, indifferent servants, delicate health, and limited means, it will be readily understood that my mother's life was no sinecure, and that from an early period a certain responsibility devolved upon me as her eldest son, a responsibility which I am afraid I did not always adequately realize.

My younger brother, my sisters, and myself began our education under a governess, Miss Margaret Cambridge, afterwards Mrs. D. B. Parnther, wife of the assistant minister at the parish church of St. Paul's, who taught us the rudiments and a little French.

From the age of eleven I attended the Prince of Wales 'College', as it was called (it was, in reality, a grammar school), until I was almost sixteen, when the state of my father's finances compelled me to set about earning my own living. I thus never possessed the advantage of a university training, a disability under which I have laboured all my life. I enjoyed, however, five years' schooling under an excellent master, Dr. Alexander Anderson. Of Professor Anderson's faculty for imparting knowledge I cannot speak too highly. On the occasion of the visit of the Prince of Wales to Charlottetown in the summer of 1919, a luncheon in honour of His Royal Highness was given by the provincial Government in the Prince of Wales College, and on this occasion I had the privilege of introducing to some of my friends the venerable gentleman who taught me, if not in the same building, yet on that very spot, fifty-four years before.

At school, while fairly proficient, I never was really first-rate. One boy in particular could always beat me, though perhaps more frequently than otherwise I was second. Mathematics appealed to me. I remember, at the age of fourteen or thereabouts, fashioning a quadrant out of cardboard, with a pendant chair-castor for a plumb line, and measuring therewith angles, with the object of ascertaining the height of surrounding trees. I was fond of astronomy too, and remember, when thirteen, saving up my money to buy a book on that fascinating science which I possess to this day.

In sport I never did much, being always more or less inclined to sympathize with George Cornwall Lewis in his remark that 'life would be tolerable if it wasn't for its amusements'! Almost the only game I indulged in was cricket, and in that I did not excel. Shooting and fishing I liked better, and I generally enjoyed such expeditions, on which I sometimes accompanied my father.

In the summer of 1870 a general election took place in Prince Edward Island, then a separate colony, resulting in the defeat of the existing Liberal Government and the incoming of a Conservative (or as it might be more properly termed, a coalition) administration under the premiership of my uncle, James C. Pope. My grandfather, Joseph Pope, who became Treasurer under the new Government, offered me a position in the Treasury at a salary of £50 a year. The staff consisted of the Assistant Treasurer (John Robins) and one clerk, I being the clerk. I shall never forget the look of dismay on Mr. Robins's face when my grandfather introduced me to him as the new appointee—my predecessor, a bright and capable lad, in accordance with the barbarous custom (to this day, I fear, still in force as regards provincial Government offices in Prince Edward Island) having been displaced at the change of Government. Later on, Mr. Robins told me his face did not half portray the despair that possessed him at that moment. Nor were his apprehensions unreasonable. I was a perfectly unsophisticated youth of sixteen, without experience of any kind, and writing a villainous unformed hand.

Such were the auspices under which I entered the service of my country. In that trying hour, however, a great resolution took possession of my soul. I was determined to show Mr. Robins that he was mistaken in his estimate of my prospective usefulness. I began with my writing. Every day, when my special work was over, I copied long extracts with such assiduity and patience that in a surprisingly short space of time I came to write a hand amply sufficient for the requirement of the occasion. I had, too, the advantage of being a rather good arithmetician, which proved useful, especially in connection with the Savings Bank attached to the Treasury, of which before long I was placed in charge. So acceptably did I acquit myself that within a year my chief would occasionally entrust the management of the office to me, while he took a much-needed day off.

The Treasury Department was on the ground floor of the Government Building which stands in the centre of Queen's Square, the very heart of the town. At one end of this square stood the parish church of St. Paul's, and at the other the Market House, both wooden structures, since replaced by handsome buildings of stone. In 1870 the new Market House had not long been opened, and was quite a fashionable meeting place for the townspeople who used to congregate there on Tuesday and Friday mornings to exchange greetings and indulge in a little bit of gossip. I well remember, too, the old Market building, anterior to the building of 1870. It was of octagonal form, having eight entrances. Inside this building, facing one of these doors issuing from the butchers' stalls, was inscribed the text from the Book of Proverbs—if I remember rightly in gold letters on a black ground—'A false balance is an abomination to the Lord.'

The Treasury was but a stone's throw from the market, through which on Tuesday and Friday mornings I generally took a turn before the business of my office began. Thus, with the Government offices round us, the Legislature upstairs, and the market place at our doors, we were quite in the thick of things, and *au courant* with the affairs of the day.

One of the first acts of the Pope government on taking office in 1870 was to develop their policy for the construction of a railway through the island. The scheme, which evoked much interest in places where the great majority of the people had never seen a railway, almost immediately took a political complexion, the opposition contending that the project was wholly beyond the resources of the Colony, and charging that it was part of a Machiavellian scheme arranged between Sir John Macdonald, the Conservative leader in Canada, and Mr. J. C. Pope and his political friends, to overwhelm the island in debt and thus compel them to come into the Confederation. 'An Act to authorize the construction of a railway through Prince Edward Island' passed in the session of 1871. Shortly afterwards the contract was let and the work of construction begun. Meanwhile, opposition to the Government's policy grew rapidly. It was alleged that the Government, the contractors, and the Government's chief engineer were involved in a conspiracy, not merely to bring about Confederation, but also to enrich themselves at the public expense, and that with this object in view the road was unnecessarily lengthened, inferior material was put into the work, and so forth—charges which, if established, would have placed those implicated in gaol. I well remember hearing a leading member of the Opposition publicly accuse the Government of having selected contractors who would be amenable to their methods. The Government bent before the storm, dissolved the Assembly, and were decisively beaten in the general elections which followed. They resigned, and were succeeded by their opponents.

One of the first acts of the new administration was to send for two American engineers whom they commissioned to investigate all matters connected with the letting of the railway contract and the progress of the work to date. These engineers duly appeared on the scene, made a rigorous examination of the work, and reported to the effect that the road was on the whole well and cheaply built for the money spent thereon. The Government were, or affected to be, thunderstruck at the result. They suppressed the report as long as they decently could, the Premier meanwhile communicating with the American engineers, who had returned home, in a vain endeavour to induce them to qualify their verdict. All this is amusingly set forth in a newspaper article by Mr., afterwards Mr. Justice, Hodgson, an intimate friend of mine. The Mr. Haythorne referred to was at the time the Liberal Premier. The allusion to his 'classical know-ledge', contained in the following extract from Mr. Hodgson's article, came vividly to my mind when forty years later I stood on the steps leading to the Capitol at Rome and looked upon the place where the geese are said to have been confined on the historic occasion referred to:

> We can imagine with what a crushing blow the report fell upon
> the Executive. We can imagine their alarm, their dread, the earnest
> anxious consultation, how best to suppress, at least for a while, the
> vindication of their opponents' honour. Time was everything to them.
> If they could but gain a few months' delay they would improve the
> opportunity by redoubling their slanders, but how could it be done?
> At last a bright idea occurred to Mr. Haythorne. He drew upon the
> resources of his classical knowledge, and remembering that the Capitol

at Rome had once been saved by the cackling of a goose, he proposed that he should write a letter. On the 14th day of October he set himself to this task, and casting to the winds every sense of decency, he begged the engineers, in almost direct terms, to condemn the railway, the late Government, and the Chief Engineer. . . .

We stated a few weeks ago that Mr. Haythorne has not the love of making scriptural characters his own, which his Attorney General has; we must now, however, retract that opinion, but then there is this difference between them, while poor Mr. Palmer is simply ridiculous as Father Abraham, Mr. Haythorne has shown an exquisite tact in choosing for his model Balak the son of Zippor. Of course, in every little detail the simile does not hold good—a simile rarely does—for instance, the King of Moab conscientiously thought he was doing no wrong in asking for the maledictions of Balaam against the children of Israel. Mr. Haythorne with better opportunities knew better. They both had public treasuries at their disposal, and while it is believed that the gifts of divination which were sent to the unhappy prophet were really magnificent, Mr. Haythorne offered little more than the annuity for which he sold his tenants to Mr. J. R. Bourke. But in other respects the simile is perfect. If it be true that those only know what danger and sickness really are who have themselves been in danger or afflicted, and then only in proportion to the greatness of the one and the intensity of the other—we may be sure that no one has ever yet been able to enter into the feelings of the son of Zippor as has the Hon. Robert Poore Haythorne. We can imagine the heathen king standing on the mountain top amid the seven smoking altars as he looked upon the white tents of the hated Israelites in the valley beneath; what rage and despair took possession of him as the magnificent prophecies foretelling the greatness of the favoured people fell from the unwilling lips of the Prophet of God. We can imagine the trembling eagerness with which, while imploring the prophet to view them from another standpoint he uttered in an agony of earnestness which Mr. Haythorne had reproduced in his letter, 'Peradventure thou mayst curse them from hence!'—but all to no purpose—Mr. Haythorne and the heathen king were both defeated in their dear desire, and truth mightier than falsehood has triumphed now, as it did 4000 years ago.

Mr. Hodgson was in the seventies a leading barrister in Charlottetown. He lived in a fine large house, with plenty of servants, and no children of his own. Of a hospitable and generous nature, Mr.

Hodgson took much interest in young men, who were always welcome to his house and befriended by him in various ways. I often stayed there, becoming a frequent and I think a welcome guest. One great bond of union between us was St. Peter's, the new High Church recently opened in Charlottetown, of which Mr. Hodgson's brother, the Rev. George Hodgson, was priest incumbent, Edward being a chief pillar. The latter was a keen politician, and a Tory of the Tories. He was also an exceedingly well-read man and possessed a fine library. I enjoyed the entire freedom of his house, to the advantages of which I was not, even at that early day, wholly insensible.

The defeat of the Pope Government in the early part of 1872 carried with it the resignation of my grandfather. The incoming Treasurer, the late Hon. James Warburton, departing from the usual custom on such occasions, asked me to continue on under him, proposing to increase my salary from £75 to £100 if I would remain, but as I naively record in my diary, 'I think I can do better,' though at the time I do not recall that I had anything definite in view. I thanked Mr. Warburton, and a few days later withdrew from the service.

Shortly afterwards, my father wrote on my behalf to one or two of his Canadian friends, from one of whom he received the suggestion that I should apply to Mr. Jackson Rae, the cashier of the Merchants' Bank of Canada in Montreal. I did so, and received in due course an offer of a clerkship in Montreal at a salary of $400 a year. This I accepted.

On the 26th of July 1872 I bade farewell to my family and friends and also to the familiar spots about my home. My dear mother packed my trunk that evening and accompanied me next day as far as Saint John. There being no Intercolonial Railway in those days, I took a steamer, the *New York*, for Portland. The Bay of Fundy is not noted for smooth water, and this passage was no exception to the general rule. As a tribute to my seagoing powers I may mention that I remember eating a lobster that night in my berth, without any ill effects, though the accommodation was not of the best and a heavy sea was running.

I arrived in Montreal on the evening of the 30th of July. Two

Charlottetown lads, Edward Haviland and Horace Hazard, who had preceded me by a few months, met me at the station and escorted me to their lodgings. Next morning I presented my credentials at the Merchants' Bank and was set to work at the deposit ledger. From this post I was ignominiously withdrawn after a short probation and given a more elementary position in which I did better, for I remember ere long being reinstated at the ledger, where I continued two years. My life in the bank was uneventful. A shy boy, knowing nobody, it was not easy for me to form acquaintances, while my lack of means compelled me to live in the quietest possible manner.

In the summer of 1873 I paid a visit to my old home and much enjoyed the holiday, during which I was present at the opening of the Prince Edward Island railway.

In the autumn of the same year I paid my first visit to Ottawa. When I first viewed those scenes amid which I was destined to pass the greater part of my life, the government of Sir John Macdonald was then sinking under a storm of obloquy which bore down all before it. In that whirlwind of political rancour and passion, all semblance of reason and argument was abandoned. 'John A.' was down at last. Let those whom he had so long kept out of place and power rejoice. Their turn had come. I was present in the gallery of the House of Commons on one of those fateful days immediately preceding the resignation of the Government, and heard the great debate: 'Heard Sir John and a number of others speak. I thought Blake the best speaker. Sir John spoke for five hours. Got tired about 11 o'clock. Went back to my hotel and to bed.'

So I wrote in my diary of the 3rd of November. Of the great speech which so impressed Lady Dufferin, my recollection is very dim.[1]

I dined that evening with a friend in a boarding-house somewhere on Victoria or Cliff Street. The occasion dwells in my memory by reason of the fact that a member of the company was Mr. Charles Drinkwater, at that time Private Secretary to the Prime Minister. I remember his coming in late and my regarding him with a species of awe, little dreaming that in a few years I should be filling his position.

---

[1] Sir J. Pope, *Correspondence of Sir John Macdonald* (Toronto, 1921), p. 230.

I was much impressed by the Parliament Buildings, which sur-
passed my expectations, but I was disappointed with Ottawa as a
whole, which struck me as 'a dirty little place'.

Early in 1874 I fell ill of rheumatic fever. The attack was severe,
and left its mark on me through life in the form of a diseased heart
which, however, I must have largely outgrown, for during the
ensuing forty-seven years, I never had occasion to ask for or obtain
sick leave, having through the favour of God uniformly enjoyed
good health, a fact which I largely ascribed to my never (speaking
generally) having consulted a doctor nor taken any medicine.
During that long interval I have several times been rejected for life
insurance, but notwithstanding have managed to give the lie to the
medical profession for well-nigh fifty years.

My illness in 1874 necessitated absence from my duties for nearly
six months. On my return to work I found that the Bank had paid
my salary regularly in the interval and given me a substantial
increase, which I thought very good of them, and never forgot.

In 1875 I joined the Catholic Church. Elsewhere I have indicated
the reasons which led to this momentous step. I shall therefore
say nothing on the subject in this place, except to record that
I have never for one moment regretted the course I then took in
obedience to a call which, in my own conscience, I felt to be
divine.

In November 1876 I exchanged from the Merchants' Bank of
Canada into the Canadian Bank of Commerce, thereby slightly
improving my position.

Of politics I did not hear much. The Macdonald Government had
gone down to defeat over the Pacific Scandal, and in a general election
had been almost annihilated. I remember once during that campaign
(in January 1874) finding myself one evening at a political gathering
assembled on the corner of St. Catherine and St. Denis streets in
Montreal. The crowd was French-Canadian, as of course was the
speaker, who seemed much excited and wore his hair very long.
One outburst of his caught my ear: 'L'opinion publique est que Sir
John A. Macdonald a vendu le pays pour un prix,' accompanied by
much gesticulation, which moved an unsympathetic Englishman present to call out derisively, 'Give him a dagger!' I knew little at that

time of Sir John Macdonald and nothing of the Pacific Scandal, but the political instinct must have been strong within me, for I recollect shedding bitter tears of rage and mortification one evening in the following December, when walking home tired and hungry on the occasion of the defeat of Tom White by Fred Mackenzie at a political election in Montreal West. I did not know Mr. White at the time—perhaps if I had, my tears would have flowed still more copiously, for I met him in after years in Ottawa, both as a member of parliament and as a minister of the Crown, and a fine fellow he was.

At the beginning of 1878 trade was depressed, manufactures languished, and prospects in the financial world were far from rosy. On the advice of a banking friend who always evinced a warm interest in my welfare, I resigned from the Bank of Commerce to accept a position, with an advance in salary, in the Bank of Nova Scotia, and took up my residence in Halifax, where I remained until the return of the Conservative party to power in the Dominion.

During the summer of 1878 I developed a lively interest in the political campaign that was then being waged. The issue was clearcut: Free Trade versus Revenue Tariff. Mr. Mackenzie's accession to office had synchronized with a period of world-wide depression, from which his government suffered greatly. The opposition urged the increase of customs duties with a view to shutting out foreign goods and building up of Canadian industries, thus securing employment to our people and keeping them in our own country. Such a policy, however, was anathema to Mr. Mackenzie, who as an ardent—almost fanatical—free-trader would have nothing to do with protection, which he denounced as an attempt to relieve distress by imposing additional taxation. The elections came off on Tuesday the 17th of September, and resulted in an overwhelming victory for the Conservative party, which converted the Government majority of between fifty and sixty into a minority of eighty-six. Such a victory was almost unprecedented, and was totally unexpected by anybody. I remember attending the meeting in the old Temperance Hall in Halifax, where on the evening of election day the returns were received and announced. As it became increasingly evident that the Government was defeated, the enthusiasm knew no bounds. Cheer after cheer rent the air. Total strangers to each other grasped hands as though they were bosom friends. For a while pandemonium reigned. It was full daylight on Wednesday morning when I reached my lodgings, and not until the following Saturday did I recover my voice, which I had begun to fear was permanently gone.

The Ministry resigned on the 16th of October. On the 18th the new administration was sworn in at Montreal by Lord Dufferin, the retiring Governor-General. Sir John Macdonald, the incoming Prime Minister, invited my uncle, James C. Pope, to accept a portfolio as Minister of Marine and Fisheries, and he in turn offered me the position of his private secretary. I accepted this and removed to Ottawa, where I have resided ever since. A few days later the new administration repaired in a body to Halifax to welcome the Marquess of Lorne and H.R.H. the Princess Louise, who almost immediately after the ceremony proceeded by a special train to Ottawa. On this train travelled the Ministers of the Crown and their secretaries, including myself. I well remember this official journey, the first of a long series of such. I recall on that occasion I had for companion in the dining-car Mr. John Kidd, Chief Clerk in the Governor-General's office at Ottawa, and very pleasant he was.

There was a formal reception to our new Governor-General and the Princess on the evening of the day of our arrival at the capital. The streets were thronged with an enthusiastic multitude, all anxious to catch a glimpse of the royal and vice-regal party. In the midst of this crowd I struggled hard to keep my feet. At the corner of Sparks and Elgin Streets stood a policeman endeavouring to restrain the crowd, in the front rank of which appeared a vigorous female, apparently of an aggressive temperament, for she kept pressing resolutely forward, intent on elbowing her way. Immediately behind her I found myself, a slight delicate youth, who, not noted at any time for aggressive propensities, had less occasion than usual for indulging in anything of the kind just then, as I had been travelling with the celebrities and had seen them several times a day for the past week. 'Keep back,' shouted the constable, pressing his baton against the chaste bosom of the lady in front who, on being addressed, turned sharply round, and directing her glittering eye

full on me, called out loudly, 'Who are you pushing?'—adding
with ever-increasing emphasis, 'Where are you pushing to?'
Thereupon the policeman shook his baton threateningly in my
direction and I shrank back, regarded by everyone as the chief
offender. How many times in after life have I seen similar tactics
employed with equal success, and an impudent cry of 'Who are
you pushing?' attain its object of diverting censure from where it
rightfully belonged to fall on one entirely blameless.

I found the position of private secretary to a cabinet minister
congenial, though my uncle was not accustomed to such a luxury
and consequently did not avail himself of my services to the extent
I could have wished. I employed my leisure in familiarizing myself
with the operations of our own Department, and learning what I
could of the science of government generally. One of the earliest
friendships I formed was with the late Martin Griffin, afterwards
Parliamentary Librarian, then Ottawa correspondent of the Toronto
Mail, to whom I am indebted for much useful advice and assistance.
Our acquaintance ripened into a lifelong friendship, which terminated
only on his death in 1921.

In the Deputy Minister of Marine and Fisheries I had a never-
failing source of interest and amusement. Mr. William Smith, a
Scotsman by birth, who had originally been connected with the
customs service of the United Kingdom, came out in early life to
New Brunswick, and was brought to Ottawa at the time of Confederation by Peter Mitchell, the first Canadian Minister of Marine.
Mr. Smith was an excellent administrative officer, thoroughly
trustworthy and as careful of public money as of his own, in respect
of which he was reputed to be far from prodigal. One day, shortly
after the change of Government, a member of parliament called on
my uncle, the Minister, in the interests of a clerk, Mr. A. Halkett,
who was in receipt of the princely salary of one dollar a day. The
Deputy Minister, being called in, justified the rate of pay, protesting
that he could procure clerks as good as the present incumbent of
the office for the same money. The Minister, however, cut short
the discussion by directing that the clerk in question should hence-
forth receive a dollar and a quarter *per diem*. Next month the M.P.
called again on behalf of his protégé, whose position had not

improved. Mr. Pope summoned the Deputy. 'How is it that my instructions with respect to Mr. Halkett's pay were not observed?' he asked that officer, who replied that he had carried them out by increasing Mr. Halkett's salary from one dollar to a dollar and a quarter a day. Further enquiry, however, elicited the fact that he had at the same time deducted the pay which the clerk had hitherto received for Sundays and holidays, with the result that Mr. Halkett found himself worse off under the new arrangement by just fifty cents a month, which necessitated a ministerial order for a further readjustment.

The Deputy's comments to the Minister on his staff were sometimes very amusing. One of these, a brother Scot with himself, and an exceedingly capable official with a weakness, had been originally brought into the Department by the Deputy, who for some reason subsequently turned violently against him. 'I took him from the gutter, and I cherished him to my bosom,' said Mr. Smith to the Minister of this clerk, 'and the viper turned and stang me,' though so far as I could ever discover the poor fellow's sole offence consisted of getting quietly and unobtrusively drunk three or four times a year.

Mr. Smith, who frequently had long talks with me on various subjects, was rather given to dwelling on his intimacy with prominent people, among others with Sir Hugh Allan, who as a shipping magnate I dare say found it convenient to be on good terms with the Deputy Minister of Marine. In fact Mr. Smith never used to tire telling me of the intimacy which existed between them—how Sir Hugh frequently had him to dine and spend the evening at Ravenscrag, where they would hold long conversations extending far into the night. I, who had been for four years a clerk in the Merchants' Bank of Canada, of which Sir Hugh Allan was President, found this somewhat difficult to understand, for Sir Hugh enjoyed the reputation among bank officials of being the most non-communicative of men, but all doubt as to Smith's success in overcoming Sir Hugh's natural reserve was dispelled by the following story, which Mr. Smith related to me in illustration of the extent to which Sir Hugh was wont to unbosom himself.

One evening they had dined together, *en petit comité*, at Ravens-

crag, and were sitting over the fire enjoying their port, when
Mr. Smith, inspired by the warmth and geniality of his surroundings,
thought it a fitting occasion to put his host's trust in him to the test.
'Sir Hugh,' said he, 'between ourselves, don't you think you rather
made a mistake in mixing yourself up with Sir John A. and that
Pacific Scandal business?' And Sir Hugh, he looked long into the
fire, and at last, says he, 'Mebbee' says he. Could further proof be
desired of intimate and unreserved confidence?

As I have already observed, my duties as private secretary to my
uncle were not onerous. He was not an office man, nor given to
regular and methodical treatment of correspondence. As far as
possible I took charge of and arranged his political letters. One
only of these I have kept. It is an application for office from one of
his constituents, so quaintly original that it deserves preservation.
Here it is, *verbatim et literatim*:

> *summerside, Jan the 26th* (1879)
>
> Dear
>
>   I wont to let you now about the lection the day of the lection in
> summerside the were asking me who I was going to vote for.
>
>   I am going to vote for John a McDonald partey. I want to get in
> Mr. J. C. Pope into office he will make the grits fly.
>
>   then the said that jim pope Cant take no office from us; now sir
> try and put the . . . . out of office if you Can, spesil gorg
> Ramsey he is bad grit.
>
>   please give me gorg Ramsey office and I will fite for you again i
> fought for Mr. Pope and i gain the battel.
>
>   now sir I wont you to get me a smawl office the light house or
> something els so to laf at them.
>
>   times is dul in summerside nothing doing onley the warf the be
> don the brush today.
>
>   no more at present
>   iam sir your obedient servant
>   Hugh McLallen *ship Carpenter*
>   *summerside*

The election referred to in the foregoing epistle was that of the
17th of September 1878, more than four months before the date
of this letter. Mr. Pope's correspondent was quite unknown to him.
The writer, however, must have possessed a goodly share of natural

cleverness, which is observable in his appeal to Mr. Pope's party
feelings, and the crafty manner in which he endeavours to incite
the Minister against his opponents by reciting their defiant attitude
towards him, and their belief in his inability to do them any harm.
My friend Augustus Power, of the Department of Justice—no mean
judge in such matters—was so delighted with the quaint recitative
style of this letter that he translated it into Latin. What I may style
Verse 3, which Power declared read like a quotation from the
Psalms of David, he rendered thus:

Tunc dixerunt, iste non potest auferre nullam officiam a nobis.

It is too bad that such literary excellence should have been barren
of result, and I dare say that if Mr. Pope had had a free hand, it
might have fared ill with 'gorg Ramsey' and others of his class, but
against the introduction of American political methods into this
country Sir John Macdonald stood like a rock. The spoils system had
never been applied in Canada, and Sir John was resolved that he
would be no party to its introduction in any part of the Dominion.
It is true that conditions in Prince Edward Island were exceptional.
There, the people had never known anything else. A general clearing-
out of officials followed upon every change of government as a matter
of course. And there was this further consideration. When in July
1873 Prince Edward Island became part of Canada, the Dominion
Government then in power filled all the offices in the Island in their
gift with their own supporters. That Government was then under
the cloud of the Pacific Scandal, and shortly afterwards resigned.
The incoming administration at Ottawa, alleging that the appointing
Government at the time they filled these offices did not possess the
confidence of Parliament, cancelled a large number of their predecessors' appointments and filled them with their own friends.
When the wheel again went round, the ejected officials naturally
clamoured for reinstatement, but to any application of this principle
Sir John Macdonald would not consent. The utmost he would
concede was that, in specified charges of alleged partisanship in
office, made on the responsibility of some reputable person, an
enquiry might be held, at which the officials charged with partisanship should have an opportunity of explaining and defending their

conduct. If proved guilty they must suffer accordingly, but so long as a man conducted himself efficiently and properly in office, neither his political proclivities before appointment, nor his party sympathies when in office, so long as his manifestation was confined to registering his vote, should be allowed to operate to his detriment. This policy caused a good deal of party dissatisfaction on the Island, but as time went on it was generally recognized as being the more excellent way, and for many years an office-holder under the Federal Government in Prince Edward Island has been universally regarded as enjoying without question the same permanency of tenure as those in any other part of the Dominion.

During our first winter my uncle gave a men's dinner at the Rideau Club, and asked me to look after it for him. He supplied me with a list of guests, all of whom were Conservatives. Among these was Senator A. W. McLelan, afterwards Lieutenant-Governor of Nova Scotia. Unhappily, I asked, instead of this gentleman, A. R. McLelan, a prominent Liberal, who accepted and came, consequently destroying the main object for which the dinner had been given, which was to afford an opportunity to these Tory parliamentarians fresh from the polls to compare notes and jubilate generally. Such a course in the presence of a single member of the Opposition would have been a breach of hospitality which my uncle could not permit. Consequently he had to give another dinner, to which Senator A. R. McLelan was *not* invited, but I did not hear the last of this episode for some time.

In 1879 I lost my dear father, whose sudden and unexpected death came as a great shock to my uncle and myself, who were both in Ottawa at the time. He died near Summerside, Prince Edward Island, of apoplexy, with which he was struck when out shooting on the afternoon of Saturday, the 27th of September. He managed with difficulty to call his manservant and regain his carriage, but shortly after reaching home lapsed into semi-unconsciousness, followed by coma. From this he never awakened, and he passed away on the morning of the 7th of October.

My father was an able, in some respects a brilliant man, of pronounced literary taste and skill, but lacking in continuity of purpose, which was fatal to him. Popular with all classes, he was an excellent guide, counsellor, and friend to many, but a poor judge in his own affairs, while his natural tendency to some form of extravagance (he must always have for those dear to him the best of everything, whether he could afford it or not) involved him in financial difficulties from which he could never extricate himself.

My father's untimely death left me with my mother and six unmarried sisters largely dependent upon my care. In these untoward circumstances, I was compelled to bestir myself without loss of time. With great efforts I secured the division of the estate of my Grandfather DesBrisay, who had died intestate, and obtained my mother's share. Shortly afterwards an uncle died, followed by an aunt, and both of these remembered my mother, who in that way and with my assistance managed to get along. I received a salary of $1000 a year, of which I gave my mother and sisters one half, living in an attic on the other moiety. About this time I taught myself shorthand, and many an evening's hard work did I put in over the intricacies of Ben Pitman. My friend and relative, Ernest Jarvis, took up the study at about the same time as myself. We used to read to each other out of Hansard every other evening, in our attic, until we were fairly competent to take correspondence, which was sufficient for our purpose.

To my uncle, my father's death proved a blow from which he never recovered. In the spring of 1880 his failing health became apparent. An acting minister was subsequently appointed, and I served him for a while. I could not avoid the reflection, however, that as President of the Council this acting minister had his own private secretary, and that my tenure was very precarious.

1881 – 1884

Sir John Macdonald / Chestnut Park /
General Elections / Appointed Assistant
Private Secretary to Sir John / Characteristics
of Sir John / His Friends and Colleagues /
Life at Earnscliffe / Marriage

MY first meeting with Sir John Macdonald was in this wise. It happened that, in the autumn of 1881, Mr. Mackenzie Bowell, the Minister of Customs, who was then acting as Minister of Marine and Fisheries in the absence of my uncle, asked me to go over to the Privy Council Chamber and bring him a packet which I would find in the drawer of his desk. I went over accordingly, and with the permission of the Clerk entered the Chamber and began looking for the papers. While I was so engaged, the door at the further end opened, and Sir John entered. On seeing me he stopped short, saying in a severe tone, 'What are you doing here, Sir?' I briefly explained, but he evidently was not satisfied. He rang the bell, and the Assistant-Clerk appeared. Looking towards me, he said sternly to that officer, 'Nobody should come in here except the Clerk of the Council,' whereupon I withdrew feeling very small indeed.

In the same autumn my friend Fred White, who, in addition to filling the office of Comptroller of the North West Mounted Police, was Sir John Macdonald's private secretary, and who as a consequence found himself greatly overworked, said to me one day that the time had come when he must have an assistant in the secretaryship, and that he proposed suggesting my name to Sir John for the position. In a day or two White told me that he had spoken to Sir John, who desired to see a specimen of my handwriting. It satisfied him, and shortly afterwards I began work with White, taking down and writing out letters from his dictation, making copies, filing documents, and so on. It was not until the following February that I was admitted to the great man's presence. White happened to be ill one day, and I was sent for to take some shorthand notes. Sir John received me most kindly at Stadacona Hall, putting me at my ease at once. I took down his letters, reproduced them to his satisfaction, and all was well. I did not, however, come much into direct contact with the chief again for some months to come.

In May 1882 a Redistribution Bill was enacted, followed by dissolution of Parliament; and at the ensuing general elections the National Policy, adopted in 1878, was sustained by a majority almost as large as that by which it had been inaugurated four years before.

The Opposition showed themselves full of fight, and both sides made extensive preparations for the fray. It was then I acquired my first experience of elections. The work of preparing, publishing, and distributing the Conservative campaign literature for Ontario was largely under the supervision of Mr. (afterwards Sir) David Macpherson, at that time Speaker of the Senate, a member of the Cabinet without portfolio, and as such acting as Minister of the Interior for Sir John Macdonald, whose duties as Prime Minister left him little time for departmental administration. Mr. Macpherson was much addicted to writing political pamphlets, and the preparation of such literature for use in the elections was to him a congenial task. His private secretary happened to fall ill, and Sir John Macdonald lent me to Mr. Macpherson, who took me up to Toronto. I stayed with him, during the campaign, at Chestnut Park, at that time in the country; and here I received my introduction into the great world.

I must not omit to relate that, shortly before I left Ottawa for

Toronto, a friend of mine who had occasion to be up late one night chanced to meet Mr. Edward Farrer, then on the editorial staff of the *Mail* newspaper and one of the most brilliant and versatile journalists of that or any other time, taking a lonely walk on Parliament Hill at dawn on a beautiful morning in May. Mr. Farrer had been engaged to do some work in the preparation of campaign literature. 'What are you doing up at this hour?' said my friend. 'Thinking over my paper in defence of the Government's railway policy,' replied he. 'Well,' said the other, 'are you satisfied with your work?' 'Satisfied, yes,' answered Farrer, 'I'm so d——d well satisfied that I don't see how I am going to answer it, and that's what is keeping me up.' He had undertaken to write the railway campaign sheets for each side, and no doubt did both superlatively well.

I recall my first morning at the office in Toronto. Mr. Macpherson and I drove in from Chestnut Park. The campaign was then in full swing. Among the early callers was a certain Mr. Piper, whom I afterwards discovered to be what Mr. Edward Blake would have styled 'a practical politician'. Mr. Piper, whose appearance—perhaps for the reason that he wore a light-coloured tweed suit and a black top hat at the same time—is indelibly impressed upon my memory, strode into the room, and after exchanging the usual greetings, bent over Mr. Macpherson's desk, and in reply to an enquiry as to how things were progressing, replied in a hoarse whisper, 'The boys in the Ward[1] are waiting to be fixed.' 'Fixed?' replied Mr. Macpherson. 'What an extraordinary expression. Good gracious, Mr. Piper, what do you mean?' Mr. Piper, however, who appeared in no mood for such pleasantry, contented himself with observing in a surly tone: 'Those chaps have got to be looked after or there'll be trouble.' Nothing more passed on the subject at the time, but a day or two later Mr. Piper called again. As he passed into the minister's room, he nodded familiarly to me, bending over my desk as he remarked confidentially, 'The boys in the Ward are all right. Harry [his brother] was down there last night and attended to them.'

Realizing the great value to me of Mr. Macpherson's report to

[1] St. John's Ward, Toronto, commonly known locally as The Ward.

Sir John Macdonald on my usefulness—for Sir John at that time knew very little about me in the way of direct intercourse—I laid myself out to please him, working hard over the accursed pamphlets, copying and recopying pages many times, reading proofs at all hours of the day and night, and generally supervising publication. I remember, in the fulness of my zeal, calling on Mr. T. C. Patteson (formerly editor of the *Mail*), the newly appointed Postmaster of Toronto, with an edition of 110,000 of these pamphlets loaded on vans, accompanied by instructions from Mr. Macpherson that they were to be dispatched at once. Mr. Patteson, desiring no doubt to impress me with the idea that in assuming his new duties he had completely shed his political sympathies, at first refused to accept the pamphlets, alleging that this was a monstrous abuse of the postal service which he would not permit, adding that he did not care a d——n for Mr. Macpherson or the whole Cabinet. After dancing about like a maniac, indulging meanwhile in the most picturesque and flaming language, he calmed down, and finally took over the pamphlets, but I had a very *mauvais quart d'heure* with him. I fancy the whole thing was staged for the edification of my young and inexperienced self, but his ultimate capitulation destroyed much of the effect upon me which he sought to produce. Realizing that 'T.C.' was right in his original attitude, I kept this little episode to myself.

Sir John and Lady Macdonald paid a visit to Chestnut Park during my stay, and were entertained with all courtesy. At that hospitable board I met for the first time many people prominent in Toronto society, among others D'Alton McCarthy, a singularly attractive personality, Christopher Robinson, W. R. Meredith, Chief Justice Hagarty, T. C. Patteson, Mr. Justice Morrison, George Allan, and some others, all of whom have since passed away.

With this visit I associate an occurrence illustrating a type of Toryism which had not then quite disappeared. A Catholic young man was dining at the table of a gentleman of the old school who was noted for the staunchness of his Protestantism. The day happened to be a Friday, a circumstance which the *chef* apparently had over-looked, as no provision had been made for such a contingency. The young man, though feeling very uncomfortable, stuck to his guns by abstaining from meat, whereupon the host, observing his embarrassment, placed his hand upon his shoulder and kindly remarked, 'Don't mind, my boy. At my time of life I am only too glad to find anybody voluntarily observing *any* law.'

With Chestnut Park as a centre, the Ministers made excursions into the surrounding ridings and generally took me with them. While Protection was everywhere the rallying cry, other questions arose, among them the absurd charge of French domination. The Government's railway, North-West, and immigration policies were also under fire. A feature of the last-named came in for some adverse criticism. This was a system of assisting female immigration to this country with the object of providing wives for the prairie settlers, among whom there was a great shortage of women. This scheme, however excellent it might be in theory, did not work well in practice. A number of loose characters took advantage of its provisions to get out to Canada, and Sir John Macdonald, who as Minister of the Interior was specially responsible for the execution of this policy, decided to discontinue it. Amongst its warmest advocates was a certain M.P., for many years a strong and consistent Protectionist, who after the National Policy had been placed on the statute book, feeling his occupation gone, took up this immigration scheme as an outlet for his surplus energy, and pressed it strongly upon the Government. One evening as the gentleman in question was waiting in my office for Council to break up, in order to learn the decision of the Government as to the continuation or abandonment of this policy of assisted immigration, Sir John walked into the room and seeing him, said, 'I'm sorry, Angus, but my colleagues and I have talked over the subject, and we have come to the conclusion not to go on with the assisted immigration, at any rate for this year.' Then, seeing the look of disappointment on his old friend's face, he put his hand kindly on his shoulder and added: 'You know, Angus, we must *protect* the Canadian w - - - - s.'

The elections went swimmingly for the Government, and on the evening of polling day I returned to Ottawa with my triumphant chiefs. Shortly afterwards I was transferred to the Department of the Interior from that of Marine and Fisheries, and promoted to be a senior second-class clerk. In the course of the following September

I was formally taken into Sir John Macdonald's service as assistant private secretary. He sent for me one day. I was shown into the room, until recently occupied by me as Under-Secretary of State for External Affairs. Briefly he explained that Fred White's health was not equal to the strain put upon it by his double duties (in addition to being the Premier's private secretary he was, as I have already stated, Comptroller of the North West Mounted Police), and that it was necessary that he obtain assistance. He added that from what he had seen of me he thought I could relieve White of a good deal of work. At any rate he had decided to make the experiment. 'There is a vote of $600 for my private secretary. This I propose to divide equally between you and White. What is your present salary?' '$1200,' I replied. 'And three is fifteen. A very good salary for a young man. Come down to Earnscliffe tomorrow morning,' he added. 'You will have plenty to do, and remember I shall require all your time.' Thus I entered upon my secretarial duties to Canada's first Prime Minister.

I desire here to record my deep sense of obligation to my friend Fred White. He it was who first introduced and recommended me to Sir John, and his invaluable experience, advice, and counsel were ever at my disposal. Sir John, to the end of his life, in matters specially calling for tact, judgement, and discretion, continued to avail himself of White's ability, loyalty, and devotion, but as regards the ordinary secretarial work I may say that for the next four years I did it alone, with no assistance, clerical or otherwise, of any sort or kind, beyond occasional advice from White, until 1886, when I had one junior assistant allotted to me. Typewriting was then by no means so general as it has since become. Sir John would not sign typewritten letters unless of a very formal character, and then only when he could not help it. All the letters had to be written by hand. Many a time in after life when I see private secretaries, associate private secretaries, and joint private secretaries, assisted by a corps of typists and file clerks, I have wondered how I managed to get along. Yet I did it alone, and I must have done so fairly satisfactorily, for a few months after I entered his service Sir John, when piloting his estimates through the House of Commons, spoke thus: 'Mr. Pope, who was transferred from the Department of Marine and Fisheries, is now my private secretary, and a very good officer he is; I could not desire a better.'[2]

In July 1883, upon passing the requisite promotion examination, I was promoted to a first-class clerkship in the Department of the Interior. Although nominally associated with that department, the association was little more than in name, and when in the following autumn Sir John exchanged that portfolio for the Presidency of the Privy Council, and I went with him to the Council office, it may be said to have ceased altogether. From then (1883) I saw but little of Mr. Macpherson, who succeeded Sir John as Minister of Interior. This, therefore, seems a fitting place in which to express my acknowledgements towards him. Mr. Macpherson was a Highland gentleman of heroic stature, in whose presence the ordinary mortal felt very small indeed. While rather pompous in manner and over-deliberate in his methods, he was a man of integrity and sound judgement—on the whole, a judicious, capable, and conscientious administrator, while to me he was ever a kindly and considerate chief. I should not say he was popular, his manner being too magnificent for those persons with whom he ordinarily came in contact.

Sir David and Lady Macpherson were blessed with a large family of sons and daughters, all strikingly handsome men and women, and quite charming in every way—Mr. W. M. Macpherson of Quebec, Mrs. Bankes, Mrs. Becket, Mrs. Dobell, Lady Kirkpatrick, and Miss Christina Macpherson, afterwards Mrs. Ridout of Toronto. I have often reflected how singularly favoured the Macphersons were, with means, position, good looks, in short everything that is supposed to conduce to happiness in the world. Miss Isabel Macpherson married during her husband's incumbency of the Speakership of the House of Commons. When Sir John Macdonald decided to select Mr. Kirkpatrick for that dignity, he signified his intention by a short note which ran:

> My dear George,
>   I purpose, if you have no objection, to knock you into a cocked hat at the opening of Parliament next week.
>   Yours always,
>   JOHN A. MACDONALD

[2] Debates, House of Commons, 1883, Volume II, p. 1175.

I cannot say that I consider Mr. Kirkpatrick to have been a good Speaker. A Tory gentleman, he was so desirous of being considered absolutely impartial that he occasionally leant backwards—that is to say, in his anxiety to be just he was sometimes not quite fair to his political friends because they were his friends, a form of weakness one sometimes encounters. At any rate that was the impression on the Government side of the House. He, however, does not appear at any time to have been conscious of the feeling in this regard, for at the conclusion of his term as Speaker he pressed his claim to cabinet office. Upon Sir John Macdonald's not acceding to his views, he addressed some rather unpleasant letters to his chief, hinting that he might possibly have to reconsider his attitude with regard to certain public questions and so forth. Sir John Macdonald, however, was not the sort of man to be moved by threats. Though an intimate friend of the Prime Minister, socially, politically, and personally, of many years' standing, Mr. Kirkpatrick never attained his ambition. The next Cabinet vacancy from Eastern Ontario was filled by the appointment of Mr. John Haggart, and Mr. Kirkpatrick had to wait until Macdonald's death before he received recognition of his services in the form of the Lieutenant-Governorship of Ontario. This is a bit of secret history, but as all the actors are long since dead, there seems to be no reason for its suppression, particularly as it affords a rather striking illustration of Sir John Macdonald's method of dealing with men.

My term of office as private secretary to Sir John Macdonald lasted from 1882 until his death in 1891. During that period, I had many experiences and encountered many kinds of men. Besides enjoying the daily society of my incomparable chief, and profiting by his instruction and example, I met in frequent intercourse his principal colleagues, among whom I may mention Messrs. Tilley, Tupper, Campbell, Pope, Langevin, Macpherson, Chapleau, Caron, Masson, White, and Abbott. I also possessed the acquaintance in various degrees of intimacy of Sir Alexander Galt, George Stephen, Donald Smith, D'Alton McCarthy, Edward Blake, Goldwin Smith, and many other distinguished men; in fact, there was scarcely a person in all Canada, prominent in church or state, with whom I was not at some time or other brought into contact.

These nine years of association with Sir John Macdonald proved of inestimable value to me. Entering his service an inexperienced youth, I knew very little of society. My father's death at the outset of my official career had compelled me to practise the severest economy, and this, to a certain extent, prevented me from mixing with my fellows. I lived in one room in a boarding house on twenty dollars or so a month. Almost my first glimpse of the great world was afforded on the occasion of the visit to Chestnut Park to which I have referred. Social clubs were unknown to me. I had no means to go out. But when the doors of Stadacona Hall and Earnscliffe were thrown open, and my financial circumstances began to improve, I issued in some measure from the obscurity in which I had hitherto dwelt. The Prime Minister's private secretary is always more or less of a *personage*, and enjoys many advantages. From the start I was treated with the greatest kindness and confidence by my chief, and came by degrees to be regarded almost as a member of his family. I remember that on one occasion, shortly after I had entered upon my secretaryship, Lady Macdonald was giving a luncheon, and I, working in the office, was not unnaturally overlooked. Quite possibly those in charge of the luncheon arrangements did not know I was in the house. Later, when my presence was discovered, my lunch was sent in to me on a tray, quickly followed by Sir John himself, who apologized for the oversight, telling me that he was much annoyed about it. He always attached importance to what many men affect to consider trifles. 'Forms are things,' he was wont to say. That a man should be given his correct style and titles he was always most careful to observe.

One day when leaving the East Block with him, I was going out by the Governor-General's door when he checked me. 'That entrance is reserved to the Governor-General,' he said, as we walked on to the main exit. The remark was a simple one, but it conveyed a lesson which I never forgot, though I am afraid the correct practice has been for many years more honoured in the breach than in the observance. 'There are few things a person resents more than to have his name mis-spelled,' he said to me on one occasion when I had inadvertently put a Mc for Mac or committed some trivial inaccuracy of that sort. To recognize the relative

importance of people, their little peculiarities, their correct modes
of address, all these things he so inculcated by precept and example
that I gradually acquired a certain aptness in such matters which
proved a great help to me in after life.

As I have said, I encountered many kinds of people during my
secretaryship—some of less distinction than those of whom I have
been speaking. One morning, not long after my appointment, as I
was sitting in the office at Earnscliffe, which had a separate entrance
for visitors on public business, a man swaggered into the room full
of the most overpowering assurance, and demanded to see Sir John.
'He is in his library,' I replied, 'but I don't think he will see anyone
this morning.' 'Oh,' exclaimed the intruder, 'he'll see *me*. You just
take my card into him, young fellow, and it will be all right.' He
fairly swept me off my feet as I hastened to comply with his request,
wondering who the great man might be, and whether I had been
sufficiently deferential to him. Sir John took the card. 'Where's
Ben [his servant]?' he asked. 'He's in the pantry, Sir,' I replied.
'And you left this fellow alone in the office?' exclaimed Sir John.
'Good God, he'll steal everything in the room!'

Having recounted my first experience of this gentleman, I think,
in justice to Sir John's estimate of him, I should supplement it by
my last. Years passed on. I profited by experience, and soon got to
know 'K', who turned up every now and then, but who never
tried his nonsense with me again. When Macdonald died, Mr.
Abbott, his successor in the Premiership, invited me to continue
on as his private secretary for a while until as he expressed it he
'got into the way of things'. One morning, shortly after Mr. Abbott
was installed, 'K' called and asked very humbly, but very earnestly,
to see the Premier. Again I took in his card, and this time, rather
pluming myself upon my experience, volunteered to Mr. Abbott
the information that 'K' was not a desirable person, accompanied
by the suggestion that perhaps on the whole he had better not see
him. Abbott smiled—that sweet smile which Macdonald used to say
was 'from the teeth outwards'—and softly replied, 'Oh, Pope, I
have known Joe K. for thirty years, and a damn'der scoundrel God
never made. Tell him I'll not see him.'

Speaking of this type, I remember once a rather big man, a

contractor of some sort, calling on Sir John Macdonald. Mr. L. R.
Masson, Sir John's sometime colleague in the Ministry, and afterwards Lieutenant-Governor of Quebec, a gentleman whom the
Premier esteemed highly, happened to be in the room at the time.
Sir John politely received the visitor, who as I remember was rather
hard of hearing, but as he shook hands with him, in some way
contrived to prevent Masson from doing likewise, saying in an under-
tone to the latter, 'I have got to shake hands with this fellow, but
you haven't.'

An important part of my duties during my secretaryship consisted
in looking after Sir John's official dinners. His desire was that each
of his parliamentary supporters should dine with him twice during
the session, and while he liked, when he could find time, to arrange
the seating at his own table, it not infrequently happened that that
duty devolved upon me, subject to his ultimate supervision. During
my first session, and when I was quite new to the job, I found these
dinner arrangements a good deal of a task. In the first place a general
election had recently taken place, and this brought together in
Ottawa a number of faces that I had never seen before. Some of the
new members were but little acquainted with the usages of society.
Many, for instance, never seemed to consider that there was any
particular need to answer a dinner invitation. After sending out the
cards and hearing nothing from a certain proportion of the invited
guests, I would sometimes station myself at the entrance to the
Houses of Parliament, and intercept the delinquents as they passed
in and out. Every culprit would aver that he had just returned from
posting his answer, whereupon, I used to suspect, many of them
would go to their desks and write it for the first time. In order to
aid me in ascertaining which of the new members were accompanied by wives and daughters, I addressed a note to such members
as I had no other means of reaching—asking them to be good enough
to favour me with the names of such ladies as might have accompanied them to town. One afternoon I chanced to meet on Parliament
Hill one of those to whom I had so applied. Upon my asking him if
he had received my note, to my surprise I saw him bristling up.
Striding towards me, he said in aggrieved and angry tones, 'I'd like
to know what in h-ll it is your business what ladies accompany me

to town.' In a flash it came to me that this gentleman was not commonly supposed to be a pattern of conjugal fidelity, and that if rumour spoke truly, any ladies by whom he might be accompanied were not likely to grace the Prime Minister's table. Upon my explaining matters and protesting that with no ulterior motive, but in the innocence of my heart, I had done this, he became mollified and we resumed our friendly relations, but I discarded then and there my method of acquiring information respecting the wives and daughters of our legislators.

In the summer of 1883 I accompanied Sir John to his country place at Rivière du Loup, where I first met my future wife, the eldest daughter of Mr. Justice (afterwards Chief Justice Sir) Henri Taschereau. It was, at any rate on my part, a case of love at first sight, and after the usual vicissitudes attendant on courtship, we were married at Rivière du Loup in the following year. Surrounded by our children and grandchildren, I realize after the lapse of forty years how abundantly blessed our union has been in all that constitutes true happiness.

Towards the close of 1883, Lord Lorne relinquished the position of Governor-General and, with Her Royal Highness the Princess Louise, returned to England. While the retiring Governor-General found the office congenial, and both he and his royal consort were popular with all classes, and while the Governor-General's term of office is commonly six, not five, years as is generally supposed,[3] Lord Lorne considered himself bound by Lord Beaconsfield's casual remark to him on leaving England, 'Remember this is a five-year appointment,' and would not on that account stay longer. He was succeeded by the Marquess of Lansdowne, the ablest of all the Governors-General under whom it was my fortune to serve. I considered him in every respect an ideal Governor, and Lady Lansdowne a fit helpmeet to her distinguished husband.

I was now fairly in the saddle, going full swing with my secretarial duties, in which I took great interest. Every day I went down to Earnscliffe, worked with the Chief all morning, and came up to town with him in the afternoon, where cabinets or attendance at the House of Commons during session kept me busy, sometimes until

[3] Colonial Office Regulations, 1908, paragraph 103.

far into the night. I remember one unusual parliamentary experience. It occurred during the prorogation ceremony of 1884. I was on hand as usual, moving about behind the Throne. The bills passed during the session were assented to in the customary manner, and the Governor-General had just unrolled and was beginning to read his speech, when I realized that the royal assent, which is signified by a special ceremony, and for which I had no responsibility, had not been given to the Supply Bill. There was not a moment to be lost. Withdrawing the curtains which hung at the side of the Throne, about which the Ministers stood grouped, I pulled Sir John's coat tail. He turned sharply round, evidently resenting the intrusion, when I whispered in his ear that the Supply Bill had not been assented to. Like a flash he took in the situation, and stopped the proceedings. The omission was speedily repaired, and the reading of the speech resumed. Had I not acted quickly, had the prorogation ceremony been suffered to take its ordinary course, as in all probability it would have done without my intervention, it would have been necessary to issue a fresh Proclamation summoning Parliament anew for the express purpose of enabling the Governor-General to accept in the Queen's name, from Her Majesty's faithful commoners, the supplies necessary to the carrying on of the public service.

1884 – 1886

*Fenian Activity | Reminiscences of Sir John
Macdonald | His Relations with Mr. J. A.
Chapleau and Sir Alexander Campbell |
His Views on the Closure | Political Effect
of Louis Riel's Execution | Completion of
the Canadian Pacific Railway | First Visit
to the Great West and the Pacific Coast |
Impressions and Incidents | Return to Ottawa*

THE winter of 1884 saw a revival of Fenian activities, quickened by
the advent of Lord Lansdowne who, probably by reason of those
high qualities which were destined to secure for him the respect,
esteem, and regard of the Canadian people, had incurred in a marked
degree the ill-will of these gentry. Special emissaries were sent on
here from Chicago to dog the Governor-General's footsteps with
murderous intent. I have seen an intercepted report from one of
these ruffians to his chief, in which he described how he lay concealed all day in the woods surrounding Rideau Hall waiting for the
Governor-General to come out, but His Excellency did not appear.
The fellow adds, 'I could have shot the boy'—meaning Lord
Lansdowne's eldest son, Lord Kerry, who was skating on an open
rink nearby—'but my heart failed me.'

Some people, particularly those upon whom the responsibility
of action did not rest, affected rather to minimize the gravity of
the Fenian reports current at that time. Among these I rather think
should be included Edward Blake, then leading the Opposition,

but from the day on which Sir John called Mr. Blake into his private rooms in the Commons, and there showed him two large sticks of dynamite sufficient to have done considerable damage to the Parliament Buildings, which had been found with wires attached immediately outside the window of the chamber in which they were then standing, and also gave him, as a Privy Councillor, communication of the report to which I have referred above, I think he became disposed to regard the matter more seriously. At any rate, those responsible for the Premier's safety saw to it that he was suitably guarded and never suffered to drive home alone, especially late at night.

One day the cabman who had come down to Earnscliffe to take him up to town told him that Mr. J. A. Chapleau, his colleague in the Government, had just died in California, whither he had gone for his health, and I, who already knew something of the difficulties which Sir John experienced owing to that gentleman's fondness for intrigue and cabal, marvelled at the tolerant and charitable way in which he spoke of his colleague, dwelling upon his many attractive qualities and passing lightly over his faults. When he reached town we learned that it was Mr. J. C. Chapais, and not Mr. Chapleau, who had just died, but the incident, for the reason I have mentioned, impressed itself on my memory. Speaking of the latter gentleman, I recall Lord Lansdowne's first New Year's levee as Governor-General—an informal affair at which people passed by in their overcoats, the Governor-General simply shaking hands with each one in turn. As Mr. Chapleau (who was at the time the Secretary of State, and as such, the custodian of the Great Seal of Canada) went by, looking very picturesque with his flowing locks and wearing a beautiful seal-skin coat reaching almost to his feet, Sir John Macdonald, who was standing near His Excellency, stepped forward, took Mr. Chapleau by the arm, bowed to the Governor-General, and said: 'Allow me to present to Your Excellency the Keeper of the Great Seal.'

Apropos of this same Mr. Chapleau, I wonder if anyone has ever realized what Sir John endured at his hands. Beneath a charming exterior there lay in Chapleau an illimitable capacity for intrigue, and an innate want of loyalty which must have sorely tried the

patience of his chief. What Chapleau most coveted was the administration of a large department with plenty of patronage at his disposal,
and this Sir John, by reason of the distrust he felt in his colleague,
was determined he should not have. At the same time, his strongly
magnetic personality rendered him a political necessity, and obliged
Sir John to put up with much at his hands. I particularly recall the
session of 1884 when the French-Canadian Conservative members,
with the connivance, it was alleged at the time, of Mr. Chapleau,
withheld their support from the bill to grant financial assistance to
the c.p.r. until they had extorted from the Government certain
railway concessions in the form of subsidies to the Provincial
Government, and also to the still more audacious 'hold-up' by
Chapleau on the eve of the general elections of 1887, when his
chief was fighting with his back to the wall in a contest the result of
which he considered doubtful. In both these instances and in others
of similar character, there was no real question of principle involved;
it was always a sordid demand for more influence or patronage or
material advantage of one kind or another. Generally the Premier
bore these threatened disaffections in silence, but I remember on
one occasion his letting himself go. On the death of John Henry
Pope, Sir John undertook the administration of the Department of
Railways and Canals, which it was well known Chapleau especially
coveted. Driving over to the West Block, in which the Railway
Department was situated, Sir John said to me, 'I am afraid I shall
have to take this Department myself.' I do not know what devil
tempted me to say it, but I could not refrain from remarking, 'What
will Mr. Chapleau do then?' The old man's eyes flashed as he turned
towards me in the carriage. 'Do?' replied he. 'He'll follow like a
dog, that's what he'll do.' And he did.

Another colleague who gave some disquietude was Sir Alexander
Campbell, a very different type of man from Mr. Chapleau, but
like Mr. Chapleau not always to be depended upon in an emergency.
This was strikingly revealed to me when preparing my *Correspondence
of Sir John Macdonald* for the press. At several critical periods in
Macdonald's life Campbell failed him by refusing to subscribe to
party funds, by absenting himself during important election cam-
paigns, even where Macdonald himself was the candidate, by failing

to support him at the Council board, and in other ways. For example, on the eve of Macdonald's election in Kingston in 1874, when opposed with extraordinary rancour by both the Dominion and Provincial Governments, Campbell wrote an apologetic letter regretting that he found himself obliged to go to New York, leaving his old partner, leader, colleague, and friend in that extremity to fight the battle alone. I had intended to print some of these letters, but the aggregate produced such an unfavourable picture of Campbell that I decided to omit them from Macdonald's correspondence. There is no reason, however, why, in justice to my old chief, I should not refer to the subject here.

'Campbell hates me,' observed Sir John in one of our drives into town from Earnscliffe. 'Hates you, sir?' said I. 'It seems to me that you have been pulling chestnuts out of the fire all your life for him.' 'Yes,' replied the old man almost fiercely, 'and that is just why he hates me. Don't you know that there are some people in this world who resent nothing so much as the sense of an obligation which they can never repay? Campbell is one of those persons. He knows he can never requite me for what I have done for him in the past, and he hates me for it.'

Among those of his supporters outside the Cabinet who latterly gave him some concern was the late D'Alton McCarthy, a charming man with a high sense of public duty, but one whose political judgement and sagacity were scarcely commensurate with his other gifts. Sir John, while at no time placing much reliance upon McCarthy as a politician, thought so highly of his legal attainments that it was commonly understood McCarthy could have had the portfolio of Justice almost any time between 1880 and 1885, had his financial position allowed him to accept it. In view of the beggarly salary paid to our Cabinet Ministers, McCarthy simply could not afford to relinquish his leading position at the bar of Ontario. The Prime Minister, however, continued to consult him with regard to judicial appointments in that province, and such regard had Macdonald for McCarthy's knowledge of bench and bar, and for the sound character of his advice in such matters, that he continued to exercise up to the year 1889 a very considerable influence in appointments to the Ontario bench.

The session of 1885 was marked by the hitherto unparalleled obstruction offered by the Liberal Opposition to the passage of a Franchise Act for the Dominion. Up to this time the provincial franchises had been in use for the Dominion House of Commons, but Sir John Macdonald had long felt that the Parliament of Canada should fix the electoral qualifications for its own body. The Opposition resisted this change, and their obstruction reached such a pitch that the Government of the day seriously contemplated imitating Gladstone in his conflict with the Irish members by introducing the closure. Sir John, however, opposed this policy, which he regarded as an interference with the freedom of debate. While admitting that the closure might eventually become a necessity, he declared that he would prefer its introduction by a Liberal rather than by a Conservative Government. He considered that on purely party grounds its adoption would be a tactical mistake.

We spent the summer of 1885 at St. Patrick, Rivière du Loup, where Sir John had a cottage. Summer holidays meant for me little more than a change of air and scene. The first thing to do on reaching the seaside was to organize an office, make the necessary postal and telegraph arrangements, and start work anew on the old lines, the principal difference from life in Ottawa being that there were fewer visitors in the country and consequently less interruptions. Moreover, Sir John did not ordinarily work in the afternoon. But I never had a whole day off. The stress, however, was less than in Ottawa, and I enjoyed the life-giving air of the lower St. Lawrence to the full. We generally arrived at Rivière du Loup during the last days of June, and remained until the first week in September.

The autumn of 1885 was likewise memorable for the execution of Louis Riel for the crime of high treason, which event caused no small stir in Canada at the time. The Government, in view of the prevailing excitement, were especially careful to see that Riel was accorded all his legal rights, and when these were exhausted, they appointed a Commission composed of three medical men, one of whom being Dr. Michael Lavell, warden of the Kingston Penitentiary, to enquire into Riel's mental condition. The Commission were instructed to proceed immediately to Regina, hold their enquiry and report to the Governor-in-Council with the least possible delay. To me was entrusted the duty of dispatching Lavell on his mission, and it was highly desirable that this should be effected without anybody knowing anything about it. Accordingly I slipped out of Ottawa by a late train one Saturday evening, bound for Kingston. I travelled via Sharbot Lake, where I had to wait several hours in the woods, reaching Kingston Junction in the middle of the night. Next morning I was early astir, and selecting a cabman to whom I was personally unknown I drove out to the Penitentiary where, I am afraid, the officials regarded me as an untimely visitor, for it was a Sunday morning. Eventually I saw Dr. Lavell, presented my credentials, and started him off by the first train for the West, I myself returning to Ottawa the same evening without any inkling of my mission getting out, though several of Sir John's friends, under cover of profuse hospitality, tried very hard to pump me. However, nobody knew anything of Lavell's connection with the Riel enquiry until he announced it himself at Regina some days later.

Riel's execution had a far-reaching political effect. Not only did it cause the overthrow of the Conservative party in Quebec at the provincial general election which came off in the following year, but the popular outburst in that province gave rise to a corresponding racial excitement in Ontario which took the form of an anti-French and anti-Catholic agitation headed by the *Mail* newspaper, and supported, amongst others, by Mr. McCarthy, who was very bitter in his attacks on the French Catholic people and their church (viewed in its political aspect). This used to puzzle me not a little, as it appeared to be at variance with the much more tolerant attitude he took on both these subjects in private life. I asked Sir John if he could account for this apparent contradiction, whereupon he replied, 'My dear fellow, it's in his blood. His father was just the same.'

The Canadian Pacific Railway was completed in the autumn of 1885, and in the following summer the Chief paid his first and only visit to the Great West, and invited me to accompany him. Our party consisted of Sir John and Lady Macdonald, Fred White, George Johnson of the *Mail* staff, myself, and two servants—old

Ben Chilton, Sir John's man, and a maid. We travelled in the
Premier's private car *Jamaica*, which had been luxuriously fitted
up by Mr. Van Horne, the President of the Canadian Pacific Railway.

I had some qualms about setting out on this long journey, my
eldest son being only two weeks old, but after talking it over, my
wife and I decided that it would not do to decline on her account
as she was doing well, and that I should go—so I went, leaving her
to close our house and go down to Rivière du Loup as soon as she
was able to travel.

Sir John had quite a reception at Winnipeg, where a large number
of people assembled to receive him. Among the crowd gathered
round the car was an enthusiastic young Tory who was cheering
with all his might. Upon Sir John's appearance the enthusiasm
became tremendous. When the lull came, the young Tory, who
evidently had never seen Sir John before in his life, remarked in a
low voice to a friend standing by, 'Seedy-looking old beggar, isn't
he?' and then resumed his cheering with redoubled vigour, as
though determined that his private impressions should not be
allowed to interfere with his party loyalty.

I did not expect to find so great a development in Winnipeg,
which seemed to have suddenly sprung up out of the prairie. In
1871, only fifteen years before, there was scarcely a house outside
the Hudson's Bay Fort. In 1886 it was a flourishing city of 25,000
people. Main Street, as I record in my diary, would do credit to
any city of equal size anywhere. 'It is excellently paved from end
to end with wooden blocks and is a long street of exceptional width
(138 feet) lighted with electricity and furnished with all the appliances of modern civilization, including a first-rate line of street cars.'
In Winnipeg I met with a surprising number of old friends who had
taken Horace Greeley's advice and gone west.

I found the same promise of development everywhere as we went
west. At Brandon, a flourishing town, Fred White told me that five
years before he had camped on its site, then the virgin prairie.
Regina had scarcely begun to be interesting, and Moose Jaw, Medicine Hat, and Calgary, save where there happened to be Mounted
Police posts, were in embryo. On this my first trip, everything was
so new to me that I did not experience a dull moment.

It was on this journey that I saw my first prairie—a strange and novel sight. I thus record my impressions in my diary: 'Imagine a boundless plain, perfectly level, covered with short wavy grass, not a tree or bush of any kind, stretching out in all directions as far as the eye can reach, nothing but grass and sky, and you have a prairie. It makes one think of the ocean in its boundlessness and the mind fancies that the occasional settler's house far off against the sky is a ship making its way across the waters.' The buffalo had disappeared some years before, but every now and then one could perceive their bones bleaching on the prairie. The rapidity with which these animals were extinguished or driven far north is remarkable. In 1882 there were 100,000 skins sold in St. Paul, and in 1883 just four! An old settler told me that he well remembered seeing the present site of Regina black with buffalo.

The whole journey partook of the nature of a triumphal progress. At almost every town and village addresses were presented to Sir John and the greatest enthusiasm prevailed. At Regina, as at Winnipeg, we remained over some days, staying at Government House, and holding receptions which in all cases were well attended. At Gleichen the Indians assembled in force, and a great pow-wow was held in our honour, attended by the Lieutenant-Governor in state, Sir John, and other dignitaries. The Indians were marshalled under Crowfoot, head chief of the Blackfeet, Three Bulls, and a third chief whose name I forget. They were gorgeous in war paint and feathers, with the exception of Crowfoot. He was in mourning for Poundmaker, who had recently died, and for that reason appeared in undress, which consisted of little more than a dirty blanket round his loins. The Indians began by smoking a filthy-looking pipe, which they passed from one to another, each warrior merely taking a whiff or two. Crowfoot, being invited to state his grievances, began by alluding to the prairie fires caused by sparks from the railway engines, against the continuance of which he strongly protested. He then passed on to the great question of food, which is the staple grievance with Indians on all such occasions.

The interpreter on this occasion rejoiced in the name of Billy Gladstone, and the circumstance suggested a similar scene held at the same place on the occasion of a visit by Lord Lorne, then

Governor-General, five years earlier, when there were no railways upon which prairie fires could be blamed. Billy Gladstone was also to have been the court interpreter on this occasion, but something occurred to prevent his attendance, and his place was taken by another whose knowledge of English was limited. Upon the Indian chief being invited to present his complaints, he began by a long harangue, illustrating his remarks by various pantomimic gestures. When at length he stopped for want of breath, Lord Lorne looked towards the interpreter who, feeling the responsibilities of the occasion and realizing the inadequacy of his linguistic attainments, hesitated, shuffled his feet, and finally replied, 'He say he damn glad to see you.' The Indian chief, no doubt wondering at the conciseness of the English tongue, then resumed his speech, and after more pantomimic appeals to the sun, sky, prairie, the Great Mother over the water, and so on, again subsided for want of breath. Again the Governor-General turned to the interpreter, who manifested renewed embarrassment, shuffled his feet as before, and finally replied, 'He say he damn hungry.' In consequence of his more copious diction, which fitted with his great name, Billy Gladstone took more time to translate Crowfoot's speech than did his former *locum tenens*. In substance, both Indians said the same thing —that their people were originally happy and free with plenty of food at all times, that the white man had come in, taken their land, killed off their buffalo, thus depriving them of their means to live, and so forth. Crowfoot went on to protest his loyalty, which he had already proved in the rising of 1885, and, Sir John having appropriately replied and having provided a banquet for the occasion together with the presents of pipes, tea, and tobacco, this picturesque gathering terminated. We rejoined our train, and were soon speeding towards the great mountains already fringing the western sky.

With the mountains I was enormously impressed. The sublimity of the scene awed me beyond measure. As I sat with some members of our party on the cow-catcher of our train at a point near the summit of the Selkirks, suspended over a foaming torrent nearly three hundred feet below, with the glorious mountains all about us, I found myself unconsciously repeating the opening words of the

Te Deum, 'Te Deum laudamus, Te Dominum confitemur,' while all around seemed to answer back, '*Te aeternum Patrem omnis terra veneratur.*'

Sir John joined us on the cow-catcher at this point, and we rode together thereon about a hundred and fifty miles, a rather risky procedure, as we afterwards learned, and any repetition of which Mr. Van Horne, when he heard of it, peremptorily forbade by reason of the land and rock slides which every now and then came thundering down the mountain slopes of the newly constructed road. Lady Macdonald, with characteristic imprudence, occupied the cow-catcher most of the way between Canmore and Port Moody, a distance of nearly six hundred miles, Fred White, George Johnson, and I accompanying her in turn. On the last morning of our western railway journey my turn on the cow-catcher came with the rising sun. We were going along over a straight piece of road near Hope at a fairly lively rate when suddenly there started up from a neighbouring ditch a number of young pigs, just in front of the train. They ran for a while straight ahead of the engine, then broke and scattered, all except one little fellow who seemed determined to try conclusions with us, for he kept on the track, running as hard as he could, and squealing at the top of his bent. We closed on him rapidly. I knew we were in great danger, but there was nothing to be done. The train rushed on. The point of the cow-catcher was a foot from the pig's hind legs. I heard the thud as the on-speeding train struck him. Squealing, he was lifted high in the air, and passed *between my body and the post I was holding!* The engine driver, who immediately above me was looking out of his window in horror, comforted me after the crisis had passed, with the assurance that if that pig had struck any of us going at the rate we were, it would have been more disastrous than a rifle bullet. I have not ridden on a cow-catcher since.

At 1 p.m. the same day we reached the terminus at Port Moody (the railway not yet having been carried through to Vancouver) and looked out on the blue waters of the Strait of Georgia. The usual address followed, and then Sir John, taking off his hat, addressed the people from the platform of his car. As I stood on the shore of the Pacific by the side of that old man, with his grey hair

blowing across his forehead, I could not help feeling what an
exultant moment it must have been for him. Here was the full
realization of his political dream of years. His chief opponent had
left on record his belief that all the resources of the British Empire
could not build the road in ten years. Here it was built, out of the
resources of Canada, in less than half that time. It was no paper
road, this. He had travelled over it himself. With his own eyes he
had witnessed the marvellous feat. Here was the car which had
brought him from Ottawa. Here, too, lapping his feet were the
waters of the Pacific Ocean. His dream had become an accomplished
fact!

British Columbia is to me the most attractive of all the provinces,
and Victoria the Queen City of Canada. There is a charm about the
latter which captures the visitor from the very start, as it did me,
and which, after the lapse of well-nigh forty years, is as potent as
ever. We took our steamer for Victoria and arrived at about 10
p.m. on the evening of Saturday the 24th of July. As we steamed
into the harbour the strains of 'The Red, White, and Blue' greeted
our ears from over the water, and sounded very prettily. We were
met on landing by a torchlight procession, and escorted to our hotel
with much enthusiasm.

We stayed three weeks in Victoria, every moment of which I
enjoyed. To me the thoroughly English character of the place and
people, as expressed in certain manners and customs, reminded me
of my childhood's home, otherwise so different. The weather too
was very pleasant.

I remember, however, when one of us was sounding the praises of
the Victoria climate, Sir John agreed, but added as an aside, 'The
day was always in the afternoon.' The intimation was plain, but I
must say I never experienced any enervating quality in the Victoria
air, though perhaps it does not possess quite the strength and vigour
of the lower St. Lawrence.

In 1886 there was not much communication between British
Columbia and what they still called 'Canada'. Until the completion
of the railway, comparatively few Canadians had penetrated so far
west, while the residents of Victoria seldom came east, so that,
with the exception of a few parliamentarians, I knew nobody. I

remember dining with Fred White at Mr. E. Crow Baker's, then member of parliament for Victoria, whom I knew chiefly by his fierce denunciation of everything Chinese, and especially of the enormity of employing Chinese labour. I was therefore rather amused on visiting his house to find the door opened by one China-man and dinner served by another!

Happily circumstanced as I was, I lacked no opportunity of making friends or of sharing in the boundless hospitality extended to my chief. I had the pleasure on this occasion of meeting a good many people, among others Chief Justice Sir Matthew Begbie, who had been sent out from England in Crown Colony days to administer justice with a firm hand, and right well did he execute his office, for his very name became a terror to evildoers. Many stories are told of his stern and unbending attitude in this regard. Once a case came before him in which he happened to take a more lenient view than was generally expected. 'Prisoner at the bar, I fine you sixty dollars.' 'Thanks, Judge,' interrupted the man, delighted with the unlooked-for leniency of the sentence. 'I have the money right here in my pants pocket.' 'And sixty days in the county gaol,' continued Sir Matthew, with a stony glare. 'Have you got that in your pants pocket too?'

I, however, had no experience of the Chief Justice's severity, as I was introduced to him on his tennis court, and our subsequent meetings were confined to social functions at which he was always most affable. And so our early days in this beautiful spot glided by swiftly until the time came to say good-bye. It seems almost ungrate-ful to say a disparaging word of a place of so much beauty and charm, but candour compels me to observe that the hotel people of Victoria, even in those primeval days, were not wholly unacquainted with the art of making visitors pay for the privilege of enjoying their beautiful city. I had had an intimation of this beforehand, so it was with some trepidation, in view of Sir John's economical views on such subjects, that I approached the counter of the Driard Hotel to pay our bill. I was one of a small queue bent on the same errand. Ahead of me, chewing a cigar, was a Yankee, wearing, like the practical politician I met in Sir David Macpherson's office in Toronto four years before, a black top hat, much tilted, and a light tweed coat. This gentleman immediately preceded me. As he got his bill, I was not reassured to hear him say, 'By G-d, I'll not pay that, I'll fight like a —— of —— first.' I do not recall how *he* came out of it, being too much engrossed with my own affairs. Our bill amounted to $1,193. There were six in our party, including two servants. We had lived on a most moderate scale, had dined *table d'hôte*, and our wine bill amounted only to ten dollars. On the matter being brought to Sir John's notice, he remarked philosophically, 'Of course you have got to pay it.' I think what riled me most was an additional livery stable charge of $37.50 for bringing our luggage up from the steamer to the hotel, a distance of about a quarter of a mile.

On the 13th of August Sir John formally opened the Esquimalt and Nanaimo Railway, and afterwards descended six hundred feet down the main shaft of a coal mine at Nanaimo, the scene a few weeks later of a terrible explosion whereby one hundred and fifty miners lost their lives. On the same afternoon we left Nanaimo for New Westminster in Mr. Robert Dunsmuir's tug *Alexander*. As I said in my diary: 'The sun was setting when we stood out to sea, and its rays lighting up the landscape, made our last glimpse of Vancouver Island a very beautiful one—only less beautiful than the mainland hills towards which our faces were now turned, while in order that nothing might be wanting to complete the scene, Mount Baker stood radiant in the southern sky, catching and reflecting the light back to us for some time after the sun had disappeared below the horizon.'

Sir John and Lady Macdonald were the guests in New Westminster of the Rt. Reverend Mr. Sillitoe, the Anglican Bishop, whose accommodation was not equal to putting up the whole party, so Fred White and I drove over to Vancouver, which, started in February and burned down in June, was just rising from its ashes. White and I approached the proprietor of the principal hotel in the place, and asked him if he could give us a bed for the night. 'Well,' said he, 'if you don't mind shinning up a ladder to it. I'll be glad to accommodate you gentlemen, but the fact is we have not yet got the stairs up in this hotel.' We willingly complied with the conditions and these are the circumstances under which I spent my first night in Vancouver.

Among the few people I knew in the town was Mr. A. W. Ross, member of parliament for Selkirk, Manitoba, then doing business as a land agent in Vancouver. He tried his best to induce us to buy some town lots on the corner of what is now Hastings and Granville Streets for $700 a lot, one of which has since sold for $475,000. Neither of us had the money to buy, nor was the offer so tempting as it sounds today. Then the whole western problem had not got beyond the experimental stage. There was no assurance, for example, that wheat would ripen on the prairies. On the solution of that problem the success of the Canadian Pacific Railway depended, and if the Canadian Pacific Railway did not succeed, what would become of Vancouver? The best evidence that we were not so silly as several of those to whom I afterwards related the circumstance seemed to think, is that George Johnson, who was a widower, with no children and plenty of money, equally with us declined the proposal, observing that three thousand miles was a long way off from one's property.

In driving over from New Westminster I was much struck by the size of the trees, and the richness of the vegetation, which seemed to me almost semi-tropical in character. As regards the trees, I quote from my diary: 'To anyone who cares about seeing big trees, I recommend this drive as affording ample gratification of his tastes in this particular. For the last six or seven miles, the road is one long avenue lined by trees, which must be seen to be appreciated. They are of enormous girth and without branches for perhaps half their height, rising 250 and 275 feet straight into the air. The vista is superb. The vegetation along the way seemed to be of proportionate size. I saw ferns, for instance, 14 feet high.

'The largest tree I saw in British Columbia was at the upper end of the Vancouver town site. About forty feet or more had been cut down, and was lying on the ground hollowed out. Into this hollow tube we walked, and, standing upright, I was just able with an outstretched cane to reach the top. A few feet from the ground the trunk measured 42 feet in circumference. It was, therefore, about 13 feet 6 inches in diameter, and was 310 feet high. This last measurement I did not verify, but it is on the word of a member of Parliament and, therefore, admits of no dispute.'

On the return trip we stopped a day or two in Winnipeg, one of which, the 24th of August, being the hottest day I have ever experienced, the thermometer reaching according to my diary 108°, with a wind like the blast from a furnace.

We arrived in Ottawa on the 30th of August, and so closed one of the most remarkable and enjoyable incidents in my life.

1886 — 1891

*Political Campaign and General Elections of
1887 | Personal Relations with Sir Wilfrid
Laurier | Irish-American Attacks on Lord
Lansdowne | The Catholic Church and Loyalty |
Mr. Andrew Macdonald Appointed Lieutenant-
Governor of Prince Edward Island | Appointment
as Assistant Clerk of the Privy Council | The
1890–91 Campaign | Sir John Macdonald's Death*

SCARCELY had I settled down again to my usual life when signs of
an impending general election began to appear in the political sky,
and the Prime Minister started out on a tour of Ontario. This
campaign—the hardest fought of all Sir John's electoral contests
of which I had personal knowledge—was hardly under way when
Mr. Mowat, the Premier of Ontario, with the object of assisting his
friend Mr. Edward Blake, then leader of the Dominion Opposition,
suddenly dissolved his legislature and precipitated a general provincial election. This necessitated Mr. W. R. Meredith, the leader
of the Provincial Opposition, taking the field. The two Conservative
leaders hunted in couples during the next few weeks.

Now Mr. Meredith, though less pronounced in expression, was
supposed to be more or less sympathetic with the anti-French and
anti-Catholic views of Mr. McCarthy and of the *Mail*, which were
injuriously affecting the Catholic adherents of the Ministry whose
support Sir John considered it important to retain. Messrs. Meredith
and McCarthy, I should add, were intimate personal and political

friends. It was during this campaign when we were somewhere in Western Ontario—I think in the vicinity of Chatham—one Saturday afternoon that I, acting in accordance with what I understood to be the arrangements decided upon, gave the order to cut off our private car and place it on the siding over Sunday. In the course of the evening I learned that we were going back to Toronto that night. Fearing that I had misunderstood him, I spoke to Sir John about this. 'Oh, no,' he replied. 'You did quite right. I had intended remaining over, but I have just learned that Meredith is going back to Toronto tonight, and I don't want him to be alone there with McCarthy over Sunday!'

An an illustration of the bitterness with which these elections were waged, and the lengths to which presumably respectable persons were prepared to go and actually went to defeat 'John A.', I may mention that on the occasion of Sir John's visits to Toronto in the early part of this campaign, the *Globe* placed a spy on his movements who followed him everywhere at all hours of day or night during his stay in town. If he drove out to Chestnut Park, about thirty yards behind his carriage one could see the *Globe* emissary following in a cab. Should the chief have occasion to visit the bank or the Bishop or the Mayor or his dentist, or to perform his devotions, or to make a social call, he was invariably shadowed by this spy who persistently dogged his footsteps. Sir John never seemed to mind this outrage, in fact he used to make a joke of it. As for myself, who was similarly honoured, I got to regard it as great fun, and occasionally made it minister to my amusement at a period not remarkable for the extent or variety of my diversions. Suddenly issuing from our headquarters (the old Queen's Hotel), I would call a cab, drive to some little-frequented quarter, get out of the carriage, dodge down a side street, return to the carriage after a short absence and repeat the performance elsewhere, with the sole object of fooling the *Globe* man, in which I at first succeeded to the top of my bent. Ultimately, however, he either realized that I was playing with him or grew ashamed of his ignoble role, for after a season he gave up the pursuit, and I was thus deprived of one of my few relaxations!

This campaign was a tremendously hard-fought battle. The

opposition put forward their supreme effort and were confident of victory. Macdonald made his principal fight in Western Ontario, supported by his colleagues, Thompson, Chapleau, Tupper, White, and Foster. Chapleau particularly created an impression with the Western Ontario farmers. I remember on one occasion, when the Ministers were getting ready to go somewhere, a big burly fellow in the crowd shouting at the top of his lungs, 'Where's the immortal Chapleau? I don't give a d - - n for Thompson or White or Foster. Where's Chapleau?' and in due time Chapleau was produced. As he came forward, a strikingly picturesque figure with his pallid features, intellectual countenance, and long grey hair artistically bestowed, he was received with expressions of welcome which grew into deafening shouts of applause as he thus addressed the crowd: 'You have heard a great deal of late about the *habitant* from Lower Canada, and no doubt you are curious to see a living specimen of the *genus*. Well, gentlemen,' advancing to the front of the platform, striking his breast, and assuming that histrionic attitude which he knew so well how to put on—'I am the offspring of a *habitant*. I come among you a farmer's son, one of yourselves, to address to you a few words on the public issues of the day.' It is not too much to say that this completely captured the meeting, and Chapleau did what he liked with it afterwards.

Sir John Thompson was an effective speaker, though of a different type from Chapleau, who was apt to be demagogic in his methods. Sir George Foster also spoke very well. I remember once Lady Macdonald saying to her husband during this campaign, 'Can you explain to me how that timid, shy, retiring man [Foster] is always so much at home before an audience, and not always a sympathetic audience at that?' I remember too his reply: 'Consciousness of power, my dear.'

I have sometimes reflected how singular it is that I, who knew Sir John Macdonald so intimately, possess scarcely any letters from him addressed to myself. The explanation of course is simple. He seldom wrote me because I was scarcely ever absent from his side. Thus the occasion for correspondence did not arise. One or two brief notes I treasure, for example his first letter, which is especially valuable as indicating the confidence he reposed in me after two years' service.

Earnscliffe,
Ottawa,
Dec. 15, 1884.

My dear Pope,

 You must lay up until quite well.

 I go up to Toronto to-morrow at noon and will take White with me—so that you can rest until I return.

 Send for the letters and open them all.

     Yours always,

      J.A.M.D.

And this line, on the occasion of the birth of my eldest son Edward.

Earnscliffe,
Ottawa, June 25/86.

Dear Pope,

 I congratulate you on the happy event. Give my love to Minette. I send you a cable to decipher.

     Yours always,

      J.A.M.D.

Two or three brief notes such as the above are all I possess from my old chief.

 And so I could go on indefinitely, but I must remember that this time I am writing my own memoirs and not another's, that I was Sir John Macdonald's secretary for little over nine years—not one quarter of the period with which I have been connected with public affairs—and that if I am to preserve a due sense of proportion in my story, I must pass along.

 From Sir Wilfrid Laurier, on the other hand, I have many letters to which I shall refer in place. I knew Mr. Laurier before I met Sir John. My acquaintance with the former dates from the beginning of the year 1879, which after my marriage in 1884 quickly ripened into friendship. My wife's mother came from Arthabaskaville, the home of the Lauriers prior to 1896. Madame Taschereau was the second daughter of Mr. E. L. Pacaud, a well-known advocate of his day, who showed Mr. Laurier much kindness at the beginning of his career. The two families grew up in intimacy, and when I entered the Taschereau family I found friends at once in the Lauriers.

When Mr. Laurier became leader of the Opposition in succession to Mr. Edward Blake, on the latter's resignation after his failure to carry the General Elections of 1887, I wrote Mr. Laurier a congratulatory note, to which he thus replied:

Ottawa, 28th June, 1887.

My dear Mr. Pope,

I thank you sincerely, most sincerely for your very kind letter. I fully appreciate the feeling of friendship which has dictated it. Minette is right, however, it is an empty honor in the way of profit, and full of thorns and difficulties, otherwise I am exactly of Minette's mind, and I long hesitated before accepting.

Tell your dear little wife that I was very sorry at being unable to go to see her before leaving Ottawa. Mr. Pacaud enquired about her the first thing when I met him. It grieved me to have to admit that I could not answer his enquiries, as I would have wished.

Yours very truly,

WILFRID LAURIER

The Lauriers and ourselves were often seen in public together. On one occasion we accompanied them to a ball at Earnscliffe, which gave Lady Macdonald occasion to say, half jokingly, at the breakfast table the next morning, 'Sir John, do you think it quite the thing for your Private Secretary to be seen so frequently in the company of the leader of the Opposition?' 'Coming to my house, yes,' replied he. There seemed to be something implied in the qualification, but he really meant nothing by it, for about the same time he said to me that he was glad we were such friends, adding, 'Laurier will look after you should you need a friend when I am gone.'

In the spring of 1887 two notorious Irish agitators, William O'Brien and Denis Kilbride, members of the Imperial House of Commons, visited Ottawa with the avowed object, as they phrased it, of 'driving Lord Lansdowne out of Canada' by reason of his alleged harsh treatment of the tenantry of his Irish estates. Lord Lansdowne had been Governor-General of Canada for upwards of three years, and during that time had so borne himself as to win in a marked degree the esteem and respect of the whole community. He was, moreover, the representative of Her Majesty the Queen amongst us, and the abominable insults sought to be put upon him by this brace of itinerant ruffians, apart altogether from his own high character and charming personality, were deeply resented by those who, whether they possessed the honour of the Governor-General's personal acquaintance or not, venerated his great office and the Sovereign whom he represented.

Now loyalty to my Sovereign has ever been with me, alike in youth, manhood, and old age, the paramount obligation, the highest duty, the dominating impulse of my life. Sedition and treason I have ever regarded as the greatest of crimes. The utterances of O'Brien and his comrade reeked with disloyalty to the Queen, to England, to the flag, to everything that I had been taught from my childhood to revere. Small wonder then that I resented the visit of these worthies to Ottawa, but my feelings may be better imagined than described when it was announced in the press that O'Brien was to be invited to make use of the hall of the Ottawa College in furtherance of his propaganda.

St. Joseph's, my parish church, was owned by the College of Ottawa, the pastor of the church and his curates being members of the Oblate Order and resident in the College. When, therefore, I learned that the Ottawa College was preparing to welcome the agitators, I felt it incumbent on me as a parishioner of the church to speak out, and accordingly I wrote my parish priest expressing the hope that the rumour was unfounded. I received a reply the same day to the effect that the report published in the press, 'that we are going to place our hall at the disposal of Mr. O'Brien was altogether groundless'.

It is true that O'Brien was not invited to speak at the College during his visit, and did not so speak. On the evening of the 20th of May, however, he was attended by a band of Ottawa College students who formed a bodyguard and escorted him from a meeting held in the Royal Rink to the Russell House. At this meeting O'Brien outdid himself in blackguardly attacks on Lord Lansdowne. As the leading newspaper of the capital remarked next morning, speaking with particular reference to a meeting held a few days earlier, in the Queen's Park, Toronto, 'Mr. O'Brien's attacks on the Governor-General will not help his mission to Canada. So atrociously unjust, so wantonly malicious, so absolutely devoid of truth, were his charges against His Excellency, that even persons who may have been disposed to accept as gospel attacks against the management of Lord Lansdowne's estates, will come to the conclusion that the statements O'Brien makes at his meetings in support of his charges that Lord Lansdowne is a cruel, exacting and persecuting landlord, should be taken with, at least, reserve.'[1]

The only result of the O'Brien crusade was to intensify and deepen the respect entertained for Lord Lansdowne. His friends took advantage of the occasion to entertain him at dinner, and on this occasion not merely his admirers but all those who stood for decency in our public life vied with one another to do him honour. In this manifestation of respect I was privileged to join.

And so this discreditable episode terminated as far as the public of Ottawa were concerned. My personal sense of propriety, however, had received a severe shock. I could not avoid the reflection that if the controlling spirits of the College had been animated by the proper feelings of respect for the Governor-General and his office no such exhibition on the part of the students as took place would have been permitted, and that the outrage must have been connived at by someone in authority. I made no claim to judge others. Many members of St. Joseph's congregation I knew to be as loyal as myself. It was not for me to reconcile their course with my conception of loyalty. I could not speak for them. As for myself, however, I felt I could no longer countenance an institution which tolerated O'Brien or any of his fellow rebels. Accordingly, when the lease of my pew in St. Joseph's expired, I did not renew it, but sought accommodation elsewhere.

We spent the summer of 1887 at the Inch Arran Hotel, Dalhousie, New Brunswick, varied by a visit to Sir Leonard and Lady Tilley at St. Andrews. One day we went up the St. John River to St. Stephen under the guidance of Mr. John D. Chipman, Lady Tilley's brother, who ran unsuccessfully for the County of Charlotte in the Conservative interest at the general elections in the preceding February. To him fell the honour of entertaining the distinguished visitors in his home town. The functions began by a public reception

[1] Ottawa *Citizen*, 21 May 1887.

at which Mr. Chipman presented those persons who desired to pay their respects to Sir Leonard and Sir John. Among these was a maiden lady of a certain age, who as she shook hands on passing, said twice, in a strongly American accent, 'So sorry our superintendent didn't get there. So sorry our superintendent didn't get there,' to each of them, and not a word more. 'Jack, what did that lady mean by "our superintendent" and "getting there"?' asked Sir Leonard of Mr. Chipman at luncheon. Jack seemed rather embarrassed by the question, but finally the truth came out. Mr. Chipman was superintendent of a Sunday school in which the lady taught, and the allusion to his not 'getting there' had reference to his defeat at the polls in the general elections six months before!

Now and then Sir John Macdonald paid me the compliment of consulting me with regard to political appointments in my native province. Before I had been with him two years, one of these occasions arose. Mr. T. Heath Haviland's term as Lieutenant-Governor of Prince Edward Island drew to a close, and the question of his successor came up for consideration. In addition to Mr. Haviland there were several aspirants to the office, one of them being Mr. George W. Howlan, then a member of the Senate. Both these gentlemen pressed their claims strenuously, Mr. Howlan in particular leaving no stone unturned to secure the appointment. Now Mr. Howlan, though owing his senatorship to the Government of Sir John Macdonald, was not supposed to have remained entirely true to his political friends when in opposition; in fact it was said that during the period of the Mackenzie régime (1873–78) he had covertly intrigued with the leaders of the Liberal party to turn the Catholic vote against the Conservative opposition, Howlan being a 'Professional Catholic'. With this object in view, he proposed his scheme to some leading members of that persuasion, including a certain Father Doyle, the parish priest of Summerside, but not meeting with success in that quarter, he switched back just before the general elections of 1878. How he voted on that occasion is not known, but he had the impudence to telegraph Mr. J. C. Pope, when the latter became a member of Macdonald's cabinet, not to make any appointments until he reached Ottawa! Years passed, his lapse was forgotten, and in 1884 he claimed the Lieutenant-

Governorship as a reward, I suppose, for his political fealty! What strengthened his claim was the fact that there had not been a Catholic at Government House for many years, and there was a very general feeling that such an appointment was due to that portion of the community, which always supported the Conservative party then in power. Sir John concurred in the expediency of such an appointment, but seemed to think that there was no available candidate for the position other than Howlan. I knew better, and when he spoke to me on the subject, I replied that I had an alternative scheme which I would like to put before him. 'Go ahead,' said he. Thus encouraged, I stated my views. 'You wish to appoint a Catholic as Lieutenant-Governor. You also desire to find a position for Mr. Brecken [then Conservative M.P. for Queen's]. Now I can show you a way in which both these objects can be attained, and more. Mr. Andrew Macdonald has been for some years Postmaster at Charlottetown. He is a devout Catholic, a gentleman as you know, and a highly respected citizen. I may remind you that he was one of the Fathers of Confederation at the Charlottetown and Quebec Conferences in 1864. In addition, he is a pronounced total abstainer, which Mr. Howlan is not. His appointment on that score alone would gratify a number of people to whom his religious belief might perhaps not be equally acceptable. He would take the office, and his appointment would provide the position you are seeking for Brecken. This in turn would make a vacancy in Queens for which Jenkins [Brecken's defeated colleague at the last elections] could run, and thus heal the breach in the Conservative ranks which has been so detrimental to the unity of the party for the past two years.'

Sir John thought well of my suggestion, and carried it out. It worked like a charm. Andrew Macdonald made an excellent Lieutenant-Governor, Brecken an acceptable Postmaster, Jenkins carried the vacant seat in the Commons. In short, everybody was satisfied—except Howlan.

There is a supplement to this story which I may as well recite here. When in turn Andrew Macdonald's period of office expired, Howlan was again in the running for the Lieutenant-Governorship, and again, I flatter myself, I had something to do with preventing or,

at any rate, delaying an appointment which seemed to me undesirable
in the interests of my native province. This time my opinion was not
directly invited, but Sir John received one day a letter from Howlan
pressing for appointment to the Episcopal See of Charlottetown of
the Reverend Father Doyle, of whom I have already spoken, and
asking the Premier to use his influence to that end with the Duke
of Norfolk, Sir Charles Tupper, and other influential people in
England. Sir John handed me over the letter to read, remarking at
the time, 'Howlan says that Doyle has always been a true friend of
ours.' 'Well, Sir,' I made answer, 'Howlan ought to know, for he
tried to seduce him himself!' and I told him the whole story. 'Ha!'
exclaimed Sir John. 'When was that?' 'About fifteen years ago,'
replied I. 'Oh,' said he, 'fifteen years is a long time,' but Howlan
never attained his ambition to be Lieutenant-Governor of Prince
Edward Island during Sir John's lifetime.

During these years I continued to perform assiduously my duties
as Private Secretary. In fact I saw very little of my family, the
younger members of which were generally not up in the morning
when I left, and in bed when I returned at night. Though by no
means demonstrative, the Chief appreciated this service, for he said
to me on more than one occasion that he felt he was keeping me
back, 'but the fact is, I can't spare you. I am an old man now, and
don't like changes.' I of course told him that I was only too pleased
and honoured to continue to serve him, and was quite willing to
take the chances of the future. In the autumn of 1889, when he
took over the portfolio of Railways, he said to me, apropos of the
Assistant Clerkship of the Privy Council, then vacant, 'I'll appoint
you to this if you would like it.' As it was then the equivalent of the
first Assistant Deputy Ministership in the service, which brought
me a substantial increase of salary, I gladly accepted and was gazetted
accordingly. This office I retained until I became Under-Secretary
of State seven years later. I recall an incident in connection with this
appointment. While the minute was in course of preparation,
Chapleau, who was late, came into the Council Chamber where
Sir John and I were sitting before Council began. 'Chapleau,' said
Sir John, 'I was just proposing to appoint Pope, my private secretary,
Assistant Clerk of the Council. What do you say to it?' 'You may

appoint him Chief Justice of Quebec [a post then vacant],' he replied, 'with my full concurrence.' And so I was appointed Assistant Clerk.

Without wishing to appear boastful, I think I may truly say that I took a good deal of more or less administrative work off the Chief's hands. I always opened his letters, and dealt with a certain number without reference to him, exercising, of course, a due discretion in that regard. I possessed the great advantage of knowing every Government supporter in Parliament, and was thus in a position to straighten out the troubles of a good many. The Ministers took their cue from the Chief, and were always most courteous and pleasant. One afternoon at Earnscliffe, Sir John was in his library when some of his colleagues arrived and joined the circle. On one of them indicating that they wished to be alone, Sir John signalled to me to remain, observing, 'Joe is one of us.'

The summer of 1888 was spent more or less uneventfully at Inch Arran Hotel, Dalhousie. It was an uncommonly cold, wet season, particularly in Ontario, chiefly remembered by me as giving occasion for a witticism at the expense of our weather prophets which appeared in a local newspaper during the ensuing September:

> The Mr. Moses Oates, now confined in Brantford gaol on a charge of indecent assault, desires it to be understood that he is not the Mr. Moses Oates who predicted a dry summer.

About this time I had the good fortune to win a prize offered by Lieutenant-Governor Angers, through the Literary and Historical Committee of the 'Cercle Catholique de Québec', of a silver medal for the best essay on 'Jacques Cartier, his Life and Voyages'. A day or two after the announcement appeared, I received this note from Mr. Laurier:

HOUSE OF COMMONS

CANADA

Ottawa, 28th Feb. 1889.

My dear Mr. Pope,

I want you to accept my most warm and most sincere congratulations. Your success affords me really more pleasure than I can express.

Very truly yours,

WILFRID LAURIER

Mr. Joseph Pope.

During the summer of 1888 Prince Roland Bonaparte visited Canada and was entertained by Sir John Macdonald. His Imperial Highness was very cordial and pleasant to me on this occasion. Bearing in mind that his special interest was in all matters appertaining to geographical research, when my little volume appeared I took the liberty of sending him a copy, and received this courteous acknowledgement:

Paris le 5 avril 1890.

Mon cher Monsieur Pope,

J'ai reçu le charmant volume que vous m'avez envoyé. Je vous remercie de cet envoi qui me rappelle le trop court séjour que j'ai fait au Canada, séjour dont j'ai gardé le meilleur souvenir.

Agréez, mon cher Monsieur Pope, l'assurance de mes meilleurs sentiments,

ROLAND BONAPARTE

The year 1890 is chiefly memorable to me as that in which the period of my association with Sir John began to draw to a close. Although fairly well and active, I could not but observe that the weight of years was beginning to tell on him, and that he looked forward to a relinquishment of the cares of state at no very distant period. During his holiday at Rivière du Loup he spoke more than usual of his early political life, and interested himself in pointing out various incidents connected therewith, evidently desirous that I should note them with a view to the future.

In August of this summer he visited Prince Edward Island, where he had not been for twenty years. On this occasion he stayed with my friend Mr. Edward Hodgson, whose house was among my most familiar haunts when a boy. Mr. Hodgson had lost his wife during the preceding autumn, and I remember very well that circumstance being alluded to in the letter of invitation to Sir John, in which he mournfully added that he could now only receive him with 'maimed rites'. It was a proud occasion, this return to my native town under such flattering auspices, and I took great pride in presenting the friends of my youth to the grand old man, who it seemed to me received them with special warmth. Now and then I am afraid I made a slip in my introductions—eighteen years is a long absence— and Sir John chaffed me unmercifully when I unwittingly called the wrong name, but on the whole I got along fairly well, and Mr. Hodgson was literally a host in himself.

Shortly after our return from the seaside, the political campaign was opened in earnest by Sir Richard Cartwright declaring for Unrestricted Reciprocity. This was adopted by the Liberal party, and formed their battle-cry in the next elections. In the meantime Sir John paid a visit to Halifax and Saint John, in the course of which he addressed several meetings on the political issues of the day.

On his return to Ottawa preparations were undertaken for his final political struggle, which it was generally realized could not be far distant. Now with this campaign I was closely associated. I was at the Chief's side from the day on which the minute advising dissolution was agreed to in Council on the 2nd of February 1891, down to the close of the polls on the 5th of March. The leading incidents of the time are ineffaceably stamped upon my memory. It was, therefore, with no little surprise that I read in Professor Skelton's recent work, *The Life and Letters of Sir Wilfrid Laurier*, an account of the 1890–1 campaign, much of which was quite new to me. I learned then for the first time that the plans of the Canadian Pacific Railway entered largely into this election; that the necessity of upholding the Government was essential to the success of the railway company's policy; that to accomplish this object the railway management had to 'shell out as never before', and so forth and so on. Where Professor Skelton learned that the Canadian Pacific Railway was in league with the Government during the elections of 1891, or that John Henry Pope was devising schemes at that period, I cannot form a conjecture.

It matters little now what were the issues in that election, but a regard for the facts compels me to say that Professor Skelton's description of the relations existing at that time between the Government and the Canadian Pacific Railway is incorrect. These elections were restricted, as completely as it is possible to confine a general election to a single issue, to the policy of unrestricted reciprocity with the United States. The Canadian Pacific Railway was not a factor in the contest. The company was not seeking financial assistance. Their claim against the Government had gone to arbitration. In this arbitration their interests were confided to

Mr. Edward Blake, the erstwhile leader of the Opposition. More-over, the relations between the Government and the railway were no longer cordial as of old. Stephen had resigned and gone to England, cherishing, we are told by Mr. Van Horne's biographer, 'a deep resentment against Sir John Macdonald for the sufferings and mortification he had experienced at Ottawa, and, having reluctantly entered upon the Canadian Pacific enterprise and made great sacrifices to patriotism, he was indignant at the unworthy motives constantly attributed to him by a section of the Canadian press. He was now intensely chagrined and disgusted by Sir John's refusal, owing to political exigencies, to redeem his promise to give the company running rights over the Intercolonial from Moncton to Saint John and Halifax; and he had made known to his friends his determination to shake the dust of Canada from his feet. The moment was well chosen. The Canadian Pacific was firmly estab-lished. Despite an exceedingly light crop in Ontario and a steady diminution in the rates for passengers and freight, the company was prospering. Numerous branches were in the course of con-struction between Quebec and the Pacific, and the connections necessary to full completion of the system were not few in number.'[2]

One has but to read the letters which passed between Macdonald and Stephen on the eve of Stephen's departure from Canada in 1889 to appreciate that the latter was not in a mood to 'shell out' at that particular time.[3] Between Van Horne, who succeeded Stephen in the presidency, and John Henry Pope there existed a personal feud so bitter that the two men did not speak for some years, and shook hands only on the latter's death-bed.

The reader is referred to the imaginary conversation recorded in Volume I, page 411, of Professor Skelton's work, to which I have already referred:

> *Before the day was over they learned that the report was correct,*
> *and that Canada was soon to be in the throes of a general election.*
> *What was still more to the point, they learned in due time that their*

[2] Walter Vaughan, *The Life and Work of Sir William Van Horne* (New York, 1920), p. 162.
[3] Sir J. Pope, *Correspondence of Sir John Macdonald* (Toronto, 1921), p. 454 *et seq.*

own necessities had been the argument that had turned the scale for dissolution. Macdonald had spoken to John Henry Pope of his promise to Stephen and Van Horne. Whereupon Pope replied: 'That makes this just the time to bring on the election.' 'How's that?' 'The C.P.R. crowd can't simply let you lose, with all they have at stake; they will have to shell out as never before.' The reasoning was irresistible.

This conversation is represented as having taken place shortly before the 2nd of February 1891. Now John Henry Pope died on the 1st of April 1889. In February 1891 Stephen was in England. Macdonald and Van Horne were in different parts of Canada, seeing each other but seldom. In fact I do not recall their having met during the campaign. It is true that Van Horne strongly opposed unrestricted reciprocity, not by reason of any particular regard for the Government, but because, according to his biographer, he was 'sincerely convinced that [unrestricted] reciprocity would irreparably damage the prospects of his company and retard the development of Canada's natural resources for a generation'. One subject, and one only absorbed public attention—our trade relations with the United States.

The campaign, though stubbornly contested, was not the desperate battle of 1886-7. Various circumstances contributed thereto. To begin with, it did not seem to me that there was in the latter year that absolute unity of sentiment and of action among the Opposition which marked the earlier conflict. Though nothing occurred in the nature of a schism, it was more or less felt that a certain number of the Liberal party was not enthusiastic over the idea of Unrestricted Reciprocity, involving as it did discrimination against England, which had been in a measure forced on them by Sir Richard Cartwright, and that their late leader, Mr. Edward Blake, did not subscribe thereto. He declined renomination in his old constituency, and throughout the campaign remained silent, but on polling day there appeared a letter in the press over his signature which confirmed the rumours associated with his name, and showed him to be adverse to the policy of the party of which he had recently been the leader.

Then there was the *exposé* caused by the publication of the Farrer pamphlet. Edward Farrer, editor of the *Globe*, had written about this time a brochure in the interest of certain American interests, in which he openly advocated the annexation of Canada to the United States, and went to the length of suggesting certain lines of policy best calculated to promote that object. The proof sheets of this scandalous document were placed in the hands of Sir John and by him given to the world at a great public meeting in Toronto on the 17th of February 1891, at which I was present. I well remember the excitement produced thereby. Farrer's treason was so flagrant that there seemed no escape from its damaging results. That it injured the cause of the Opposition there is little doubt, though to what extent it was difficult to say. For as against Farrer's conduct there could be adduced the undoubted loyalty of numbers among the Liberal party, of Messrs. Laurier, Mowat, and others, who, it was well known, were true to British interests, and had no thought of bartering their allegiance for Yankee influence or gold. Farrer's declaration, however, that Sir John Macdonald's disappearance from the stage would be the signal for a movement in Canada towards annexation, proved, in what was generally recognized as Macdonald's last fight, of immense assistance to the old chief.

But if the prospects of the Government were somewhat more favourable in 1891 than in 1887 as far as I personally was concerned, I shall always look back on Sir John's last election campaign as the most arduous experience of my life. We left Ottawa for Toronto on the 15th of February. On the night of the 17th took place the Farrer *exposé*, with all its attendant excitement. After a short stay in Western Ontario, Sir John left for Kingston where his presence was urgently required both in his own and surrounding constituencies. His strength proved unequal to the task, and after a few days he was obliged to take to his bed. To me this period was one of undiluted anxiety. To begin with I was alone, and the task was too much for one man. Sir John stayed with Dr. Williamson, his brother-in-law, a widower who lived in a desolate-looking house with the minimum of comforts of any kind, painfully lacking the evidence of a woman's touch, and was besieged by politicians who thought only of their immediate interests, intent only on extracting from him the last measure of service. 'Joe,' said Sir John to me one afternoon as he lay half dozing in his cheerless room, 'if you would know the depth of meanness of human nature, you have got to be a Prime Minister running a general election!'

Every day presented fresh difficulties. Sometimes he was so weak I dared not trouble him with the letters and telegrams which were pouring in from all sides, and frequently I knew not what course to pursue. In the absence of anyone to consult, I could only take each day as it came, and deal with the circumstances as they arose, but the anxieties of the period were great. Added to my troubles, a severe cold brought on attacks of nose-bleeding, and altogether I was very wretched. Sir John, even when better and able to be up, was notably less energetic than formerly, disposed to be languid and apathetic, which was a new role for him. His Kingston supporters, however, worked like Trojans, and re-elected him by a thumping majority, which gratified him exceedingly.[4] On the eve of election day he rallied sufficiently to leave Kingston for Ottawa where he took to his bed, and so did I. But whereas I was a young man, he was an old one 'broken by the storms of State'. A short period of rest restored me to my normal health, but his course was run. Elsewhere I have related the story of his last days. On the 30th of May he was stricken with paralysis, and after lingering eight days in a semi-conscious condition, he passed away quietly and painlessly on the 6th of June. His death, while not unexpected, evoked a universal manifestation of sorrow such as is seldom witnessed. For myself, I mourned for him as a father, and shall ever hold his memory in grateful and affectionate remembrance.

[4] In 1887 his majority in Kingston was 17; in 1891, 483.

1891 – 1893

*Mr. J. J. C. Abbott Succeeds to the Premiership/
Memoirs of Sir John Macdonald / The Bering
Sea Arbitration / Canadian Delegation in London/
Houses of Parliament, Westminster Abbey and St.
Paul's / Charms of Oxford / Paris / Personnel
Composing the Arbitration Tribunal / The Quai
d'Orsay / Recollections and Impressions of Paris/
The Award / Return to Canada*

ON the night on which Sir John died, Lady Macdonald addressed
a letter to Lord Stanley of Preston, the Governor-General, begging
His Excellency, in the interests of Canada and of the Conservative
party, to send for Sir Charles Tupper to form the new administration
made necessary by the death of the Prime Minister. Whatever may
be thought of the propriety of Lady Macdonald's course in thus
volunteering her advice to the Crown upon a matter of this kind,
there exists no doubt in my mind that her counsel in itself was
sound and should have been followed. Sir Charles was by all odds
the man for the occasion. Though he had filled the office of High
Commissioner for Canada in London during the previous seven years,
he had kept in close touch with the Dominion and its affairs, and
by reason of his experience, energy, courage, resourcefulness, and
boundless optimism, he was, in my judgement, undoubtedly the
best man to take up the mantle of leadership. He happened to be in
Vienna at the time, attending an international postal conference, but
he would have responded to the call if requested to do so. That he

was not invited is, I have understood, due to the personal relations existing between the Governor-General and himself. It is right also to say that there were those in the Cabinet opposed to his selection. A leading member of the late Government told me at the time that not one of his colleagues would have followed Sir Charles Tupper had Lord Stanley called upon him to form a Government, but, with all deference to the ex-minister, this could scarcely have been the case because, when five years later their unskilful administration of affairs had well-nigh wrecked the Conservative party, those who remained were only too ready to serve under Sir Charles Tupper when invited to do so. At the time of Macdonald's death the political outlook for that party was far from rosy. In addition to the usual disintegrating forces at work, the Opposition confidently looked forward to obtaining power, within a short period, by what were known as the Tarte-McGreevy charges of corruption brought by the late Joseph Israel Tarte against Sir Hector Langevin, then Minister of Public Works. Owing perhaps to a certain cirumstance which I shall proceed to relate, I was not so much impressed as the majority of people by the inherent gravity of these charges, nor by the remorseless and implacable attitude manifested in their regard by Mr. Tarte and his friends.

One day during the Chief's last illness, Mr. Tarte called at Earnscliffe and told me that he particularly wished a few minutes of private conversation with Sir John; that he had a matter of great urgency and importance to communicate to him. Mr. Tarte, whom I knew very well as an old-time Conservative, went on to hint that a settlement of the Langevin-McGreevy affair was not beyond the bounds of possibility. He did not at the time know how near Sir John was to his end, nor indeed did any of us. At his pressing request I went upstairs and repeated the substance of this conversation to the sick man, who simply said, turning his face to the wall as he spoke, 'It is too late now', and would not see him.

The man best fitted by his intellectual attainments to succeed Macdonald was Sir John Thompson, but though recognized as very able and bearing a high character for probity, it was generally realized that the fact of his being a convert from Methodism to the Church of Rome would prove a fatal bar to his political ambitions.

He was, nevertheless, the first choice of the Governor-General. On his declining the office, and on his advice, the Governor-General sent for Mr. J. J. C. Abbott, and thus the man who Sir John Macdonald less than three years before declared to me 'had not a single qualification for the office' became his successor. Mr. Abbott's motives in accepting this responsibility were of the most disinterested character. A first-rate commercial lawyer and long in public life, politics had ever played a secondary part with him. Upwards of seventy years of age, of indifferent health, and without any special aptitude for the post, he accepted office only from a high sense of public duty, with the intention of relinquishing it at the earliest moment consistent with his obligations. In fact he spoke of himself, openly and habitually, as a 'stop gap', and during the period of his administration he relied largely upon Thompson.

On the evening of Sunday the 14th of June, a day or two after the return of the Macdonald funeral party from Kingston, an elderly gentleman of unpretentious appearance called and asked to see me. On being told that I was not at home, he requested to see my wife, and on receiving some unsatisfactory reply asked if he might come in and rest a little while, the day being warm and he tired. My wife coming downstairs at that moment was surprised to find sitting in the hall the new Prime Minister. He had called, he said, to ask me if I would act as his private secretary until he could familiarize himself a little with his new duties and surroundings. I, of course, was only too glad to be of service to him in that or any other capacity, and I remained with him some months until he was suited, when I took up the duties of Assistant Clerk of the Privy Council, to which Sir John had appointed me two years before.

During the years 1891 and 1892 I employed most of the time I could spare from my official duties in sorting, classifying, and arranging Sir John Macdonald's papers, which were very voluminous and required much going over.

The question of when and by whom his memoirs were to be written soon came up for consideration. Though fearing that I could not avoid the responsibility, and while in other circumstances I should not have been unwilling to assume it, I realized that I was not a free agent in the matter, and that in undertaking the task of

Sir John's biographer, I might find myself as a civil servant in an embarrassing position in the event of a change of Government, a by-no-means-improbable contingency. It is true that a Prime Minister's private secretary occupies a privileged position as regards politics, and from the day I ceased to fill that office I detached myself from all political associations and devoted myself exclusively to my official duties as Assistant Clerk of the Privy Council. Further, when in politics, I had so borne myself as to make friends of the 'Mammon of unrighteousness' in the shape of the Opposition, to which, doubtless, I was largely indebted to the personal friendship of Mr. Laurier. Notwithstanding these advantages I realized that it behoved me to walk warily. Apart from prudential reasons, I thought it too early to begin. I felt that it would be better on every ground, including that of adequate performance, to allow some years to elapse, when political animosities should have died down, so as to be afforded a better perspective in which to view Macdonald's life and work. It was all very well, I argued, for irresponsible persons to take advantage of the present wave of sympathy and interest inspired by Macdonald's death, to get out 'lives' while the great leader's memory was green. I could not approach the subject in any such commercial spirit. With this thought in my mind I declined several tempting offers from enterprising publishers in the summer of 1891. I found, however, a very general desire among the members of Sir John's family and immediate friends that I should not delay the preparation of what was represented to me as a duty to my old chief's memory.

There could be no doubt as to Sir John's general wishes in the matter. Indeed, he said to me in so many words, 'I want you to be my literary executor.' In order to make quite sure that by 'literary executor' he meant to include the preparation of his biography, I consulted Dr. S. E. Dawson, at that time Queen's Printer, an old and intimate friend of Macdonald's, and asked him for his views on the subject. He replied:

Ottawa, 22nd March, 1892.

Dear Mr. Pope,

Your letter of the 21st of March is just to hand, and in reply I beg to say that it was most distinctly arranged between the late Sir

John A. Macdonald and myself that you were to be the writer of the projected political biography. Several names were submitted to him, but he selected yours, for he said that he could speak with much more freedom to you than to anybody else, because you stood almost in the relation of a son to him on account of your intimate knowledge of his political life and having been so long his Private Secretary.

This was so clearly understood that if you remember, I drew up an outline of the proposed work, and even came up to Ottawa and selected from the Library several works to serve as models of the projected memoirs. Sir John promised that he would dictate to you as he found leisure. It was put off from time to time but finally arranged that when he went to Rivière du Loup he would take an hour a day for the purpose; and with the notes thus given and the papers which he proposed to entrust to you, he thought that the work could be compiled.

I always felt sorry that Sir John had not time to complete his intentions: he spoke of many things of which he alone had the threads and which he intended to explain. There are many passages in the history of Canada which he alone could have elucidated; and I am afraid that now he is gone these matters can never be made clear.

If you have occasion to use this letter pray do so. The whole thing was carefully talked over, and there are one or two other persons who are aware of the fact besides myself.

Sincerely yours,

Joseph Pope, Esq.   S. E. DAWSON

Lady Macdonald was also of the same mind as Dr. Dawson.

Ottawa, Canada, July 8th, 1892.

Dear Mr. Pope,

I read with much interest the letter of Mr. S. E. Dawson to you, of date March 22, 1892, and I share with him to the fullest extent the desire therein expressed that you should undertake the preparation of a political memoir of my dear husband.

I feel the more anxious that you should be the author of this work because, not many weeks before he was called hence, when the advantage of such a memoir was brought before him, Sir John himself said to me that he wished you to write it, as you had been for many years closely associated with both his public and private life.

In recalling the events of that time and the intimate relation in which you stood to Sir John during the last ten years of his life, I feel *sure that no one is better, or perhaps so well, qualified to deal with subjects so important in the history of our country, as yourself.*

Sir John held you in high esteem and regard, and I know spoke to you fully and unreservedly on many points which you will thus be able to deal with satisfactorily, and the daily intercourse which drew you so near to him will give, no doubt, an additional value and interest to what you may say.

To further, as far as possible, the adequate preparation of these memoirs, I have, in view of Sir John's desire that you should write them, given you free access to the mass of valuable letters and papers which he had so carefully preserved during his long and eventful life, and you have my warmest wishes for the successful completion of what will I feel sure be an important and valuable literary effort.

I hope, if this letter can be made useful, that you will not consider it as a private communication.

Believe me to remain,

Yours very sincerely,

MACDONALD OF EARNSCLIFFE

Joseph Pope, Esq.

Finally, with many misgivings I consented to attempt the task, first stipulating that I should be the sole judge of what the memoirs should or should not contain, and further that my story should not come down as a connected narrative later than 1873. The nearness of time and the presence amongst us of so many active participants in the scenes of only eighteen years before, rendered this an essential condition so far as I was concerned. To this Lady Macdonald agreed, and while naturally desirous to see the work begun, she never sought to hurry its progress, but was most considerate to me in this respect throughout. I set to work in the autumn of 1892, and my work appeared in November 1894.

Towards the close of the year 1892, I became associated with preparations then going forward looking to the holding of an arbitration for the purpose of adjusting certain differences which had arisen between Great Britain, on behalf of Canada, and the United States, in respect of the Bering Sea. In the year 1821 the Emperor Alexander of Russia issued a ukase granting exclusive fishing and whaling rights to Russian subjects, and prohibiting all foreign vessels from approaching the coasts of Russian territories in the North

Pacific Ocean within one hundred Italian miles. Both Great Britain and the United States protested against this extravagant claim of maritime supremacy, the result being that the United States made a convention with Russia dated 5/17 April 1824, and Great Britain a convention with Russia dated 16/28 February 1825, agreeing to the abandonment of these pretensions.

On the 30th of March 1867, the United States and Russia made a further treaty by which Russia sold Alaska to the United States for the sum of $7,200,000 in gold. In 1886 the United States revived the old Russian claim of seizing vessels in the open sea until the point was decided against them by the Bering Sea Arbitration Tribunal sitting in Paris in 1893. In the same year (1886) certain British vessels were seized in Bering Sea by the United States authorities when pursuing their calling seventy miles from land, and were subsequently condemned by the district Court of Alaska, the masters and mates being imprisoned and fined.

Great Britain protested against this action on the part of the United States, and negotiations took place which resulted in a treaty between the two countries, dated 29 February 1892, by which they agreed to submit the question to a tribunal of arbitration to be composed of seven arbitrators, two British, two American, and one each to be named by the President of the French Republic, the King of Italy, and the King of Sweden and Norway. This tribunal met in Paris in the early part of 1893, and its award, which was adverse to the pretensions of the United States as regards their claim to consider Bering Sea a *mare clausum*, was delivered on the 15th of August following. Mr. (afterwards Sir) Charles Hibbert Tupper, then Canadian Minister of Marine and Fisheries, was appointed Her Majesty's agent before this tribunal. His secretary falling ill, he asked me to accompany him to Paris in that capacity, to which I gladly consented, as I had never crossed the Atlantic. I note in my diary, 'Everything comes to him who waits, and I am off for England and France.' Our party consisted of Mr. and Mrs. Tupper, Miss Caron, my wife and myself. We sailed from New York for Liverpool on Wednesday, the 25th of January, in the White Star steamer *Majestic*, between 9,000 and 10,000 tons, then accounted a miracle of size and speed. In size, of course, she has been far outclassed, but as regards speed the disparity is not so great, for even at that time we made a roughish January voyage in a week, docking at Liverpool just seven days after leaving New York.

The only drawback to what would otherwise have been an enjoyable passage was my wife's severe and persistent sea-sickness. It was her first ocean voyage, and it well-nigh proved disastrous, for she was extremely ill throughout, and did not appear on deck until we entered the Mersey. On landing at Liverpool we took the boat-train for London and on arrival at Euston drove at once to Sir Charles Tupper's house in Cromwell Road, where we were most hospitably received and lodged during our stay in London. Next morning I drove with Mr. Tupper to the Foreign Office to meet those officials with whom I was to be associated and also to get an idea of our work.

Mr. Tupper, who had been over several times during the past year arranging for the arbitration, and who was consequently quite at home in the Foreign Office, introduced me to several men of whom I was destined to see a great deal, e.g., Messrs. R. P. Maxwell, W. C. Cartwright, Charles Russell (son of the Attorney-General), Ashley Froude (son of the historian), and others. I also met my dear friend Dr. George Dawson, a universal favourite there as everywhere else. As I found time, my wife and I 'took in' the regulation sights, the Abbey, the Tower, the Houses of Parliament, and so forth, with all of which I was greatly impressed. Everything was much as I had pictured save that St. Paul's somewhat exceeded my expectations. The sum of the impressions produced on me by my sight-seeing in London during the first month of my stay was a feeling of pride and exultation that I belonged to a country of so much glory and greatness, that I had a part and share in this proud heritage which nothing could take away.

Through the kindness of Mr. Munro Ferguson I obtained a seat in the Distinguished Strangers Gallery, where I saw and heard several eminent personages, among others Gladstone, Morley, Churchill, Harcourt, Asquith, and others. I thought Gladstone looked very old. He was then eighty-four and lived five years longer. We also visited the House of Lords. Lord Kimberley and the Marquess of Huntly were speaking at the time, and I had my first look at Lord Salisbury, for whom I had always entertained a strong admiration. Shortly after reaching London we dined at the Leonard Courtneys' (to whom we brought letters from his brother, Mr. J. M. Courtney), where we met Lord and Lady Ripon, both of whom spoke at length and most appreciatively of Sir John Macdonald, whom they had known in Washington in 1871, Mr. Munro Ferguson, Mr. Leveson Gower, and others, from several of whom we experienced much kindness.

Our arrival in England coincided with a period of great political excitement. I find in my diary under the 16th of February, 'Nothing is talked here but Gladstone's new Home Rule Bill which he recently introduced.' Public opinion in London was largely opposed to the G.O.M. and all his works. Apropos of this I received a well-deserved rebuke from Sir Charles Tupper. After returning from dining somewhere, some of us were recounting what had taken place, and I happened to mention that round the dinner table we amused ourselves with composing epitaphs on the G.O.M., such for example as 'Here lies W.E.G.: he always did', or indulging in such witticisms as 'This must be true, for Mr. Gladstone has since denied it', when Sir Charles Tupper suddenly interposed with, 'And don't you think you young men might be better employed than in publicly disparaging the Prime Minister of England?' The reproof was just, and during the remainder of my stay in England I kept my opinions concerning the G.O.M. strictly to myself.

Early in February we paid a brief visit to Oxford, where Mrs. Tupper's sister, Mrs. Jordan and her husband, lived.

I experienced many consolations at Oxford, the greatest attractions of which of course centre round its colleges and churches. These venerable buildings possess for me an inexpressible charm. We visited St. Michael's Church, the Church of St. Mary Magdalen, and many other places of interest, particularly Newman's haunts, Oriel, the Church of St. Mary the Virgin, and Trinity—'My Own Trinity' —as well as those of the saintly Keble and a multitude of others eminent in every walk of life.

My wife and I attended High Mass on Sunday at the Catholic Church, a modern red brick structure with a fine altar, the gift of the Marquess of Bute. The service was admirably rendered, giving the impression that those in charge were English gentlemen, a class for whom I confess my partiality. I was much gratified by the intonation at the end of the Mass of the prayer *Pro reginam nostram Victoriam*, which is not always remembered in Canada.

Upon our return to London from Oxford we plunged into work again at the Foreign Office, where I suffered a good deal from cold. In fact, I wore my heavy overcoat frequently at my desk during the winter months. The absence of a uniform temperature to which I was accustomed I found at times rather trying. We dined out quite often, and attended several very pleasant theatre parties at which we saw Penley in *Charley's Aunt*, Toole in *Walker Bondon*, *Our Boys*, *Liberty Hall*, and a number of other amusing plays and play-actors. I remember dining on one of these occasions with my wife and the Tuppers at the Berkeley Hotel, the guests of Messrs. Maxwell and Froude of the Foreign Office, and afterwards going to the Garrick, where we heard *Diplomacy*, a very powerful play, excellently performed. Our dinner too was uncommonly good, and I note in my diary, 'Altogether this has been one of the most pleasant evenings we have spent since we left home.' I derived great pleasure from my visits to St. Paul's and Westminster Abbey, where I sometimes attended Sunday afternoon service. On Sunday the 18th of February we went to Low Mass at the Brompton Oratory, and then attended service in the Temple Church with Mr. Russell Roberts, a friend of the Tuppers.

Meanwhile it was arranged that the arbitration should be held at the French Foreign Office (known as the Quai d'Orsay), where the Government placed two spacious chambers at our disposal. The tribunal, as I have said, consisted of seven members—two English, Lord Hannen and Sir John Thompson, the Canadian Prime Minister; two American, Mr. Justice Harlan and Senator Morgan; one French, Baron de Courcel; one Italian, the Marquis Visconti Venosta; and a Norwegian, M. Gregers Gram. Our leading Counsel were Sir Charles Russell, the Attorney-General; Sir Richard Webster, ex-Attorney-General; and Mr. Christopher Robinson of Toronto. It was settled that the Tribunal should assemble in Paris on the 23rd of February, but in view of the impossibility of Sir John Thompson's being there on that date, an adjournment for a month was arranged for. We went over to Paris, however, for the formal opening which took place on the 23rd of February, the date originally fixed, and which lasted just half an hour. We were present the same evening at a ball given by President Carnot at the Elysée for which several hundred invitations had been issued (a case, I presume, of *post hoc, sed non ergo propter hoc*). The crush was overpowering, so much that it took us an hour to get in. We found there only the *bourgeoisie*, as the French aristocracy would scorn to go to the Elysée during a Republican régime.

An example of this class was afforded in the person of the Vicomte H. de Manneville, who if my memory serves me aright had some post in the French Foreign Office. This dapper little gentleman, while very friendly to us, resented the familiar attitude of some of our journalistic retinue. I remember one occasion when a London reporter, not particularly distinguished for his modesty of demeanour, addressed the Vicomte as 'my dear fellow', the little man turning on him with, 'Sir, I vish you would not call me a fellow!'

We remained a few days in Paris sight-seeing, returning to London on the 26th, where we remained until the 17th of March when we all returned to Paris to attend the first full meeting of the Tribunal, summoned for the 23rd. On the 20th the Tuppers and ourselves went down to the Gare de l'Ouest to meet Sir John and Lady Thompson and Lady Caron, who were putting up at the Hôtel du Jardin overlooking the Tuileries Gardens. The evening before leaving London, Mr. Tupper entertained the whole Bering Sea party at dinner at the Windsor Hotel, Victoria Street. Twenty-three of us sat down, and a pleasant evening it was.

The formal opening of the Tribunal took place at the French Foreign Office on Thursday, the 23rd of March, being prefaced by a gracefully worded address of welcome from Mr. Jules Develle, the French Minister of Foreign Affairs, after which the meeting was convened under the presidency of Baron de Courcel, and promptly adjourned until the 4th of April. On completion of these formalities we all drove to the Elysée, and were presented to President Carnot. My wife and I then called on Lady Dufferin, the wife of our Ambassador, who was gracious and charming as she used to be in Ottawa fifteen years before.

I visited the Madeleine, of course, and was much impressed by the solemn and affecting manner in which the ceremonies of Holy Week were carried out, being particularly moved while gazing on the beautiful statue of Mary Magdalen over the high altar, at the chant of the words of the Passion: *Amen dico vobis, ubicumque praedicatum fuerit hoc Evangelium in toto mundo, dicetur, et quod haec fecit in memoriam ejus.*[1]

Our party put up at the Hotel Chatham, rue Daunou, where we secured suitable accommodation and were quite a happy family for some months to come.

The Hon. C. H. Tupper, as British agent before the Arbitration Tribunal, was our recognized chief. Sir Charles Russell (afterwards Lord Russell of Killowen), at that time Attorney-General of England, a forceful domineering man of great brilliancy and power; Sir Richard Webster (later Lord Alverstone), both eminent in their profession; and Mr. C. Robinson, Q.C., of Toronto, were the leading British counsel. Between the first and last named there existed the greatest possible contrast. Russell was bold, aggressive, and could at times be impatient and irritable in manner to the point of rudeness; Robinson was a mild, timid, retiring man, of singularly modest mien. Sir Richard Webster was of a type different from the other two, and in my judgement decidedly inferior to either in intellectual force. His leading characteristics appeared to be extreme industry, coupled with an abnormal love of detail which showed itself in many ways and seemed at times scarcely compatible with the sense of dignity which should appertain to one who had recently filled the high office of Attorney-General of England.

On the working staff I was perhaps most intimate with Mr. R. P. Maxwell of the Foreign Office, with whom I became associated shortly after my arrival in England, and for whom, together with Ashley Froude, I formed a high regard. Maxwell and I were destined to meet on subsequent occasions, but Froude I have never seen since the day I bade him farewell at the Hotel Chatham in the summer of 1893. Another friendship I formed at that time was with Charles Russell (afterwards the Hon. Sir Charles Russell, Bt.), son of the

---

[1] Verily I say unto you, Wheresoever this gospel shall be preached in the whole world, there shall also this, that this woman hath done, be told for a memorial of her.—St. Matt. XXVI, 13.

Attorney-General. While in many ways the younger Russell was gifted with a goodly share of his father's ability, and while of an equally warm-hearted, impulsive, and generous disposition, he possessed a somewhat gentler nature than the elder man, which rendered him a special favourite in all quarters.

The American party lodged at the Hotel Continental in the rue de Castiglione, the Hon. John W. Foster, sometime Secretary of State, being the agent of the United States Government. Though considered a rather pronounced anti-Britisher in those days (in after years he proved sound to the core), his bark was always a good deal worse than his bite, and both he and Mrs. Foster became warm friends of ours, both on this trip and afterwards in Quebec, Washington, and elsewhere. The leading American counsel were Messrs. Phelps, Carter, Blodgett, and Coudert, together with Messrs. William Williams and Robert Lansing, the last-named destined to be Mr. Wilson's Secretary of State during the greater part of the Great War (1917–19). Mrs. Lansing was the daughter of Mr. and Mrs. Foster, and we all became fast friends.

My duties as private secretary to the British Agent were not unduly onerous, though we all did a good deal of work behind the scenes. The Tribunal began its regular sessions on the 4th of April, convening at 11.30 a.m. on Tuesdays, Wednesdays, Thursdays, and Fridays, suspending operations for *déjeuner* at one o'clock and adjourning until four. The arbitrators sat on a dais slightly elevated above the floor of the chamber. I forget the precise order of seating, but I remember that the Marquis Venosta was placed between the two American arbitrators, each flanked by a huge spittoon which was not merely for ornament, and I used to derive a certain degree of amusement in watching the trepidation manifested by the stately old Italian on hearing any warning signals of impending use of these articles, lest at any time one or other of his American colleagues should fail either in directness or accuracy of aim.

We occupied two spacious and lofty rooms in the Foreign Office, in one of which the Tribunal held its sittings, and the other in which the *déjeuner* was served, a sumptuous repast provided daily for forty or fifty people. Various little incidents connected with this Tribunal impressed themselves on my memory. I recall the absence of blotting paper, its use being supplied by sand which one lightly spread over the letter; the exclusive employment of quill pens instead of steel nibs; and so on. In the proceedings before the Tribunal I could not help noticing the overbearing manner which the leading English barristers habitually manifested towards their juniors. I used often to wonder how the younger men took it all so much as a matter of course, but then I had no experience of the English bar.

The American counsel led off in a series of elaborate speeches, going at great length into the questions before the Tribunal, treating exhaustively of the seals from every point of view—international, legal, historical, diplomatic, and zoological. Though true to their custom on like occasions of claiming everything in sight, I think the American lawyers must have been so far conscious of the weakness of their case on what were known as questions of juris-dictional right, as to rely largely upon the existence of an alleged right of property in the seals visiting the Pribylof Islands, that is, on a proprietary interest accruing from the American doctrine of 'husbandry' of the seals in Bering Sea. Considerations of space and perhaps of interest forbid that I should give the merest outline of the leading speeches on the occasion, but I remember particularly amid all the wealth of argument on the part of brilliant counsel in support of the 'husbandry' claim, the happy contention of Mr. Robinson, to which I shall refer later on.

Leaving the precincts of the Quai d'Orsay for the present, let me recall a few of the lighter incidents of our stay in the gay capital in which I found myself. Needless to say, Paris had for me much of interest—the Eiffel Tower, the Arc de Triomphe, Napoleon's Tomb, the Louvre, the Madeleine, which I went through for the second time, and to which I occasionally resorted at the close of a busy day. These and many other objects I very much enjoyed.

I had quite looked forward to hearing High Mass at the Madeleine on Easter Sunday, but in this I was disappointed, for though I arrived in good time, I found the church already filled to overflowing, and I had to give up my seat to a companion. The same difficulty as regards seats happened on more than one occasion, which afforded me much satisfaction, as tending to disprove the idea prevalent in

some quarters that the churches of Paris were almost empty, or at
any rate were frequented only by women. I particularly noticed
that while a majority of the congregations were women, there was
always a fair proportion of men.

During the afternoon of Easter Sunday my wife and I drove through
the Bois de Boulogne, a lovely day with everything at its best.
During this whole spring we were favoured both in France and
England with exceptionally warm sunny weather of which we took
full advantage. On Low Sunday nearly our whole party, including
my wife, went on an excursion to St. Cloud. I did not go, being
incapacitated by an attack of gout which used to bother me occasionally in those days, principally in the way of interfering with my
locomotion. On one occasion I tripped and fell headlong down a
long flight of stairs in the Chatham, fortunately without injury.
I do not think that there could have been any connection between
these attacks and my mode of life, as I was always very moderate
both in eating and drinking, but the subject recalls to my mind
many hospitable occasions during that Paris visit. The official
entertainment started with a dinner given in the Chatham by Sir
Charles Russell and Sir Richard Webster, as joint hosts to the
American counsel in the arbitration. I remember the ceremonious
manner in which Sir Charles, who presided, pronounced the old-
fashioned Oxford grace (rather an unusual proceeding nowadays):
'*Benedictus benedicat*'. Entertainments and excursions of various
kinds followed in quick succession. I remember the occasion of my
first meeting with the Attorney-General. Arriving at the Chatham
the evening before, Sir Charles ordered breakfast for 9 o'clock next
morning—an English breakfast, at the English time, and in the
English way. In consequence, nothing quite suited him, the *chef*
probably being in bed at that time. 'What is that?' said he to the
waiter, turning over with a spoon something which purported to
be an omelette, 'Looks like a geological formation!' Once he went
for a drive on the top of a bus. He mounted at random, not knowing
anything about the vehicle or where it was bound. As it happened,
this bus when it reached its destination stopped there, and the driver
told Sir Charles so, suggesting at the same time that he descend,
which he refused to do. It was in vain that the driver represented to

him that the bus was not going farther. 'No, I'll not budge,' replied he. '*J'y suis, j'y reste.*' How he got back I do not remember.

On another occasion, he and Mr. Robinson were together at a theatre for which Sir Charles had taken seats. Owing to a misunderstanding, some time later a lady and gentleman arrived holding tickets for the same seats. With characteristic modesty Mr. Robinson rose to give way, but Sir Charles restrained him, saying, 'Don't stir. We paid for these places and I propose to occupy them'—the lady and gentleman standing by all the time. After saying, '*Mais, Monsieur, c'est impossible,*' two or three times without producing any effect, the usher went away and shortly afterwards returned with a superior official of some sort who was no more successful. Finally, the head man said to the other, '*C'est un Anglais,*' and gave up the attempt to dislodge our friends. It was as though he had said, 'He is an Englishman, there is no use arguing with him.'

These little anecdotes may serve to illustrate one phase, and that not the most attractive, of Sir Charles Russell's composite character. He at the same time possessed many of the attributes of a great man. To commanding ability and boundless courage, energy, and resource, he joined much generosity of feeling and kindness of heart which compelled regard and admiration and must, in the case of those who knew him intimately, have inspired much genuine affection.

Though I was not particularly drawn to Sir Richard Webster at any time, I must say I admired his loyalty to the Attorney-General during the whole of the arbitration proceedings. At the time of their first association in the case, Webster was the Attorney-General and Russell the associate counsel. When the Government changed at home, their roles were reversed: Russell became Attorney-General and Webster associate counsel, yet the latter accepted the fortunes of war with equanimity and bore with exemplary dignity and self-restraint the little eccentricities of his somewhat peremptory and exacting colleague.

On the 2nd of May Mr. Carter concluded his argument before the tribunal, having taken nine days.

On the 6th of May I attended a large dinner given by the British Chamber of Commerce at the Hotel Terminus to the British side of the Bering Sea Commission. Sir Edward Blount, an Englishman who had resided in Paris for sixty years, and was president of the Chemin de Fer de l'Ouest, presided. Mr. Tupper spoke very well as did Sir Charles Russell and Sir R. Webster.

On Sunday the 7th, after early Mass at the Madeleine, my wife, Miss Caron, Maxwell, and I went out to Versailles, and spent the day there, lunched, drove, and saw the fountains play. We also visited the two Trianons, in which I was rather disappointed. I note in my diary under that date that 'the long-looked-for rain has come at last. The drought has lasted seventy days and is quite unparalleled.'

To return to the Quai d'Orsay. On the 10th of May Sir Charles Russell opened the case for Great Britain with a long speech of great brilliancy and power. His closing peroration seemed to produce a visible effect upon the members of the Tribunal. Sir Charles, after speaking twelve days, thus concluded:

> There are two Great Powers before you: One a representative of the civilization of the Old World, great in its extent of dominion, greater still in its long-enduring traditions of well-ordered liberty and in the stability of its ancient institutions. The other, a young but stalwart member of the Family of Nations, great also in its extent of territory, in the almost boundless resources at its command; great, too, in the genius and enterprise of its people, possessing enormous potentialities for good on the future of the human race. These Powers are in difference. Great Britain conceives that she has been wronged by these seizures, as we submit justly so conceives that her sovereignty has been invaded; her rights upon the high sea, represented by her nationals, set at nought. Happily the dread extremity of war was avoided. These nations have not sought to turn their ploughshares into swords to settle their differences. They are here before you, friendly litigants, peaceful suitors in your Court, asking by pacific means the adjustment and the determination of their rights in times of peace. This is, indeed, a fact of great moral significance.
>
> Peace hath her victories not less renowned than war.
>
> This arbitration is—who will gainsay it? who can gainsay it?— a victory for peace. Will your award be a victory for peace? You, Gentlemen of this Tribunal, alone can answer.
>
> It will be, it must be, a victory for peace if, as I cannot permit

myself to doubt, it conform to and leave untouched and undoubted the principles of that law which have been consecrated by long usage and stamped with the approval of generations of men: that law which has, after all, grown up in response to that cry of humanity heard through all times, a cry sometimes inarticulate, sometimes drowned by the discordant voices of passion, pride, ambition, but still a cry, a prayerful cry, that has gone up through all the ages, for peace on earth and good will amongst men.

On Sunday the 14th of May, after nine o'clock Mass at the Madeleine, we all drove out to Neuilly, where on an island in the Seine we attended a luncheon party given to the British counsel engaged in the arbitration. The day was pleasant, the company agreeable, and everything passed off charmingly.

Thus passed the time pleasantly, favoured all the while with ideal weather, until it was necessary that some of us should begin to think of home. Mrs. Tupper had already gone, and a month later saw my wife making similar plans. In anticipation of her departure, many friends gave farewell entertainments in her honour. My wife's last public appearance in Paris was at a reception given by the Minister of Foreign Affairs at the Foreign Office. Her departure was greatly regretted by every one of our party, some of whom I think would have said good-bye to me with greater equanimity, but it had to be as it was. We left for Havre on Friday the 19th of May. The Attorney-General, who was holding a conference at the time, adjourned the meeting, and he, together with the counsel, came to the station to say good-bye. At Havre we met Mr. and Mrs. Rainville of Montreal and Mr. A. E. Forget (afterwards Senator) of Regina, who were crossing on the same steamer, *La Bretagne*, a fine big ship. We slept that night in the Hotel Continental, and were awakened by the wind next morning, which sounded ominous for my poor wife, who greatly dreaded the voyage.

Meanwhile the argument before the Arbitration Tribunal had been proceeding leisurely along. The Attorney-General was followed by Sir Richard Webster, and after him Mr. Robinson who, though the briefest, was by no means the least effective speaker, notwithstanding that he was all the while travelling over a well-gleaned field. Speaking with particular reference to the American claim to property in the seals, derived from what is known as 'husbandry', and addressing his remarks to the American counsel, he said in effect:

> *You speak of the care and protection you gave to the seals, and you attempt to deduce from that a certain proprietary interest in these animals. Well, what do you do for the seals? You do not feed them, if you confine them they die—all you do for the seals is at certain seasons to drive them, who are marine animals, on land over sharp stones, a toilsome and painful journey, and club them to death when they reach the end of it. Let us suppose that owing to some great convulsion of nature every man, woman, and child in the United States was drowned tomorrow. How would that adversely affect the seals on the Pribylof Islands? Would they not prosper at an unheard-of rate and flourish as never before?*

One day in June, Mr. Gladstone, who was beginning to grow impatient over the long-drawn-out absence of Sir Charles Russell from the House of Commons, where he was supposed to have charge of the Home Rule Bill, telegraphed *en clair* from Brighton to Lord Rosebery at the Foreign Office:

> *Russell's continued absence is an outrage. Cannot that extra-ordinary Tribunal sit on Mondays? Such a display of childish indolence as they exhibit surely was never witnessed in this world before. If Russell is not in his place in the House on Tuesday night to assist in the debate over the 4th clause it will be an intolerable scandal.*
>
> GLADSTONE

My informant added: 'And yet there are people to be found who say the G.O.M. is not mad.'

All the same, I find in my diary under date of Tuesday, June 13, 1893: 'Sir Charles Russell left Paris this afternoon for London whither he has been summoned by Mr. Gladstone to take part in the Home Rule debate.' And *The Times* of the following morning recorded that on the preceding evening the Attorney-General walked into the House of Commons, where he was received with applause.

Mr. Phelps finished his argument on the 8th of July, on which day the Court took the case under consideration until such time as they were ready to give their decision, which was not until the 15th of August.

In the interval everybody who could do so left Paris, until only the arbitrators, Messrs. Tupper, Maxwell, Dawson, and myself remained to receive the judgement.

During these warm evenings Mr. Robinson and I frequently dined together, sometimes at the Richelieu restaurant on the boulevard— a capital place for a three-franc dinner. Occasionally we patronized the English Tavern in the rue Amsterdam near the Gare St. Lazare, where we had capital roast beef and cherry pie—excellently cooked in the English manner—for four francs. On the solemnity of the feast of St. Mary Magdalen, Sir John Thompson entertained forty or more French-Canadian students at the Café Marguéry, where we ate of the famous sole *à la Marguéry* and otherwise enjoyed ourselves. During the warm evenings we dined frequently in the Eiffel Tower, the coolest place one could find, and also the English Tavern. Meanwhile our party kept dwindling. Dr. Dawson left on the 20th of July amid general regrets. He was followed by Charlie Russell and others until our party was reduced to Mr. Tupper, Maxwell, and myself. We three, to vary things a bit, used latterly to dine at the Café Rougemont on the Boulevard Poissonière, an excellent restaurant and not dear.

I myself did not quite see the end, as I left Paris via Dieppe and New Haven on the evening of the 14th of August and the Award was not delivered until the following day. The channel crossing was beautifully smooth, and I sat up most of the night thinking out how to complete my *Memoirs of Sir John Macdonald*.

I dined next evening with Charlie Russell at the Reform Club, and later went with him to the House of Commons, where I was fortunate enough to hear Balfour, Chamberlain, Harcourt, and Asquith.

On the 15th of August the long-looked-for Award was pronounced. It was, as generally expected, adverse to the pretensions of the United States upon what were known as the five points or questions of right, which were:

1. What exclusive jurisdiction in the sea now known as the Bering Sea and what exclusive rights in the seal fisheries therein did

Russia assert and exercise prior and up to the time of the cession of Alaska to the United States?

2. How far were these claims of jurisdiction as to the seal fisheries recognized and conceded by Great Britain?

3. Was the body of water now known as the Bering Sea included in the phrase 'Pacific Ocean', as used in the Treaty of 1825 between Great Britain and Russia; and what rights, if any, in the Bering Sea were held and exclusively exercised by Russia after said Treaty?

4. Did not all the rights of Russia as to the jurisdiction and as to the seal fisheries in Bering Sea east of the water boundary, in the Treaty between the United States and Russia of the 30th of March, 1867, pass unimpaired to the United States under that Treaty?

5. Has the United States any right, and if so, what right of protection or property in the fur-seals frequenting the islands of the United States in Bering Sea when such seals are found outside the ordinary three-mile limit?

This decision, though sounding very well, was generally regarded at the time by those who knew as a barren victory, for the Treaty of reference further provided as follows:

> If the determination of the foregoing questions as to the exclusive jurisdiction of the United States shall leave the subject in such position that the concurrence of Great Britain is necessary to the establishment of Regulations for the proper protection and preservation of the fur-seal in, or habitually resorting to, the Bering Sea, the Arbitrators shall then determine what concurrent Regulations, outside the jurisdictional limits of the respective Governments, are necessary and over what waters such Regulations should extend;
>
> The High Contracting Parties furthermore agree to co-operate in securing the adhesion of other Powers to such Regulations.

By virtue of this agreement the Americans had us tied and bound, for there was a general disposition among the neutral arbitrators, shared in with true British magnanimity by Lord Hannen, now that we had triumphed on all the questions of right, that we could afford to be generous as regards the regulations.

Sir John Thompson, however, who in addition to being a member of the Tribunal was Prime Minister of Canada, did not see it in that light. He disputed the regulations one by one on their merits, and

when they were finally adopted by Lord Hannen and the neutral arbitrators, they lacked the signature of the Canadian representative. The differences of opinion over the framing of these regulations were sometimes acute. I remember it was said at the time that Sir John Thompson, who could be a very passionate man, in a moment of excitement, pulled Senator Morgan half-way across the table. On another occasion when the Foreign Minister was having a critical conference with Lord Dufferin, our ambassador, over the Siamese difficulty, just then very acute, Mr. Develle sent a polite message to the members of the Bering Sea Tribunal with the request that they would make less noise! A main reason for high feeling was that Canada considered the regulations of such a drastic nature as seriously to interfere with the sealers in the pursuit of their calling. They were forbidden to take seals within a zone of sixty miles round the Pribylof Islands. In addition, a close season was established from the 1st of May to the 31st of July, and this was felt to be fatal. Like many another case, however, the expectation of trouble proved worse than the reality. It was found that the seals went far outside the sixty-mile zone in search of food, and our hunters still managed to secure a profitable return. I will again refer to this subject. This, however, was then in the future, and we left Paris with the impression, an erroneous one as it turned out, that while we had won the arbitration, the victory was a Pyrrhic one.

I left London next morning (which was my thirty-ninth birthday) for Liverpool in company with Sir Charles, Lady and Mr. Tupper, and on the following morning we sailed for home in the *Parisian*, spending some hours at Moville which gave me the opportunity of riding in a jaunting car, buying a blackthorn, and gathering some shamrock. Arriving at Rimouski on the morning of the 25th, we found a special train awaiting us. I reached Rivière du Loup at 10 a.m., where my family were awaiting me, thus bringing to a close a pleasant and profitable trip.

I found Mr. Tupper a kind and considerate chief throughout, and am grateful for the opportunity he gave me of seeing something of the world and of extending my list of friends. As for his father and mother, they were hospitality itself, at all stages of my visit. Shortly after our return Mr. Tupper was created a K.C.M.G., and Messrs.

Russell and Webster each given the Grand Cross of that Order. Mr. Robinson at the same time declined the honour of Knight Bachelor, it is said, because he did not see his way to accept a dignity so manifestly inferior to that bestowed upon his colleagues. What truth there may have been in this, I do not know. He never told me so himself, and it was very unlike Mr. Robinson. Whatever might have been the reason, the fact remains, however, that he declined the honour, and his refusal gave great offence to Queen Victoria, for his acceptance had been taken for granted and the formalities were far advanced. Since then steps are always taken to make sure that the offer will be accepted before it is actually made.

About this time I received a letter from Sir Charles Russell which gratified me very much and which I print here. In one of those generous impulses of which he was full, it probably occurred to him that I had worked hard, and had kept more or less in the background, and that a letter from the Attorney-General of England might be of service to me. And so he wrote it:

Attorney General's Chambers
Room 543,
Royal Courts of Justice,
Strand, W.C., London.

10 *New Courts,*
Lincoln's Inn, W.C.

4th October, 1893.

Dear Mr. Pope,

I want to be allowed to tell you in a word how much I was impressed in Paris with the zeal, ability, and untiring industry with which you did all that lay in your power to secure and defend the interests of Canada. I must say that the labours of our colleagues—including yourself—did much to render effective and at the same time to lighten the efforts of those who, like myself, were charged with the more public share of our joint duties.

I beg that I may be kindly remembered to Mrs. Pope.

Believe me,
Dear Mr. Pope,
Faithfully,
C. RUSSELL

In addition to the more formal letters of thanks from our respective governments, with which I will not trouble the reader, I received the following very kind and appreciative note from Mr. Tupper:

MINISTER OF MARINE AND FISHERIES

OTTAWA, CANADA

September 20th, 1893.

My dear Mr. Pope,

In reporting upon the services rendered by me in connection with the presentation of the British Case to the Tribunal of Arbitration in Paris, I brought your name to the notice of Lord Rosebery, and it gives me a great deal of pleasure to enclose herewith a copy of a communication from Lord Rosebery, in which His Lordship expresses his gratification in reading the testimony I bore to the efficient aid received by me from you and the other gentlemen employed at Paris.

Yours faithfully,

CHARLES HIBBERT TUPPER

This I acknowledged as follows:

Ottawa, 21st Sept., 1893.

Dear Sir Charles,

I beg to acknowledge receipt of your letter of yesterday's date, and enclosure. I have to thank you for bringing my name to the notice of Lord Rosebery and for all the kindness and consideration I experienced at your hands during my association with the work of the Bering Sea Arbitration.

Yours sincerely,

J. POPE

1894 — 1899

Memoirs of Sir John Macdonald / Sir John
Thompson's Death / Decline of the Conservative
Party / Sir Mackenzie Bowell's Administration /
The Shortiss Case / Sir Charles Tupper Succeeds to
the Leadership / Appointed Under-Secretary of
State / General Elections of 1896 / Mr. Laurier
Becomes Prime Minister / Personal Relations with
the Lauriers / Origin of the Canadian Archives /
Mgr. Merry del Val / The Alaska Boundary /
Atlantic and Bering Sea Fisheries / International
Joint High Commission / Meetings at Quebec
and Washington / Unsatisfactory Termination
of the Proceedings / Death of Lord Herschell

MY leisure, during the year succeeding my return from Paris, was largely occupied in preparing for the press my *Memoirs of Sir John Macdonald*. I used to work at it as a rule from 4 or 5 p.m. until dinner time, and again in the evenings, often on Saturday afternoons and holidays, and sometimes, I am sorry to say, even on Sundays. It was a great labour, though a loving one. The work appeared in November 1894, and was favourably received, in fact more favourably than it deserved, viewed apart from the limitations by which I was surrounded. Without aspiring to any high degree of literary excellence, I have always felt that had I been quite untrammelled at the time, I could have produced a better book than the one which actually appeared. I have already referred to these disabilities. There is no occasion to do so again, but apart from all other considerations, it is manifest that the life of a statesman which does not profess to deal with the last twenty years of his public career must leave a good deal to be desired. Of its inadequacies I am very sensible. The kind, though too flattering, notices which greeted the appearance of the

Memoirs must in large measure be ascribed to the greatness of the subject, and to feelings of personal consideration for myself, rather than to any inherent merit in the work itself.

The close of the year 1894 was saddened by the death of Sir John Thompson at Windsor Castle. He had gone over partly to be sworn in as a Privy Councillor, and partly for reasons of health. That his health was in an unsatisfactory condition he knew well, though I do not think he realized how far the disease had progressed. While I knew Sir John fairly well, I cannot say that we were ever really intimate, and I saw less of him after he became Prime Minister than before. He never said anything to me on the subject of his health, but the late Martin Griffin, between whom and Thompson there existed a life-long intimacy, told me that Sir John, on the eve of his departure, said to him that he knew he was a doomed man, but trusted that with care he might count on a few years. Sir John Thompson was a gifted man, high-minded and honourable, and his untimely death was widely deplored. He will never be appreciated at his true worth in this country because his term of office was too short. It was especially unfortunate that, at the time of this national loss, the office of Governor-General should have been held by a man so little fitted for its responsibilities as the Earl of Aberdeen, or to give him his present title, the Marquess of Aberdeen and Temair.

In the last four years death had been busy among the leaders of the Conservative party, Macdonald, Abbott, and now Thompson. All the chiefs had disappeared with the exception of Sir Charles Tupper, who on Thompson's death should have been summoned without delay, but who for some inexplicable reason was passed over by Lord Aberdeen in favour of Mr. Mackenzie Bowell, a worthy, loyal man, but one as little qualified to be Prime Minister of Canada as Lord Aberdeen was to be Governor-General. Then followed days which I never recall without a blush, days of weak and incompetent administration by a cabinet presided over by a man whose sudden and unlooked-for elevation had visibly turned his head, a ministry without unity or cohesion of any kind, a prey to internal dissensions until they became a spectacle to the world, to angels, and to men. At one period during the summer of 1895, I remember it was almost impossible to get public business transacted

at Ottawa. The session sat late. As soon as Parliament rose, the
Ministers scattered. Weeks passed without a Treasury Board being
held. When at last a necessary quorum was obtained, the Governor-
General had gone out to his country place in the mountains of
British Columbia, and the papers had to be sent out after him.
The place took fire, and the Treasury Minutes, while lying there
awaiting the vice-regal approval, were consumed. When at length
fresh papers were procured, signed, sent to British Columbia and
returned to Ottawa, the Auditor-General of the day held up many
of them by reason of some obscure feud between himself and the
Deputy Minister of Finance, with the consequence that public
business during that unhappy summer was well-nigh paralysed. Of
these things I had intimate personal knowledge, for during this whole
period I was Assistant Clerk of the Privy Council.

I cannot go into the general subject of the administration of
public affairs at this period in any detail, but will content myself
with an allusion to the Shortiss case as illustrative of what Lord
Aberdeen and Sir Mackenzie Bowell appeared to regard as an act of
high statesmanship in the affairs of the Dominion.

On the 1st of March 1895, a man named Valentine Shortiss
murdered two men, the motive being robbery. He was arrested,
tried, and condemned to be hanged on the 3rd of January following.
The case was duly considered by the Government, having before
them a special report from the Minister of Justice, who, after a
careful review of the whole subject, advised that the law be allowed
to take its course. The Cabinet, after consideration, announced
themselves as equally divided on the subject, and the First Minister
so reported the fact to the Governor-General, stating that in the
circumstances he and his colleagues had no advice to give. Lord
Aberdeen so cabled the Secretary of State for the Colonies, who
replied that in the circumstances he must act according to his own
judgement, whereupon the Governor-General, acting on his own
authority, promptly commuted the sentence to one of imprisonment
for life. The affair created a great sensation at the time. It was very
generally felt that a grave miscarriage of justice had taken place,
for which the ministry was primarily responsible. I myself heard
the Prime Minister openly announce, with the air of having done

something clever, that the Cabinet were equally divided in the case, and that in the circumstances they had no advice to tender the Governor-General, who should have replied that if his present advisers could not guide him, it became his duty to provide himself with ministers who could. Moreover, the alleged reason for shirking the performance of their duty appeared the more futile when it was considered that a member of the Cabinet, Mr. Donald Ferguson, was not present at the Cabinet Council at which the Shortiss case was considered. Mr. Ferguson was in his home in Prince Edward Island at the time, whence a telegram could have brought him to Ottawa in a few hours, thus breaking the deadlock and enabling the case to be dealt with one way or the other. But this course was not taken. The whole proceeding had the appearance of being deliberately planned to save the neck of an atrocious criminal, in whose behalf no redeeming plea could possibly be offered.

I remember attempts being made at the trial of Shortiss to prove insanity, which were on a par with other efforts on his behalf—the most harmless eccentricities, such for example as his practice when a boy on horseback of sitting backwards on the horse, being put forward as evidence of unsound mind—all of which the jury disregarded, finding the prisoner guilty of murder and responsible for his actions. I have no desire to attribute motives or to apportion blame in this matter. The Governor-General and his Prime Minister doubtless acted according to their lights, but in the words of Lord Rosebery when criticizing Hudson Lowe's treatment of Napoleon, 'The acting was poor and the lights dim.'

Meanwhile the Bowell Ministry went from bad to worse. In the summer of 1895 they lost a Minister (the Hon. A. R. Angers) over their irresolution on the Manitoba school question. A few months later Clark Wallace, then Comptroller of Customs and, though not in the Cabinet, an influential personage of the opposite school of thought from Mr. Angers, followed suit, and a day or two after the opening of Parliament in January 1896, half the Cabinet deserted the ship on the ground of the impossibility of continuing to serve longer under the leadership of Sir M. Bowell. Sir Charles Tupper, who had arrived in Ottawa shortly before (having been summoned, I presume, by those who realized that he was the only man in the emergency) was the unanimous choice of the Conservative party. He consented to act if called upon, but he insisted that the proprieties of the occasion must be duly observed. It was arranged that Sir Mackenzie Bowell should continue as Prime Minister until the prorogation of Parliament, when he should resign in favour of Sir Charles, the recalcitrant members of the Cabinet resuming their portfolios until the resignation of the Prime Minister. This programme was carried out, and on the resignation of Sir Mackenzie Bowell, Sir Charles was sent for by the Governor-General. Promptly he set to work, and with his usual courage and resolution succeeded in forming a Cabinet which, though far from ideal, was the best possible in the circumstances. Among the last acts of the moribund Government was to appoint me Under-Secretary of State of Canada, an appointment which, though made nominally under Sir Mackenzie Bowell, I feel and have always felt that I owed to Sir Charles Tupper. The ministers were unanimously of the opinion that I had earned this promotion. The Prime Minister himself (Sir Mackenzie Bowell) told me that he knew it was the place Sir John had destined me for; but, though personally most friendly, he had not the courage to act, because my appointment would involve the displacement of a French Canadian by an English Canadian. There was no question of fitness for the office, or of the extent of my claims, which were generally recognized, but I was not a French Canadian, and therefore ineligible. Sir Adolphe Caron told me himself that, friends as we were, he simply *could not* in the circumstances consent to my appointment, and his French-Canadian colleagues, while personally most friendly and equally recognizant of my claims, found themselves for the same reason obliged to take the same course. Though the appointment of a Deputy Minister was always held to be in the gift of the Prime Minister, Sir Mackenzie Bowell would *do* nothing, and I bade fair to be sacrificed to this ignoble racial prejudice, when as a *dernier ressort* I called on Sir Charles Tupper, laid my case before him, and sought his powerful aid. No man knew better than he how I stood to Sir John Macdonald, and what Sir John's intentions were with regard to myself. He took the matter up most warmly, and when everything else failed, insisted upon the appointment of a French Canadian to succeed an Englishman as Deputy Head of another Department. This plan was adopted, and I was duly gazetted Under-Secretary of State of Canada to the contentment of everybody, on the 25th of April 1896—the day on which Sir Mackenzie Bowell resigned in favour of Sir Charles Tupper, who took the portfolio of Secretary of State, being influenced in his choice, he was good enough to say, by a desire that he might have me for his deputy.

Shortly afterward, the moribund Parliament—the House of Commons whose election in 1891 had cost Sir John Macdonald his life—was dissolved by Proclamation, a few hours before its expiry by effluxion of time, and the general election was fixed for the 23rd of June.

During the ensuing two months I saw very little of my chief, who was absent from Ottawa almost the whole time fighting like a lion, as I have explained, against tremendous odds. Through no fault of his, he had no chance. Had he been called upon when Thompson died, the outcome might have been, and probably would have been, different, but the late Government had made such a mess of everything they had touched that nothing could have saved their successors.

The proximate cause of Sir Charles Tupper's reverse at the polls in June 1896 was primarily the failure of the Bowell Government to deal with the Manitoba school question in the session of 1895. Owing to their inability to agree among themselves as to the course to pursue, they suffered it to go over into the session of 1896, and it was not until the day after Sir Charles Tupper entered the House of Commons as member for Cape Breton, and assumed the leadership of the House, that the Remedial Bill, providing a measure of relief to the Catholics of Manitoba, was introduced. At that date Parliament had but a few weeks to run. The Opposition were well aware of this, and realized to the full that they had only to practise a little obstruction to render its passage impossible. Thus, owing to the fatal weakness of the former Prime Minister, and the lack of cohesion in his cabinet, the measure failed to become law. When this was seen to be inevitable, the Remedial Bill was withdrawn, and the fate of the incoming Government thereby sealed.

While naturally sympathetic with the Conservative party, with which I had been associated all my life, I studiously avoided during the whole of this campaign any interference in their interest, and was careful to hold aloof from anything that could by any possibility be afterwards construed into a charge of partisanship. I did this on several grounds: firstly, by reason of the inherent propriety of such a course—a course which, I may say, I have always followed during my whole term of office in the Civil Service, save of course when filling the position of the Prime Minister's private secretary, who, it is generally recognized, cannot dissociate himself from his chief; secondly, because I felt in my bones that the Government was going out. I realized that a dead set would be made on my position by the multitude who for eighteen years had been dwellers in the wilderness of Opposition. While I also knew that I had a friend in Mr. Laurier, who there was little doubt would be the next Prime Minister, I was resolved that no act of mine could be adduced to render his efforts in my behalf more difficult than they otherwise would have been.

Under Sir Charles Tupper, then verging on his seventy-fifth year, whose courage and amazing vitality evoked the strongest admiration alike from friend and foe, the Conservative party made a tremendous fight, but in vain. I shall never forget the jaunty air with which that intrepid old man came down to his office the morning after the battle, nor the brave and resolute manner in which he faced the reverse which he must have realized at his age meant the death-knell of his ambitions and hopes. This was especially noticeable in his correspondence with the Governor-General, in which Lord Aberdeen, who had refused to permit the retiring administration to fill certain vacant positions before resignation, had very much the worst of it, as anyone can see who takes the trouble to consult the records.[1] Sir Charles was easily able to show that in filling vacancies before retiring from office he was acting conformably with English practice since the beginnings of responsible government, a practice which had always obtained in Canada. But far more open to criticism than his refusal to comply with the advice of his Ministers were the reasons alleged by Lord Aberdeen in support of his action, particularly as regards vacancies in the Senate and on the Bench—that there was already a large majority

[1] *Session Papers*, Vol. xxx, *2nd Session of* 1896, *No.* 7.

of Conservatives in the Upper House and on the Bench, as though the political sympathies of those recommended for judicial or senatorial positions was the concern of the Queen's representative. Was it to be accounted a disqualification for high office that a man should be a Conservative? The Governor-General possessed the constitutional right of declining to accept the advice of his Ministers on any subject at any time. Had he simply done so in July 1896, while the act would have been ungracious and unusual, Sir Charles Tupper could not have disputed Lord Aberdeen's abstract right to take such a course if he saw fit. It was, however, when His Excellency proceeded to give the reasons for his action that he exposed the weakness and partiality of his course. 'James,' said Lord Macaulay, as he bade goodbye to a friend who was leaving for India to accept a judicial position about which he felt some doubt as to his capacity to fill, 'never give a reason for your judgements. According to the law of chances, your judgements may sometimes be right, but your reasons never.' I recalled this anecdote to Sir Charles as he was addressing his resignation to Lord Aberdeen. He laughed heartily as he sent for a candle and wax and, removing his signet ring with great deliberation, carefully sealed the letter, quoting at the same time Nelson's remark in sealing a letter to the Crown Prince after the battle of Copenhagen: 'This is no time to appear hurried and informal.'[2]

On the morning of the 9th of July, as Under-Secretary of State, I accompanied Sir Charles Tupper to Government House, whither he was summoned for the purpose of tendering his resignation to the Governor-General and of surrendering the Great Seal, which he held as Secretary of State. In view of the treatment which the outgoing Prime Minister had received at the hands of Lord Aberdeen, it need scarcely be said that the proceedings on this occasion were of the most formal description. Sir Charles briefly tendered his resignation of the office of Prime Minister and Secretary of State. He then returned into the hands of the Governor-General the Great Seal of Canada, which Lord Aberdeen handed to me for safe custody, and the interview was over. In the afternoon of the same day I accompanied Sir Charles to the railway station, where we said

[2] R. Southey, *Life of Nelson* (London, 1861), Vol. 1, p. 284.

goodbye, and having discharged my full duty towards him, prepared to greet the new Prime Minister.

I was not kept long in suspense regarding the attitude of the new Government towards myself. From the very first Mr. Laurier almost went out of his way to show me that I had nothing to fear from the change. When forming his Cabinet, as soon as he had decided on his Secretary of State, Mr. R. W. (afterwards Sir Richard) Scott, he acquainted me of his choice, adding that he hoped I had a Minister to my liking, which was very much the case, for Mr. Scott and I were old friends, and I esteemed myself indeed fortunate to have him for my chief. At the ceremony of the swearing-in of the new ministry, at which I was present in charge of the Great Seal, Mr. Laurier introduced me to Sir Oliver Mowat as 'the man who wrote Sir John Macdonald's biography', at which Sir Oliver smilingly observed, 'I wish he would write mine.' A few weeks later Mr. Laurier addressed me this note:

PRIVY COUNCIL
OTTAWA

21st Aug. 1896.

Private
My dear Mr. Pope,
   In writing the life of Sir John Macdonald, did you notice the history of the navigation of the St. Lawrence. If so, could you refer me to the authorities.

Yours very sincerely,
WILFRID LAURIER

Mr. Joseph Pope

I have no recollection of following up this enquiry at the time and have sometimes thought that Mr. Laurier, in raising it, was influenced less by any special interest in the subject of the navigation of the St. Lawrence than by a spirit of friendliness towards myself.

Meanwhile the general impression outside leaned to the view that my tenure of office was precarious. It seemed almost impossible that a man so close to the late Conservative leader as I had stood could escape. I remember a high Government official safely volunteering his opinion that the members of the Civil Service would continue to hold their positions unaffected by the change of Government, 'except perhaps Joe Pope, who', he rather thought, 'would have to go.' He himself has gone long since.

About this time the *Globe* published an exceptionally vicious article on 'The Tory Deputy Ministers' or an article with some such heading, in which a general cleaning-out was advocated. It so happened that on the evening of the day in which this article appeared, my wife and I dined with the Lauriers. As we entered the drawing room, my wife made a sweeping curtsey to the Prime Minister, exclaiming, '*Ave Caesar Imperator, morituri te salutant.*' 'Why *morituri*?' said he. 'Ah, the *Globe's* rubbish.'

A few weeks later, Blanche (my wife's sister) and I were invited to dine at the Lauriers'. My wife said to Madame Laurier that there was no occasion to include me on this occasion as we had dined so recently, and that my place should remain available for another. This suggestion, however, did not commend itself to Mr. Laurier, who lost no time in writing me this note in which his characteristic delicacy is clearly shown:

PRIVY COUNCIL
CANADA

Nov. 7, 1896.

My dear Mr. Pope,

   My wife went to your house yesterday to ask Blanche and yourself to dine with us tonight. You have perhaps been told of it already. Blanche accepted. Will you now let me know if you will also accept.

Believe me, as ever,

Yours sincerely,

WILFRID LAURIER

Joseph Pope, Esq.

With such a friend at court, there is not much wonder that I felt tolerably secure.

About this time there occurred an incident which afforded me some quiet amusement. The Governor-General and Lady Aberdeen apparently belonged to that class of persons whose idea of impartiality consists of being alternately unfair to each side. How unfairly His Excellency treated Sir Charles Tupper I have endeavoured to show. It so happens that I am in a position to demonstrate his apparent lack of confidence in the Premier of his own selection. Shortly after the

change of Government there was a dinner at Rideau Hall to which
Mr. J. M. Courtney, the Deputy Minister of Finance, was invited.
In the course of the evening Lady Aberdeen backed Mr. Courtney
into the Governor-General's private office, showed him the Treasury
minutes, passed at a recent meeting of the cabinet, and asked him
whether he thought they were such as His Excellency could properly
be asked to sign. Mr. Courtney, rather a choleric gentleman at all
times, a radical with a high sense of honour, was furious at being
made the recipient of this confidence, giving the lady to understand
that in the first place she should never have seen those minutes, and
secondly that if Lord Aberdeen had any doubts as to the propriety
of the recommendations they contained, his proper course was to
consult his Prime Minister, whose name stretched half way across
the page submitting the cases for approval, and not a permanent
official like himself. This story was related to me by Mr. Courtney
at the time, almost word for word as it is here set down. I kept it
to myself for years. One day I told it to Sir Wilfrid. He simply
laughed, and said nothing.

The opening of the year 1897 found me very pleasantly situated.
My relations with my Minister were all that could be desired, and
the same might be said of my staff, who of course were of different
degrees of usefulness. My accountant, Mr. F. Colson, was a particularly capable man to whom I was much indebted for advice and
assistance.

Our relations with the Lauriers continued to be of the most
cordial description. For some time past I had been awaiting his
convenience to bring before him a subject in which he used to
manifest interest when a private member. Thus he arranged the
meeting:

PRIVY COUNCIL

CANADA

16th January, 1897.

Dear Mr. Pope,

  I understand that you and Minette are to be with us to-morrow
evening. May I suggest to you that we might take advantage of the
occasion to discuss the plans which you have in view and which you
mentioned the other day.

*When the high revel of card playing will be in progress we may
retire to some quiet corner, and talk business. If you have anything
written on the subject, please bring it with you.*

Ever yours sincerely,

WILFRID LAURIER

The subject which I desired to lay before the Prime Minister
concerned the state of our public records. Agreeably to his suggestion, I had prepared a memorandum which I brought with me on
this occasion, dwelling on the insecure and perilous condition in
which these documents were housed, and the total inadequacy of
the measures available for their preservation in the event of fire.
Mr. Laurier showed himself a most sympathetic listener, thanked me
for bringing the matter to his notice, and promised to consult his
colleagues as to the steps which should be taken to remedy this
state of things, which he agreed with me was discreditable to the
country. Our conversation took place on the evening of the 17th
of January. On the ensuing 11th of February a fire broke out in the
West Block of the Parliament Buildings, resulting in the total
destruction of the top storey of the whole building. My recollection
is that on this occasion the loss was great and irreparable. The
Government took prompt action by appointing a departmental
commission, consisting of Mr. J. M. Courtney, the Deputy Minister
of Finance, Mr. J. M. McDougall, the Auditor-General, and myself,
to examine into and report upon the condition of the records of the
several departments and to make such recommendations as appeared
to be called for. While I welcomed this recognition of the interest
I had always taken in the subject as a fresh mark of confidence on the
part of the Government, I was not unmindful of the difficulties of
the position which confronted me, principally from the circumstance
that neither of my colleagues on the Records Commission was on
speaking terms with the other. Besides which, both were elderly
gentlemen who would naturally be inclined to let their junior
colleague do most of the work, which was largely one of laborious
detail. However, I was young and strong, and hard work agreed with
me, so I took hold of the job and carried the enquiry to a successful
issue. At times I needed all my diplomacy to avoid a rupture, but
patience and a policy of conciliation prevailed. In November 1897

the three commissioners signed a joint report which ultimately bore fruit in the present Archives Department, and which, under the efficient administration of Dr. Doughty, is a credit to the Dominion.

In the spring of 1897, Mgr. Merry del Val, Apostolic Delegate, arrived on a mission from the Holy Father to enquire into the Manitoba school question. He bore letters of introduction to me from certain friends of mine, but I was not in a position to afford him any information on the subject of his mission. My personal sympathies on this question were opposed to those of the Government of the day, yet loyalty to them, as well as ordinary prudence, restrained me from opening my lips on the subject. I told Mgr. Merry del Val frankly that, as a permanent official, I had nothing to say in regard to political questions, nor could I discuss our public men, though we talked on general subjects very pleasantly. I found him suave and diplomatic to a degree. He spoke English perfectly— indeed, he is half English or Irish—and was a man of the world who understood my position perfectly, and told me so.

I remember Queen Victoria's Diamond Jubilee very well, or rather the celebration of the solemnity in this country. The Jubilee celebration proved a great demonstration of loyalty, which was very gratifying to me. What I chiefly recall, however, was the fuss made over Sir Wilfrid's acceptance of the G.C.M.G. 'A democrat to the hilt', he had always described himself. Years afterwards he spoke to me about this, in explanation of his course. He said that when he got over to England, he found all arrangements made for his acceptance of the honour, that his acquiescence was taken for granted by the Queen, and that to refuse at the last hour would have been a boorish act and one deeply resented by Her Majesty. I quite believed him when he said that, in the circumstances, he could not have done anything else, much as he would have liked to. Many members of his political supporters were greatly chagrined, though on the other hand many of his personal friends were, I think, rather gratified than otherwise at the honour paid to the representative of Canada.

Opinions were of course much divided on the course pursued by Sir Wilfrid Laurier at the Imperial Conference held in London that same summer. His action in granting a preference to the goods of the Mother Country as a free gift, without desiring or expecting a return of any kind, shattered the whole scheme of an Imperial Zollverein or Customs Union within the Empire, which was the Conservative policy, or at any rate their dream. However, I must not travel out of my beat.

Sir Wilfrid's homecoming on the 1st of September was most enthusiastic. He was the lion of the hour, and would have been so no matter what his fiscal policy might have been.

I spent a good part of this summer, as I did the previous year, at Stanley Island near Cornwall, where my family and I enjoyed ourselves very much in a quiet way, bathing, boating, fishing, and so on. Its proximity to Ottawa enabled me to visit my office when any occasion arose, so that I came and went a good deal during July and August.

During the spring of 1898 I learned to ride a bicycle, and became quite proficient therein, deriving great pleasure from the exercise, both in Ottawa and during my frequent visits to Washington at that period. Indeed, I rode a bicycle steadily, when the snow was not on the ground, for upwards of twenty years, until I came to realize that the exercise was becoming a little too strenuous for one of my age.

About this time there became manifested, both in the United States and Canada, a disposition to adjust the various questions in difference between the two countries. The suggestion appeared to be favourably received on both sides of the line. In the Dominion the recent discoveries of gold in the Yukon had rendered a means of ready access into that region, such as is furnished by the inlets on the northwest coast, eminently desirable to Canadians, while the Americans had for some time been pressing for a revision of the Bering Sea sealing regulations, which they complained were not sufficiently restrictive. The President of the United States was believed to be favourable to the negotiations, and altogether the time was felt to be opportune for a settlement of these controversial questions. With this object in view, a protocol was signed at Washington on the 30th of May 1898 by certain leading statesmen of Canada and the United States arranging for the creation of an International Joint High Commission which should consist of five British representatives and five American. It was further arranged

that of the five British members, four should be Canadian. I had
not thought at all of the matter, but one summer's day in June,
Sir Wilfrid sent for me and told me that he proposed availing
himself of my services at the approaching conference, which was to
meet at Quebec during the course of the coming summer. He
added that the subjects of reference would be mainly four: the
Atlantic fisheries, the Bering Sea fisheries, the Alaska boundary, and
matters of trade. The first he entrusted to me, the second to
Mr. R. N. Venning, the third to Mr. W. F. King, and the fourth to
Mr. W. G. Parmalee. He asked me to prepare a special memorandum
on the Atlantic fisheries. He further told me to consider myself the
agent of the Canadian Government for the purposes of this Commission, to take full charge of all the arrangements for the Conference, and to meet him in Quebec on the 18th of August. As I
remark at the time in my diary: 'Is it not singular that I, Sir John's
right-hand man, should be performing the same functions for his
successor?'

I immediately set to work on the fisheries memorandum, prepared it at Stanley Island, and then took an early opportunity of
handing it to Lord Herschell, the Imperial Commissioner, whom I
met at Quebec, and who, at the first meeting of the Commission,
was unanimously elected President. Of Lord Herschell I formed a
high opinion from the start. To a remarkably alert and vigorous
mind he united high gifts of style and manner which rendered him a
singularly attractive personality. He was, moreover, a warm friend
of Canada at every stage of the negotiations, ever constant in his
friendship and in his desire to promote our interests in so far as
was compatible with his duties as President of the Conference.
In fact, I was told his only hesitation in accepting the Presidency
arose from the fact that it might render him of less use to Canada
than he might otherwise have been.

On this occasion I renewed several old friendships, among others
Chauncey Cartwright of the Foreign Office, whom I had met at the
Bering Sea Arbitration gathering in London in 1893, and General
and Mrs. Foster.

Mr. Cartwright acted as secretary to Lord Herschell, who was also
accompanied by his son, at that time a stripling, and Sir Hedworth

Williamson, Bt., a most amusing fellow and a general favourite. Of Cartwright, my wife (who accompanied me) and I saw a good deal, both in Quebec and afterwards at Washington, and we became fast friends. We were also destined frequently to meet Mr. Chandler Anderson, of the New York bar, who acted as American secretary to the Commission, Cartwright being the British secretary, and Henri Bourassa, M.P., the Canadian secretary, at that time accounted a warm friend of Sir Wilfrid Laurier, and a young man of great promise, which however he scarcely appears to have fulfilled. Mr. Bourassa and I have not met for many years, but I entertain most pleasant recollections of the time I spent in his agreeable society— now twenty-five years ago. The Commission met then at Quebec, and after some leisurely proceedings there followed a long adjourn-ment in the course of which my wife and I took General and Mrs. Foster fishing in the mountains north of Quebec, and otherwise provided for their entertainment. During the adjournment my wife and I also paid a visit to my old home in Prince Edward Island, where we spent some days with my mother, returning to Quebec in time for the resumption of proceedings before the Commission. Owing to the fact of my not being at the meetings, I did not hear very much at first hand of what was going on, though enough to render me dubious as to the amount of progress being made.

Sir Wilfrid gave it to be understood early in the day that he could not agree to any settlement which did not include the Alaska boundary. After a certain amount of preliminary discussion on various subjects, the conference adjourned to meet at Washington on the 1st of November.

Meanwhile our sojourn at Quebec had been everything that could be desired. The weather was delightful. Dinners, receptions, and functions of every kind followed each other in quick succession. Among our hosts I specially remember the Dobells, who royally maintained their traditional name for graceful and charming hospi-tality. Then we had Spencerwood, at that time occupied by Sir Louis and Lady Jetté; the Provincial Government, Her Majesty's ships of war in port at the time, and much else. Our American friends also gave a very fine entertainment, regarding which the only criticism I had to offer was that at it they drank the President's health before that of the Queen, which was a mistake, for the rule in such cases is that the health of the sovereign in whose dominions one is at the moment should always be honoured first. It is a simple rule, and one easy of observance. I made a mental note at the time that when the opportunity offered I would show our friends the etiquette of the occasion, but this I was not permitted to do, for when the corresponding dinner was given in Washington, Lord Herschell, with that excessive consideration which marked all his relations with the Americans, insisted on the loyal toasts being drunk jointly, 'President and Queen'.

Meanwhile I had transferred my energies to Washington and was busily engaged in making preparations for the resumption of the conference. Our patronage was largely sought by hotel managers. Finally we decided on the Shoreham, notwithstanding the fact that its principal rival very considerately offered me, as an inducement to favour them, complimentary accommodation for both my wife and myself during the continuance of the Commission! To Washington, then, we repaired at the appointed time, and began work in earnest. On arrival I called upon Sir Julian Pauncefote, who however was not in. I bore a letter from Sir Wilfrid Laurier and was thus led to recall the circumstances that in 1894 I had presented a letter at the Embassy from Sir John Thompson to this same Ambassador, so that I have been twice introduced by Prime Ministers of Canada to Sir Julian Pauncefote without having met him. I subsequently did so, however, and found that both he and Lady Pauncefote were most agreeable.

Of friends whom I made in Washington at that time I desire to include Mr. (afterwards Sir) Reginald Tower, then Second Secretary at the British Embassy, to whom I was much indebted for kindly advice and assistance of various kinds.

Shortly after reassembling at Washington, the commission dined with President and Mrs. McKinley at the White House. The guests numbered about fifty, and included the members of the commission, Sir Julian and Lady Pauncefote, Chief Justice Fuller of the Supreme Court, the members of the Cabinet, and their wives. The President and Mrs. McKinley received in the East Room, she seated, being an invalid, and he standing by her side. I was struck by the blending of dignity and simplicity which characterized this entertainment.

On the 26th of November a large number—in fact almost the whole—of the Commission accepted an invitation extended to us by Senator Faulkner (I think when in Quebec) to visit his place at Boydville in West Virginia, about two hours from Washington. Here we enjoyed southern hospitality in its most profuse form, including the Senator's own particular brand of mint juleps which constituted a prominent feature of the occasion.

From time to time, as the state of public business permitted, we made excursions in the neighbourhood of Washington; to Mount Vernon, Arlington, Annapolis, the astronomical observatory at Georgetown, at which I enjoyed the privilege of looking through the great reflector at certain objects visible at the time. I also ascended the monument, and afterwards attended the opening of Congress, with which latter ceremony I was not impressed. I also visited the State Department and inspected their system of keeping records in which I was much interested at the time, having recently served on our own Government's commission. I mention in my diary having been shown a machine adapted for copying into registers, then the *dernier cri* in typewriters.

On Saturday, the 11th of February, the thermometer at Washington fell to seventeen below zero, breaking all records, and on the following day a snowstorm set in which raged with such violence as utterly to eclipse in its fury anything I had ever experienced in Ottawa or elsewhere. The snow drifts were phenomenal, but a day or two later the streets were running water. I had been invited a fortnight before to dine with Mrs. Horstmann, a prominent Washington hostess, on Monday the 13th. Not only was I unable to go, but I could not even send word, as the storm was so violent that no cabs or messengers were to be had for love or money. Of the twenty guests invited only one, in addition to the members of the family, sat down to dinner—that one being Mr. Bourassa, who arrived in Washington after New Year's with full Canadian equipment—blanket coat, snow-shoes, and the rest. We all laughed at him for bringing these, but they proved very convenient on that occasion. 'Is it not a little strange', I note in my diary, 'that the worst snow-

storm I have ever seen should be in Washington in Lat. 38° while
the hottest day I have ever experienced was in Winnipeg in Lat. 50°?'

In the early days of the Conference it was intended that the
subjects for discussion should be confined to four, but insensibly the
list grew until at last they numbered a dozen or more, the principal
ones in addition to the original four being:

1. Alien labour laws.
2. Mining rights.
3. Revision of the agreement of 1817 as to naval vessels
   on the Great Lakes.
4. Reciprocity as to wrecking and salvage.
5. Transit privileges.

All these questions were debated, some at great length, and I believe
that touching several a certain amount of progress was made, but in
regard to the question of immediate primary importance—that of
access to a port on the Lynn Canal—agreement was found to be
impossible, for in all their proposals the Americans persisted in
assuming the point at issue, which was supreme dominion over that
region. Lord Herschell in one of his confidential dispatches of the
period does say that the American commissioners, while maintaining
their claim to sovereignty over the head of the Lynn Canal, offered
to grant Canada a fifty-year lease of Pyramid Harbour with a strip
of land running back to the British hinterland as a right of way to
the Yukon. This proposal would also have enabled American vessels
to trade between American ports and Pyramid Harbour. There was
a rumour to the effect that a Canadian cabinet minister so wrote
to his son, then stationed at Skagway, who incontinently repeated it.
Immediately the Pacific coast took fire. Deputations poured into
Washington protesting against any 'cession of American territory',
and the whole thing came to nothing. Whether the Canadian commissioners would have accepted this proposal if formally made to
them or not, I do not know. My impression is that they would not.
I know that, in one of my visits to Ottawa at that time, a member of
the Government, speaking to me confidentially, expressed the hope
that his colleagues on the Commission would not agree to anything
of the kind, and I rather fancy that would have been the prevailing
attitude, though it was not mine.

During the whole of these negotiations, which extended well into the month of February, Lord Herschell proved himself indefatigable, both in conference and in committee, in his endeavours to exhort, persuade, and induce his American colleagues to take a more reasonable attitude than they seemed disposed to adopt. Perhaps one might question the policy of his course in devoting himself so exclusively to Senator Fairbanks rather to the neglect, some of us used to think, of certain American members of the Commission who had social aspirations and would have appreciated a little attention on the part of Lord Herschell, more perhaps than Mr. Fairbanks, but how far this might have contributed to the failure of the negotiations, I do not know.

The Alaska boundary proved the stone of stumbling. Sir Wilfrid all along showed himself unwilling to come to any settlement until agreement had been reached on that head, or at any rate a decision arrived at to refer it to arbitration. This the Americans would not consent to on any terms which our side could accept; and so the Conference came to nought.

For some days a break-up was seen to be inevitable. On the 13th the newspapers announced that General and Mrs. Foster were leaving that day for Florida.[3] On the same day an American gentleman, closely associated with the commission, told me that the members were getting tired of one another and were losing their tempers, and that he would not be surprised if the Commission were to terminate at any time.

On the 15th of February Lord Herschell had the misfortune to slip and fall in the street, breaking a small bone in his hip—an accident which eventually proved fatal. On the 20th the Commission met for the last time, and on the following day we left Washington for Ottawa.

On the evening of the 21st I called on Lord Herschell to say good-bye, and spent twenty minutes or so at his bedside. On knocking at his door, I asked if I might come in. 'By all means,' replied he. 'I am always glad to see my friends.' I did not expect quite so cordial a greeting, as I did not very often meet him, and could not be

[3] The protocols show that General Foster was present at the meeting of the Joint High Commission held on the 15th of February, the proceedings at which, however, were purely formal.

considered at all intimate with him. On this occasion I chatted with
him very pleasantly for a while. He was lying in bed smoking a
cigar and had been reading a novel. He told me of a difference he
had had with General Foster at the Conference, and how in subsequently alluding to it, with a desire to smooth things over, he
referred to General Foster's remarks on the occasion, which had the
appearance of being offensive. General Foster interrupted, 'They
were meant to be offensive,' said he. This amused, though I think
rather surprised, Lord Herschell.

The only low-spirited remark he made to me was that he had
laboured hard for six months and got nothing for it but a broken
leg. Whereupon I observed that fortune had been kind to him many
times, and he must expect a little reverse now and then. He laughed,
and said that was quite true, and that he did not complain. On my
leaving, he said to me to tell my wife that if she would take pity
on his loneliness and write him some of the gossip of Ottawa, he
would be very grateful. Poor fellow, in a week he was dead.

It appears that on the morning of Wednesday the 1st of March
he awoke about five o'clock and complained of weakness. He had
another attack about six, this time suffering from pain below the
heart. He speedily became unconscious and died at five minutes past
seven. My diary closes with the words, 'This Commission has
indeed been unfortunate.'

1899 — 1902

Visit to England re *Alaska Boundary Matters* /
Glencoe / *Diversions in London* / *Correspondence
with Professor Goldwin Smith* re *Sir John
Macdonald* / *Queen Victoria's Death* / *Duke of
York's Visit to Canada in 1901* / *Mr. Spring-Rice
and the Alaska Boundary* / *The Coronation* /
Mr. J. Israel Tarte / *Sir Wilfrid Laurier's Ill
Health* / *Vicomte de Fronsac*

I HAD not long settled down after my extended absence from
Ottawa when Sir Wilfrid Laurier sent for me and asked me if I
would prepare for him a history of the Alaska Boundary controversy,
exposing the contentions of Canada with respect thereto. I replied
that, although possessing little knowledge of the subject, I would
endeavour to discharge this duty. I did my best, and in about three
weeks presented him with the fruit of my labours in the form of a
draft memorandum, which he was good enough to say he liked very
much. In discussing it he told me that Mr. Chamberlain, then
Secretary of State for the Colonies, was extremely desirous that he
should visit England in connection with this business; that if he
went, he would take me with him, and that if he found it impossible
to go himself, he would advise whoever of his colleagues might
undertake the mission to avail himself of my services. A few days
later Sir Louis Davies came into my office and told me that he was
shortly sailing for England on Alaska matters, and that the Prime
Minister had expressed the wish that I should accompany him. While

I should have liked above all things to have accompanied Sir Wilfrid Laurier, there was none of his colleagues, failing the First Minister, that I would have preferred to Sir Louis. Sir Wilfrid also associated with us in this business Dr. W. F. King of the Dominion Observatory, who was one of my intimate friends. Miss Ethel Davies and Miss Ursula Davies, Sir Louis's daughter and niece, respectively, were of our party, as also was Mr. W. C. Gordon, his private secretary, since deceased.

Gordon was my secretary before he went to Sir Louis in that capacity, and a more loyal, faithful, and devoted fellow it has never been my good fortune to meet. We sailed by the new Allan steamer *Bavarian* on the 7th of September, and reached Liverpool on the 16th instant and London the same evening.

A day or two after reaching London Sir Louis had an interview with Mr. Chamberlain. I saw John Anderson of the Colonial Office, who did not appear to be impressed with the strength of our case, which we afterwards discussed at length with him and the Hon. F. H. Villiers, c.b., the Assistant Under-Secretary of State for Foreign Affairs, and brother of the Countess of Derby, whom I had known in Canada. I had met Anderson in Paris in 1893 and had formed a high opinion of his ability, though he was not at that time, as I remember, officially connected with the Bering Sea Arbitration. I also renewed acquaintance with Maxwell, Cartwright, and a number of friends. Soon after our arrival, Sir Louis, King and I devoted ourselves to the preparation of a revised memorandum of our case, giving to it a more legal turn than it originally possessed, and otherwise enlarging and improving it.

When the Joint High Commission broke up in February, it had been arranged *pro forma* that the Tribunal should reassemble at Quebec on the 2nd of August. Nothing of the kind happened, but during the summer the Americans manifested a desire that it should reconvene at a convenient date in the near future, to take up certain points which had engaged its attention before the rupture, leaving to future negotiation the question of the Alaska boundary. Now the Canadian Government, on the other hand, in view of the recent gold discoveries in the Yukon Territory, regarded the use of the Lynn Canal ports as a question of pressing urgency, and were most anxious that, failing any other mode of settlement, the Alaska boundary should be referred to arbitration speedily, upon the lines agreed to in the Venezuela dispute. At the same time the Government also expressed its readiness to proceed with the other questions at issue as soon as arbitration on Alaska had been decided on. To this the Americans declined to agree, or rather they insisted that any arrangement for arbitration must except from its operation settlements made by American citizens in good faith under the authority of the United States Government, i.e. Dyea, Skagway, and Pyramid Harbour. To this we would by no means consent, and therefore there was nothing to be done at the time except to prepare and place our case before Her Majesty's Government. Inasmuch as when I come to discuss the events of 1903 I shall have something personal to say in regard to Alaska, I forbear from alluding further to the subject in this place.

We had commodious rooms at the Metropôle, though they did charge us unmercifully, which Sir Louis was apt to resent. Coming downstairs one morning in a critical mood, he was somewhat mollified by the sight of certain bouquets of flowers tastefully displayed about the room, and so expressed himself to me. 'Ah,' replied I, 'these are but the garlands with which the victim is crowned!'

Besides those I have mentioned, I met many old friends: Lady Derby (who on all occasions was most kind to me), Sir George Stephen, Lord Strathcona, the latter of whom invited Sir Louis and myself to visit him at Glencoe where we spent a week most pleasantly with Lord and Lady Strathcona, their daughter the Hon. Mrs. Howard, her husband, Dr. R. J. B. Howard, Mr. Garson, Lord Strathcona's Scottish agent, and Russell Stephenson, whom I remembered very well as Lord Dufferin's brother-in-law, and who is an amusing and entertaining fellow. On the morning after our arrival at Glencoe, some of us drove through the historic glen, noted Ossian's cave, the Lord Chancellor, the stone from which the signal for the massacre was given, and other points of interest.

I found the mountains which guard this valley of surpassing grandeur, the ever-varying lights and shades passing over them lending greatly to their charm. The rolling clouds, the purple mists, the yellow brackens, and the deep shadows of the surrounding hills unite in imparting constant variety to the scene. After a pleasant visit we left Glencoe by yacht, dined with Lord Strathcona at the Station Hotel, and returned by train to London, where we resumed our interviews with Anderson and the rest, and completed the revised edition of our memorandum on the boundary between Canada and Alaska.

During this stay in London, I made it my business to visit several old churches, such as St. Olave's, Hart Street, where Pepys is buried. I noted particularly Pepys's statue, which is built into the wall, just where he was accustomed to enter the church. Pepys is buried under the altar. Over the altar on one side is a bust of Mrs. Pepys, facing the statue seemingly to fit the old rascal's remark that on entering the church he used to feel that his wife was looking at him. All Hallows, Barking, also is most interesting. Archbishop Laud is buried there, or was, for his remains have been removed to Oxford.

I spent the time altogether very agreeably in London. As on the occasion of my last visit six years before, I dined quite often with Lord Strathcona, Maxwell, Cartwright, Colmer, and others at the Constitutional Club, Boodles, the Travellers, and elsewhere. We saw some capital plays too—*King John*, *Richard* III, etc. One, an amusing performance entitled *My Daughter-in-law*, I particularly remember.

I was also a regular attendant at the Brompton Oratory, and the Jesuit Church in Farm Street. Sometimes on Sunday afternoons I went to the Abbey and St. Paul's, which I much enjoyed. Before leaving London I spent a week-end visit with Lady Macdonald and Mary at their hotel, about halfway between Bushey and Watford, where we went to Mass on Sunday and afterwards took a long tramp across country, with its lovely hedges and sweet lanes. I remember seeing some boys playing football under the guidance of their curate. Such a thing would not have been seen in England twenty-five years ago, nor am I particularly enamoured of it at any time, for I like the quiet repose of an English Sunday.

A day or two before leaving London I attended the opening of

Parliament, where I heard the debate on the address, which was moved by the Marquess of Granby and seconded by Lord Barnard in very ordinary speeches. Lord Kimberley then spoke very well, followed by Lord Salisbury, to whom I listened with extreme interest. War had been virtually declared against the Transvaal in view of the indescribably insolent *ultimatum* which the Boers had addressed to England. What struck me during this debate was the brevity, courtesy, and moderation of the speeches I listened to.

Shortly before leaving London, Sir Louis, in acknowledgement of the many hospitalities shown us, gave a dinner at the Metropôle, with which I had something to do. Things went off very well, with everybody in good humour.

On the 21st of October, Trafalgar Day, we left London, sailing from Liverpool the same afternoon by the s.s. *Campania*, and reached New York on the 28th, where my wife met me. We remained over Sunday, took the train for Quebec, and arrived there just in time to say goodbye to my sister Georgie, who was sailing as a nursing sister on the s.s. *Sardinian* with the first contingent en route for South Africa. At 4 p.m. the *Sardinian* cast off and proceeded down the river amid salvoes of artillery, the blowing of whistles, and the acclaim of the populace generally.

A few days after my return to Ottawa, Lord Minto sent for me and we discussed several subjects, e.g., His Excellency's exact style and titles, the procedure to be followed as regards the appointment of an administrator when he left the country, and other similar subjects. His Excellency then touched upon Alaska. I told him I felt low-spirited about it and almost despaired of a satisfactory issue. He then asked me if I would write an article on the subject for the *Edinburgh Review*, of which his brother was editor. I agreed, and the article duly appeared in the *Edinburgh Review* for April 1900.

The closing year of the century was spent uneventfully by me in the administration of my department, in which I took much interest. Among my multifarious duties was that of preparing all sorts of addresses to various descriptions of people on all kinds of subjects. Here is a case in point.

PRIVY COUNCIL OFFICE
CANADA

6th June, 1900

My dear Pope,

Have you time to prepare an address to the Queen, to be presented by Senate and H. of C. on the success of the war and the fall of Pretoria—for tomorrow.

Yours,

W. LAURIER

This address to Her Majesty duly appeared in the Journals of the House of Commons on the 7th of June 1900.

During this period I derived great pleasure from my telescope which I brought into use almost every fine evening. In particular I remember witnessing a fine occultation of the planet Saturn by the moon, which was most interesting and instructive indeed. I also made several observations of Venus, then emerging from the sun's rays. The phases of the moon, the transits, occultations, and eclipses of Jupiter's satellites, the planets, Venus, Mars, Mercury and many other celestial phenomena were to me a constant source of delight.

The reassembly of the Ministers was shortly followed by the dissolution of Parliament, and a general election from which the Ministry issued triumphant, many of the leading members of the Opposition, including Sir Charles Tupper, the leader of the Opposition, experiencing defeat at the polls. I felt particularly sorry for Sir Charles, but consoled myself with the reflection that he had had a long and successful public career, and could well afford to retire in his eightieth year with honour and dignity to himself and credit to the country he served so long and well. Following the precedents set by the late Colonel Bernard and Mr. J. M. Courtney, who as Deputy Ministers did not vote, I likewise abstained, though perfectly free to exercise the franchise had I felt so disposed. In view, however, of the confidential relations in which I stood towards both sides, I considered it better to hold aloof.

About this time I had a short correspondence with Professor Goldwin Smith, which speaks for itself.

Ottawa, 13th December, 1900

Dear Mr. Goldwin Smith,

In 'Bystander's' ever delightful comments on current events I read in this week's issue of the *Sun* that my 'misplaced delicacy' has led me to conceal Sir John Macdonald's intemperate habits and thus to spoil the good story which you relate.

It had not occurred to me that I concealed this failing in writing his life. On the contrary (*Vol.* 1, p. 325) I avow it in words which seem to me sufficiently clear to prevent any misunderstanding on the subject. In the lifetime of his wife and children it would be difficult for me to be more outspoken, particularly as the weakness we are discussing was merely a tradition during my association with him. Again, how do I spoil the story? I tell it almost in the words you employ and, if I do not explicitly fasten it on Sir John, I do not deny it as his.

Pardon my troubling you with this note, but I am so completely a captive to your charm of style that your slightest censure is no light matter. Among the many obligations I am under to Sir John Macdonald, not the least is that to him I owe the honour of dining at your table and of enjoying your conversation of men and things.

Believe me,

Yours faithfully,
JOSEPH POPE

Professor Goldwin Smith,
 The Grange,
  Toronto.

The Grange,
Toronto
December 14th, 1900.

Dear Mr. Pope,

I am much obliged to you for your note. I see that my words, which were intended only to apply to the particular anecdote, might, if construed as applying to your work generally, create a wrong impression. There will be a correction which I hope will satisfy you in the new 'Bystander'.

Yours very truly,
GOLDWIN SMITH

FROM THE *Farmer's Sun*, DECEMBER 1900

In his last letter, the Bystander, recounting an anecdote of Sir John Macdonald, referred to Sir John's biographer as having with

*misplaced delicacy omitted a reference to a well-known infirmity,
thereby impairing the point of the anecdote. His attention has been
called to the fact that in other passages of the biography the infirmity
is duly recognized. He had no intention of disparaging a conscientious
and important work.*

A BYSTANDER

The year 1901 opened with the death of Queen Victoria, and, as
on the occasion of the South African victory, it devolved upon me
to draft the parliamentary address to the new Sovereign. My wife
told me at the time that she did not think very much of my effort,
but when I mentioned her opinion to Sir Wilfrid on submitting the
document to him, he said emphatically, 'That is where I do not
agree with her. I think it exceptionally well done.' Here it is.

To The King's Most Excellent Majesty:
MOST GRACIOUS SOVEREIGN:

*We, Your Majesty's dutiful and loyal subjects, the Senate and
House of Commons of Canada, in Parliament assembled, humbly
beg leave to approach Your Majesty with the expression of our deep
and heartfelt sorrow at the demise of our late Sovereign Lady Queen
Victoria.*

*In common with our fellow subjects in all parts of the Empire, we
deplore the loss of a great ruler whose manifold and exalted virtues
have for three generations commanded the respect and admiration of
the world.*

*As representatives of the Canadian people, we mourn for the
beloved Sovereign under whom our Dominion first rose into being,
and to whose wise and beneficent sway are due in no small measure
its growth and prosperity.*

*May we venture to add that above and beyond these sentiments
which the sad occasion naturally calls forth, there has come to each
one of us a sense of personal bereavement which, we say it with all
possible respect and duty, makes Your Majesty's sorrow our own.*

*We pray the God of consolation may comfort Your Majesty and the
members of the Royal Family in their affliction.*

*It is with feelings not less deep and sincere than those to which
we may have just given utterance that we hail Your Majesty's accession
to the Throne of your ancestors. We beg to assure Your Majesty of*

our devoted attachment to Your Majesty's person and Government,
and to express our unclouded confidence that the glory and the
greatness of the British Empire abroad, and the happiness and well
being of Your Majesty's people at home, will suffer no diminution
under Your Majesty's gracious rule.

During the closing days of December it was arranged between
Her Majesty's Government and the Government of Canada that the
Duke and Duchess of Cornwall and York should pay an official visit
to the Dominion on their way home from Australia, whither they
were about to proceed in order to inaugurate the new Commonwealth. The death of Queen Victoria somewhat disturbed these
arrangements, but the original plan was finally reverted to, and it
was known early in the season that the Duke and Duchess of York
were coming.

On the 5th of June I first met Major F. S. Maude, the new
Governor-General's Secretary, who informed me at the start that
it had been settled between Lord Minto and Sir Wilfrid Laurier
that he (Maude) and I were to have charge of the arrangements
connected with the approaching royal visit. A few days later the
Governor-General sent for me and asked me if Sir Wilfrid Laurier
had said anything to me on the subject of acting with Maude in
connection with this business. Upon my saying, 'No, Sir,' he
remarked that the omission to do so was singular, inasmuch as Sir
Wilfrid himself had indicated that I was to be the man. I could
only repeat that I had not heard from anyone on this subject, save
from himself and Maude. To tell the truth, I was not particularly
keen about tackling this job. I had had no experience with royalty,
was naturally timid, and thought more might be expected of me
than I should be able to perform. Above all, I had no idea that Maude
would turn out such a tower of strength as he proved himself to be.
Meanwhile I heard nothing direct from Sir Wilfrid. A few days
later I lunched at Government House, and Lord Minto again asked
me if I had heard from the Premier. I could only reply that I had
not, with this qualification, that a day or two before Mr. Scott
(my Minister) had hinted to me that perhaps it might be as well for
me to see His Excellency, but so vaguely and indefinitely was this
expressed that I did not feel like taking any action thereon. Within

the next day or two Mr. Scott sent up two telegrams to my house, one from Sir Wilfrid requesting him to send me to His Excellency at once, and the other from Mr. Scott saying that he had done so, and that I should work conjointly with Major Maude. While I never had any warrant for thinking so, I have sometimes felt that possibly there might have been some difference of opinion in the beginning in regard to this selection, though Sir Wilfrid could scarcely have been a party to it, for Lord Minto distinctly told me that Sir Wilfrid had indicated to him that he wished 'Pope' to be the man.

Lord and Lady Minto being absent from Ottawa, Maude and I worked at Government House, lunching every day at Rideau Cottage, where we enjoyed the pleasant society of Mrs. Maude, a lady no less charming than her husband, and more I cannot say. Later we transferred our energies to the Citadel at Quebec, where we laboured assiduously for some weeks. I wish I could convey an adequate idea of the extent to which I felt indebted to Major Maude for his invaluable assistance and co-operation in this whole affair. His energy and zeal were prodigious. He never seemed to spare himself or to think of himself at all. All his thought and consideration were for others. If he had a fault, it was perhaps to be found in his conspicuous frankness and sincerity. For example, I believe he has been known to hint to certain members of a civic deputation that top hats and brown boots are not ordinarily worn together on ceremonial occasions, and other elementary suggestions of a like nature, which were in all cases prompted by the most disinterested of motives, and which when profited by could not fail to prove of advantage to those concerned.

In all the arduous labours connected with these preparations and especially those which related to military reviews, escorts, processions, guards of honour, and like functions, of which I scarcely knew the names, Maude was always to the fore, organizing and directing everything down to the minutest detail, sometimes after I was comfortably asleep. In saying this I have no desire unduly to disparage myself. I had plenty of energy too, and undoubtedly possessed a good deal of local knowledge which came in usefully on this occasion, and if I lacked experience in royal tours, I knew something of tours which were not royal. I knew people, too, all over the country, and had a good perception of their relative importance, but I have no hesitation in saying that after giving to everyone concerned his full due, much of the success which attended the royal tour of 1901 is due to the energy, capacity, resourcefulness, industry, patience, and supreme unselfishness of Frederick Stanley Maude.

Many persons contributed to the success of this occasion. Among those to whom I feel we were indebted, I would especially recall the late Lord Shaughnessy, the President, and Mr. W. R. Baker, the Secretary of the Canadian Pacific, who placed the resources of the railway unreservedly at our disposal, and who spared no pains to make the tour a success.

I was much struck by the Prime Minister's dignified and courtly bearing towards Their Royal Highnesses, whom he met at Quebec, and attended in person across the continent. He travelled in a special train with Lady Minto, Major Maude and Mrs. Maude, Mr. Arthur Guise, Comptroller of the Governor-General's household, Miss Alice Grenfell, and myself, always saying and doing the right thing in his own inimitable way. To Colonel Sherwood and his Police much credit was due for faithful and efficient service, which nobody commonly hears about, but upon which the safety and comfort of many depend.

I may mention here what turned out to be a little misunderstanding which occurred on this tour. The question early arose as to who should take precedence, the Duke of Cornwall and York or the Governor-General. Lord Minto, realizing that the point was one of some delicacy, referred the matter to the Colonial Office, who replied that it was the King's pleasure that His Royal Highness should take precedence during the tour. Now this turned out to be a mistake. Lord Minto told me himself that when he next visited England he made it a point to enquire into this matter, and found that the Secretary of State gave no such direction, which was based on a misunderstanding of a clerk at the Colonial Office. I was glad of this, because I had all along taken the ground that the Governor-General, as representing the King's Majesty, should yield first place to no one under the King himself. This had been inculcated in me from a very early period. In an earlier chapter I have mentioned that one of my first recollections is the landing of King Edward at Charlottetown in the summer of 1860, and, though a mere child at the time, I recall that on that occasion the Lieutenant-Governor of Prince Edward Island took the place of honour, for I can remember His Excellency sitting on the right of the carriage and the Prince of Wales on his left as they drove up the street.

The royal party told me on landing in Canada in 1901 that they were very much surprised to find out what had been arranged here in this regard, adding that Lord Ranfurly never gave up his precedence in New Zealand, and if Lord Hopetown did so in Australia, it was only because the Duke held a special commission from the King authorizing him to do a specific act in the performance of which he represented His Majesty. In 1919, on the occasion of the visit to Canada of His Royal Highness the Prince of Wales, the ancient custom was reverted to. It was then arranged that while the Governor-General and the Prince of Wales should meet as seldom as possible, when they did meet, the Governor-General was to have the *pas*. Lord Minto quite agreed to the propriety of this course in 1901, but having made the enquiry, he felt himself obliged to abide by the ruling, with the consequence that a fine object lesson in ceremonial observance was lost to the people of Canada.

One day when I was at work at the Citadel in Quebec, Lord Minto sent for me and told me that he proposed to recommend Maude and myself for a c.m.g. if I had no objection. I replied that I felt honoured to accept any mark of royal favour which it might please His Majesty to confer upon me. I added that I was especially grateful to His Excellency for the recommendation in question, which I knew must have emanated from him. We were duly invested with this dignity at Government House, Ottawa, on the 21st of September, and our names appeared in the London Gazette of the 11th of October following, Maude, with characteristic modesty, placing mine at the head, and his own at the foot of the list, though on every ground he should have been first.

While at Quebec, shortly after the landing of Their Royal Highnesses and before their departure for the West, Sir Wilfrid invited me to accompany him on the trip across the continent. Regarding this merely as an invitation, I declined it, feeling that I had been long enough away from my office and my family. While on the way from Quebec to Ottawa, he spoke to me again upon the subject, telling me that he would very much like me to come. On my saying that if I thought I could be of use to him, I was quite ready to go anywhere, he replied that I would be of the greatest use to him, whereupon, of course, I said I would gladly go.

As many years ago I published a circumstantial account of this tour, I do not think it devolves upon me to refer to it further in this place, save perhaps to add one or two personal touches which the lapse of twenty-odd years render permissible. In his farewell letter to the people of Canada, His Royal Highness wrote:

> We wish to record our sincere thanks to the Dominion Government, the provincial authorities, the municipal bodies and private indivi- duals, for their generous hospitality, their kind forethought, and the extreme care and trouble they have bestowed upon all the arrangements for the reception and accommodation of ourselves and our staff. I feel that we are especially indebted to Mr. Pope, by whom so much of the detail was ably dealt with.

In my diary of the period occurs this note: 'I understand, in fact I know, that the mention of my name in the Duke's farewell letter was the personal act of His Royal Highness. The draft submitted to him did not contain it, and he added in pencil in the margin with his own hand, "Say something about Pope", "Say something about Maude". This of course greatly enhances the value of the reference, and this is the fact.'

I do not recall the particulars of this incident, and while I know that I must have had some precise warrant for my statement, I cannot help feeling that my dear friend Maude in some way stands behind the original mention of my name in His Royal Highness's letter.

On the day before the sailing of the royal party from Halifax, I was invited to luncheon on board the *Ophir* with a number of others. After luncheon, Derek Keppel came to me and told me not to go just yet, as Their Royal Highnesses wished to see me, so I remained. At last my turn came, and I was ushered into the royal apartments by Lord Wenlock. The Duke and Duchess were both standing when I entered. After shaking hands, the Duke proceeded to say that they had sent for me to express their satisfaction with the arrangements which had been made for their tour, with which they had understood I had much to do. On my modestly disclaiming any special credit for this affair, which I said was due mainly to Major Maude, the Duke replied, 'We understand otherwise,' and continued the expression of his thanks. He added, speaking in the plural as including the Duchess, 'We have enjoyed ourselves immensely, and we feel that we are greatly indebted to you for the arrangements that have been made for our comfort.'

'The Duchess,' I continue in my diary, 'is a charming woman, bright, clever and sympathetic, and the cordial and unaffected manner in which she devotes herself to gratifying the loyalty of so many people won my unqualified admiration. They say she is not very much of a conversationalist. As to that I do not know. I never spoke with her long enough to tell, but her gracious demeanour on all occasions quite captivated me.'

Of the suite, Sir Arthur Bigge (now Lord Stamfordham), the Duke's private secretary, was a model of courtesy on all occasions, as were Sir Donald Wallace, Commander Godfrey-Faussett, and the rest. I remember Lord Crichton as a charming, merry-tempered soul. Lord Wenlock I found somewhat crusty at the start, but he thawed out. Sir John Anderson was an old friend. Derek Keppel was always pleasant, as was also Canon Dalton; in fact, I met with nothing but courtesy from every member of the staff, though of course I saw more of some than of others.

I spent the year 1902 tranquilly at my post in Ottawa. In May I had a visit from Mr. Spring-Rice, afterwards a close friend of mine, at that time Secretary of Embassy at Washington. He had recently been staying with Theodore Roosevelt, with whom he was on intimate terms. He talked of Alaska, and this is a memorandum of what he said on that occasion:

> Spring Rice told me that the Americans will never agree to arbitration nor to any arrangement which would give us a port on tidal waters, and that the best thing we can do is to come to terms at once,

so as to remove the question from the arena of controversy. He say *he*
enemies of England, and particularly the foreign element in the United
States, want the question to remain a running sore, in the hope that it
may some day produce a rupture between the two countries—that
Roosevelt and all those who are at heart friendly to England, want it
settled for the opposite reason. He adds that we should accept anything
they offer on condition that the question is finally disposed of.

I saw Spring-Rice off at 4.10 p.m. for New York and wrote a
memo of our conversation to Sir Wilfrid Laurier.

A day or two later Sir Wilfrid sent for me and asked me to draft
two telegrams, one to the King and the other to Lord Kitchener,
conveying the congratulations of the Canadian Government on peace
having been declared.

I sent him the following:

> 1st. *My Ministers hasten to offer to His Majesty the King the*
> *humble and loyal congratulations of the people of Canada on the*
> *restoration of peace in South Africa, and they regard the announcement*
> *on the eve of the approaching solemnities of the coronation as forming*
> *a happy augury for the long continued prosperity and greatness of His*
> *Majesty's reign.*
>
> 2nd. *Canada rejoices and congratulates you and army on the con-*
> *clusion of what we all feel will prove a lasting and honourable peace.*

Both of these he accepted.

Sir Wilfrid also spoke to me on that occasion in a vague sort of
way about seeing Mr. Fielding as to my going to England with him
to the Coronation, but I could make nothing of it, except it showed
me that the idea was in his mind. I did not wish to press him,
however, or to ask any questions. In fact, I was not particularly
anxious to go. The press, however, had me booked for the Coronation, in which they were wrong.

In the course of the summer, part of which was spent as usual at
Rivière du Loup with my family, I visited my old haunts in Prince
Edward Island in the company of my youngest son and we had some
fishing and shooting.

On the 18th of October, Sir Wilfrid Laurier returned from
England after four months' absence at the Coronation. He was

received by the Mayor and Corporation of Ottawa and made one
of his taking speeches. Physically, he had grown very thin; indeed,
my recollection is that he told me he had lost sixty pounds in weight
during his absence, which scarcely seems credible in a man who at
the outside I should say never weighed more than one hundred
and eighty pounds.

During the days following Sir Wilfrid's return, speculation was
rife as to the course the Prime Minister intended to pursue with
regard to his colleague, the Minister of Public Works, who had
sorely tried his leader's patience by openly advocating the policy
of protection during Sir Wilfrid's absence in Europe, and by
numerous acts of insubordination. People had not long to wait.
While Mr. Tarte's resignation is dated one day in advance of the
Premier's letter demanding it, the latter in the circumstances
amounted to summary dismissal, which Tarte richly deserved for
presuming in the absence of the head of the Government to lay
down a policy for the Ministry, and particularly the policy of protection, which he well knew was anathema to most of them. There
can be little doubt that Mr. Tarte was deceived by the newspaper
reports which reached this country from time to time during the
summer of 1902 into thinking that Sir Wilfrid's health was irretriev-
ably shattered, and he deluded himself with the idea that the mantle
of Elijah was about to fall upon him. While the justice of his treatment was generally acknowledged, an impression prevailed in
certain quarters that Tarte had been treated somewhat harshly in the
form of his dismissal, an impression which I did not share. If the
critics meant its manner was at variance with Sir Wilfrid's habitual
courtesy towards his colleagues, in fact towards everybody, they
were undoubtedly correct. That Mr. Tarte's fault did not deserve
the penalty, I am not prepared to say. To me it only showed that
the provocation must have been very great to have called forth from
a leader possessing so much gentleness and charm such prompt and
vigorous action, and after all in turning him out of his Cabinet
whether he followed, in doing so, the more ceremonious phraseology
employed by Lord North to Fox[1] on a like occasion or summarily

---

[1] 'Sir, His Majesty has thought proper to order a new commission of the Treasury
to be made out, in which I do not perceive your name.'

ejected him as he did, the result was much the same. My feeling was that Tarte richly deserved all he got for his manifold treason, and I think most people agreed with me. Never was a downfall more sudden and complete. Tarte spluttered for a while, but his light soon went out, and Sir Wilfrid by his swift and dramatic course found himself happily delivered from what had grown to be an intolerable nuisance.

Whilst Sir Wilfrid's unwonted severity towards Mr. Tarte was most exceptional, it was not absolutely unprecedented. Two years before the date of the Tarte episode, the Dominion Government removed from the office of Lieutenant-Governor of British Columbia Mr. T. R. McInnes, who had been guilty of various improprieties, and whose official conduct was such as richly merited dismissal. It did not seem to me, however, a question of such extreme urgency as to call for anything beyond the usual mode of notification. Yet not only was the offending Lieutenant-Governor dismissed by telegraph, but he was directed by the same channel to deliver forthwith the Great Seal of the Province into the hands of the Chief Justice, who had been nominated Administrator of the Government pending the appointment of a new Lieutenant-Governor. I merely record both these instances without in the smallest degree questioning the propriety of the Prime Minister's action in either, but in both his course was very unlike Sir Wilfrid Laurier.

Meanwhile the Prime Minister's health continued very precarious. Accompanied by Lady Laurier, he went down to Hot Springs, in Virginia, to which address I telegraphed him on his birthday, the 20th of November, my customary salutation 'Ad multos annos.' He thus replied:

> *The Homestead,*
> *Hot Springs, Va.*
> *Nov. 22, 1902.*

My dear Pope,

Many thanks for your very kind wishes. The telegraph received here instead of writing down the latin: 'ad', has substituted the saxon 'add'. It is just as well, as conveying your own thought. I would willingly add multos annos to sixty-one, if they were coupled with good health. Without that most precious of all human gifts, I would not care for multos annos, *they would simply be a burden.*

I expect much good from my stay here: it is a delightful spot. The atmosphere is balmy, the sun almost as warm as June with us. Every day I walk in the open air without an overcoat. In Ottawa, I suppose it is winter, and if not winter, it is even worse

Remember us to your wife,

Ever yours sincerely,

WILFRID LAURIER

About this time there was referred to me, as Under-Secretary of State, for examination and report, a fantastic claim by a person styling himself 'le Vicomte de Fronsac', who represented himself as one of the 'members of the nobility of Canada', 'a descendant of the ancient French noblesse', and so forth. I thus reported thereon to my Minister, Mr. R. W. Scott:

MEMORANDUM FOR THE SECRETARY OF STATE

ON THE SUBJECT OF THE CLAIM OF THE 'VICOMTE DE FRONSAC'

The undersigned, with reference to certain communications which have recently been received by the Secretary of State for the Colonies from the 'Vicomte de Fronsac' on the subject of the recognition of a nobility of Canada and Acadia, has the honour to report for the information of the Secretary of State that diligent enquiry on his part fails to disclose anything of the 'Vicomte de Fronsac' beyond the fact that a person so styling himself, some years ago addressed letters from Halifax, Nova Scotia, to some gentlemen in Montreal, inviting their co-operation in the formation of a club which the undersigned presumes subsequently developed into 'L'Ordre Aryen' mentioned in the papers under consideration. From various considerations the undersigned is disposed to conjecture that the 'Vicomte de Fronsac' is not a French Canadian at all, but originally an Acadian, long resident in the United States, so long indeed as to have grown unfamiliar with the salient facts of Canadian history. As an illustration of this it may be pointed out that he grounds his claim to recognition as a descendant of the ancient noblesse, on what he terms the 37th article of the Treaty of Paris of 1763. Now there are only 27 articles in that Treaty, and none of these contains any reference to the matter in hand. The 37th Article of the capitulation of Montreal guarantees to the seigniors peaceable ownership and possession of their property, but says nothing as to ceremonial rights or privileges.

Mr. Scott will doubtlessly infer from the foregoing that the undersigned does not consider the memorial of the 'Vicomte de Fronsac' worthy of further consideration; but inasmuch as the Secretary of State for the Colonies asks for a report on the subject, he may be permitted to observe that in none of the treaties or compacts between England and France, with respect to Canada, is there any pledge of recognition of an order of nobility as the term is understood in England. In considering this question it is necessary to bear in mind that the order of noblesse established by Louis XIV in Canada offers no analogy to the British peerage, but resembles the various continental orders of nobility in being rather a caste than a rank, the nearest equivalent to which is perhaps afforded by the English expression 'of gentle blood'. These nobles or seigniors individually enjoyed certain territorial feudal rights and privileges which were uniformly respected by the British Crown, until extinguished by the Parliament of Canada in 1854, on the basis of compensation to the holders.

The undersigned has no disposition to ignore the fact that there exist today, in what was formerly Lower Canada, French Canadian families who justly pride themselves on their distinguished lineage; but these do not form a corporate entity: they claim no distinctive privileges, nor do they possess, as such, any legal status.

The claim of the Baron de Longueuil cited by the 'Vicomte de Fronsac' rested upon a different footing. His ancestor, in addition to being numbered among the noblesse, was created a Baron by Louis XIV, and this title was formally recognized by Her late Majesty Queen Victoria, but such recognition was accorded on the individual merits of the case, after diligent research by the Heralds' College and the authentication of the claim to the satisfaction of the Garter King of Arms.

The undersigned can only call to mind two French Canadian families dwelling in Canada today, descendant from the holder of a specific title like the Baron de Longueuil, neither of which, he need scarcely add, is represented by the 'Vicomte de Fronsac'.

All of which is respectfully submitted.

JOSEPH POPE

Under Secretary of State

Ottawa, 30th January 1902.

In due course my report came before the Garter King of Arms, who thus expressed his views thereon:

69 St. George's Road,
Warwick Square, S.W.
30th April, 1902.

Sir,

In returning the files of papers forwarded by the direction of Mr. Secretary Chamberlain for my information as to the correspondence with Monsieur de Fronsac upon the subject of the French Nobility of Canada and Acadia, I beg leave to state that after a careful perusal of all the documents, I entirely concur in the view expressed in the Reports signed by Mr. Joseph Pope, Under-Secretary of State, to the Governor-General of Canada.

At the same time I have formally replied to the letter addressed to me by Monsieur de Fronsac indicating to him the reference which must be adduced in the event of a reference to me through the proper Department of the State of a claim by a British subject to the use of a Foreign title; and I have the honour to enclose a copy of such reply for the information of your Department.

I am, etc.

ALBERT W. WOODS
Garter

1903 – 1905

THE year 1903 is known in my annals as the Alaska Boundary year,
I having been twice to England and also to Washington on business
connected with that international question.

One January afternoon Sir Wilfrid sent for me to tell me that a
treaty was on the point of being signed between Great Britain and
the United States, providing for the establishment of an arbitral
tribunal to determine the questions at issue between the two
countries in respect of the boundary between Alaska and Canada.
He added that if the arbitration came off, as it probably would,
I would certainly go in full charge as Agent. He mentioned very confidentially certain names of counsel as then likely to attend. I was
naturally elated at the news as regards myself, but when I came to
consider the matter more calmly, I realized very fully my own inadequacy for the position of Agent. To begin with, I was not a
lawyer. It is true that neither Tenterden at Geneva nor Ford at
Halifax were lawyers, but while perhaps not absolutely indispensable, I could not help feeling that a legal training was a great

qualification for such a position. What tempered my ardour, however, more than anything was the feeling that our case, in respect
of its really important feature, the ownership of the heads of inlets,
was not overstrong, being dependent on the interpretation of
language confessedly ambiguous and prejudged by years of neglect
and delay in asserting the British claims. While, therefore, I made
up my mind that if the Government offered me the position I would
accept it and do my best to justify their selection, I confess to a
feeling of relief on hearing that they had reconsidered their judgement, and that Mr. Clifford Sifton, the Minister of the Interior,
would go as Agent. Mr. Sifton was a lawyer, and a good one too.
He was also much better fitted than myself to make the best, before
an international tribunal, of a case not conspicuous for its strength.
Moreover, he was a cabinet minister with all the prestige appertaining to that rank. Altogether there was no comparison between
our respective qualifications for the post, and the result justified the
selection, for so far as the issue depended upon the Agent, no man
could have done better than Mr. Sifton.

Our party consisted of Mr. Sifton, Mr. F. C. Wade, counsel, the
Agent's staff, Messrs. W. F. King, J. J. McArthur, A. P. Collier,
and myself. We were to have sailed by the s.s. *Cedric*, but at the last
moment our arrangements had to be changed, and we took passage
by the s.s. *Kron Prinz Wilhelm*, a large ship admirably managed
throughout. Sailing from New York on the 24th of March we
landed at Plymouth on the 30th, and reached Paddington late the
same evening. We put up at the Hotel Cecil, and lost no time in
unpacking and getting to work. At the start the Agent asked us to
abstain as far as possible from making any social engagements that
would interfere with our work until our case had been completed
and delivered. We all agreed to this, and stuck to it, though it
involved a good deal of assiduous application. What with discussions
with Sir John Anderson and researches at the Colonial Office, and
with Mr. Villiers at the Foreign Office, conferences with Mr.
Edward Blake and Mr. Christopher Robinson, our leading counsel,
visits to the Records Office, the Hudson's Bay House, the British
Museum, and much hard work in our offices in the hotel, I had
quite enough to do.

Before I had been in London many days I had the good fortune to discover hidden in the recesses of the Foreign Office three maps for which we had long been searching: the Arrowsmith map of 1822, the Faden map of 1823, and the Russian map of 1802. As Mr. Sifton said to me at the time, 'That was a great find of yours, Pope.' I should add that a large part of my time was taken up with the drudgery of reading proof. We had much to do in little time, and we all put our shoulders to the wheel in any capacity in which we might be of service. In April I had a rather sharp attack of gout which confined me to bed for a few days, but I soon recovered, and the enforced rest did me no harm.

At length, on the 1st of May, almost the last day fixed for the purpose, I waited upon Mr. Choate, the United States ambassador in London, and formally delivered to him the British case and appendices; thence I went to Lord Alverstone's, where I left a copy for the Lord Chief Justice, and then to the Foreign Office, where I left one for Lord Lansdowne, adding in my diary, 'A great load off my mind.' I was much struck by Mr. Choate's courtliness and dignity of bearing, and have always looked back on that brief interview with him as one of the most memorable in my life. Lord Alverstone, too, was very pleasant, while Lord Lansdowne was an old friend.

Mr. Sifton was most appreciative in his remarks. When thanking me for my services, he told me that without my assistance they could not have managed to get the case ready in time, which was very nice of him to say and very pleasant for me to hear.

Previous Agents had been agreeable men to work for, but Sir Charles Hibbert Tupper and I were life-long friends, as was Sir Louis Davies, while Sir Clifford Sifton (to anticipate his honours) and I were strangers a month before our association in this work began, yet nobody could have habitually treated me with more kindness and confidence than he.

I was fortunate, too, in my associates. Mr. F. C. Wade was an eminently genial person, and we speedily became great friends. His love of Dickens and of Shakespeare established a double bond of union between us, and many a pleasant hour I spent in his company investigating places, particularly on the south side of the Thames, which have been immortalized by the great novelist. Mr. W. F.

King, Dominion astronomer, who accompanied the mission as principal technical officer, was an old and intimate friend.

While we faithfully observed the Agent's wishes in the matter, still every day during the preparation of the case we realized that we had to lunch and dine somewhere, so with that intent we sometimes repaired to the Constitutional and Reform Clubs, and now and then to one or other of the various well-known places of entertainment such as the 'Cock' in Fleet Street. Mr. Sifton and I dined sometimes together, more often with Wade and King, always a pleasant *partie carrée*, even though we merely suspended operations for dinner to resume our labours later. We also dined with Mr. Blake at the House of Commons, with Mr. Rowlatt, one of our English counsel, at the Oxford and Cambridge Club, and with Mr. Duff-Miller at the Constitutional. At the latter place I met Sir Edward Clarke, who related to me an interesting story about Lord Beaconsfield (which rather agrees with one Sir John Macdonald used to tell about Disraeli putting forward his Jewish lineage) to the effect that the last words he was heard to utter on his death-bed were, in the Hebrew tongue, 'Hear, O Israel, the Lord thy God is one God.'

Among the friendships I formed on this trip was that with the Hon. Arthur Elliot, brother of Lord Minto, and editor of the *Edinburgh Review*, for which I had written an article on the Alaska boundary three years before.

I spent a pleasant afternoon with Mr. and the Hon. Mrs. Howard (the present Lady Strathcona) at Ranelagh, dined, and drove back in the evening.

At Lord Lansdowne's I took into dinner on one occasion Lady Rodd, whom I afterwards met in Rome, where her husband, Sir Rennell Rodd, was British Ambassador.

On the afternoon of Ascension Day, at the special invitation of Lord William Seymour, Lieutenant of the Tower, a party of us paid a visit to that memorable institution, which we thoroughly inspected, and afterwards drank tea with Lord and Lady William Seymour.

I saw quite a number of theatres on this visit, among others *A Chinese Honeymoon* at the Strand—very good; *Whitewashing Julia*; Daly's Theatre, *The Country Girl*—fair; The Duke of York's, *The Admirable Crichton*—excellent; and Ellen Terry in *Much Ado About*

Nothing, where I went as the guest of Mr. and Mrs. C. Robinson and which I vastly enjoyed.

When I was lunching one day with Lord and Lady Mount Stephen, Lady Mount Stephen told me that the Princess of Wales knew I was in London, that Her Royal Highness had told her so. Accordingly I went and wrote my name at Marlborough House, as I should have done long before, but the preparation of the Alaska boundary case must bear the blame.

I saw quite a little of my old Bering Sea friends, Maxwell and Cartwright, and spent a Sunday at Brighton with the latter. I also visited Greenwich Observatory, where I was kindly received by Mr. Maunder who showed me over the building and explained the uses of the various mechanisms I saw there. Referring to some instrument of precision, I remember remarking that I suppose it could measure down to a tenth of a second. 'Oh,' replied he, 'a tenth is very rough work. A hundredth of a second is better.' Very likely a thousandth is rough work now, but a tenth is still sufficiently precise for my requirements.

I dined with the Baroness Macdonald of Earnscliffe and her daughter Mary quite frequently, and spent some time with them, with Lord and Lady Lansdowne, Lord and Lady Strathcona (rather often), the Mount Stephens, Colmers, and other old friends, including Lord and Lady Derby, who upon all occasions were most kind to me. The latter was good enough to tell me that there was always a place for me at luncheon whenever it might be convenient for me to come in, an invitation which, while I much appreciated it, I did not take too literally. I spent a week-end at Knebworth, the guest of Lord and Lady Strathcona, where I slept in one of Queen Elizabeth's numerous beds.

On Whitsun Monday, Wade, King, and I had a delightful day at Canterbury, where the Cathedral greatly impressed me. We visited the scene of St. Thomas à Becket's murder, and also the spot where his shrine stood before it was violated by that sacrilegious ruffian Henry VIII. We also visited the Black Prince's tomb, and saw his helmet, sword, &c. suspended above. We heard evensong beautifully sung by the choir in the presence of the archbishop. Then we drove to St. Martin's, the oldest church in England, which we could only view from the outside, and so back to town. Altogether a most pleasant day.

On reaching my hotel I found that Sir Arthur Bigge had telephoned me an invitation to lunch next day with the Prince and Princess of Wales at Frogmore. I telegraphed my acceptance, and left on the 1 p.m. train from Paddington. A royal carriage met me at Windsor station and drove me to Frogmore, where I shook hands with Sir Arthur Bigge, Sir Charles Cust, Lord Hyde, and another A.D.C. Then I met Lady Airlie, and afterwards the Prince and Princess of Wales came in. Her Royal Highness at once thanked me for my book on *The Royal Tour in Canada*, which had recently appeared. Then luncheon was announced, and we all went in. The Princess motioned me to sit on her left hand. The conversation which followed was very pleasant and free. We discussed Windsor, Canterbury, Slough, Stoke Poges, and of course Canada. Soon the children came in, shook hands, and the little boy of three (Prince Henry) put up his face to be kissed. I kissed him, patted the wee baby's cheek (Prince George), smiled at the little girl (Princess Mary), and then they ran away, the eldest boy (Prince Edward) first hanging over his mother, evidently begging some favour which she granted, and he tripped merrily away.

After luncheon the Prince spoke with me a lot of Canada, dwelling particularly on the loyalty of the French Canadians. Turning suddenly round to me, he said, 'Have you any French blood in you?' 'No, Sir,' replied I. 'My ancestors came from Cornwall.' 'Then how is it you are a Roman Catholic?' 'Oh,' I said, 'part of my family are Catholics.' Her Royal Highness was going out, and when she said good-bye to me, asked if I would care to see the Mausoleum. I of course said I should be very glad of the privilege, whereupon Sir Arthur Bigge took me over. It is beautiful beyond words, this large circular chapel with the two recumbent statues of the Queen and the Prince Consort lying side by side in the centre, and the Princess Alice and her baby at one side. At the four cardinal points, Isaiah, Solomon, Daniel, and David look down upon them. It appears that when the Mausoleum was erected for the Prince Consort, the Queen had her recumbent statue made at the same time, so that she appears not as an old woman, but as she looked in 1861. The rest and peace of that sanctuary are beyond words of mine to express. Then Sir Arthur Bigge and I returned to the house, he showing me on the way the old Queen's summer house, where she spent her mornings in fine weather. On our return I was ushered into the royal presence, as the Prince wished to say good-bye. He asked me how I liked the Mausoleum. 'Isn't it peaceful?' said he. 'Such a feeling of restfulness it produces,' which was what particularly struck me. I should say that the public are not admitted to this Mausoleum, so that it was a special privilege accorded to me, which I much appreciated. Then the royal carriage came round and I drove off to the station, reaching Paddington about 5.15 p.m. I dined with Wade at the National Liberal Club, and spent the next day leaving P.P.C. cards. My farewell dinner was with Lord Strathcona, and I left London on Friday the 5th of June for Liverpool, sailing for New York in the s.s. *Cedric*, at that time the largest ship in the world.

As I record in my diary, 'I leave England with mingled feelings—regret to separate myself from this dear land, and pleasure at the prospect of seeing my wife and children soon again.' On the 15th of June after a favourable voyage, I reached New York, where my wife met me, and my second visit to old England passed into history.

I had not long returned from England when I visited Washington on Alaska boundary business, with the special object of procuring photographic copies of certain documents bearing upon the ancient international controversy between Great Britain, Russia, and the United States respecting the Oregon boundary, in which the parallel of 54° 40' north latitude formerly bore a large part. The National Democratic Convention of 1844 demanded the reoccupation of the whole territory of Oregon, up to 54° 40' 'with or without war with England', and this agitation in popular parlance became widely known as 'Fifty-four forty or fight'. On the present occasion I brought with me a secretary and a photographer, and having transacted our business at the old Arlington Hotel, we slipped out of Washington as quietly as we had entered. On leaving, I asked the clerk at the desk for my bill. He passed it out under the wicket—I picked it up and read '$54.40', at which I nearly collapsed.

The Alaska Boundary Tribunal met in London in September. In

August we sailed for England, Mr. Sifton and party, to attend its
sittings, my wife and I in the good ship *Pretorian*. The Tribunal
assembled on the 3rd of September in the Diplomatic Reception
Room of the Foreign Office, under the presidency of Lord Alverstone, whose attitude towards the United States side of the case
filled us with misgivings which were destined to be realized. After
certain formalities, the Tribunal adjourned till the 15th. On the
afternoon of Saturday the 12th my wife and I went down to Cranleigh
to spend the week-end with Lord Alverstone, whom we knew
intimately, having passed six months together in Paris at the Bering
Sea Arbitration ten years before. Of what happened during this
week-end visit, I do not consider myself at liberty to speak, he
having bound me to the strictest secrecy beforehand, but I may say
that I kept before me the whole time the paramount duty of being
absolutely loyal to my chief the Agent. The position, at times, was
most embarrassing, and Lord Alverstone very improperly took
advantage of old personal friendship to put to me questions he should
not have asked, but having given my word beforehand not to divulge
what passed between us, I could not break it. As I told him at the
time, the person to whom his enquiries should have been addressed
was the Agent, who was also a member of the Canadian Government,
and not to a permanent official like myself. I was strongly tempted to
refuse to receive his confidence, but I reflected that such a course
of action might have precipitated an open rupture, and I could not
see how it would have been in the interests of the Canadian Government that I should start the proceedings by a quarrel with the president of the Tribunal, whom it was to our interest to conciliate in
every way. Moreover, I knew the Lord Chief Justice, and was very
careful what I said to him, by no means gratifying his curiosity to
the extent he could have wished. The subject has long since lost
whatever interest it might have originally possessed, but I may say
that subsequently I received the fullest assurance from Sir Wilfrid
Laurier that in a trying situation I had borne myself as he would have
wished me to do. Mr. Sifton too, to whom I related the circumstances, told me that I was not to blame. I found when I got back
to town that Lord Alverstone had been talking to others besides
myself, and that his views as to the ownership of the heads of inlets

were more or less known. I left Cranleigh on Monday morning, the 14th of September, by no means sanguine as to the probable result of the forthcoming arbitration as regards the main contention, though I was not prepared for the scurvy trick Lord Alverstone played on us on that occasion in giving Sitklan and Kannaghunut Islands to the United States by diverting the boundary, after passing Wales Island, to the Tongass Passage, instead of continuing it along that passage to the north of Sitklan and Kannaghunut Islands.

The Alaska Boundary Tribunal was composed of the following members: British—Lord Alverstone, Lord Chief Justice of England, Mr. A. B. (afterwards Sir Allen) Aylesworth, K.C., of Toronto, and Sir Louis Jetté, Lieutenant-Governor of Quebec; American—the Hon. Elihu Root, the Hon. Henry Cabot Lodge, and the Hon. George Turner. Our counsel were Sir Robert Finlay, K.C., M.P., the Attorney-General of England, the Rt. Hon. Sir Edward H. Carson, M.P., the Solicitor-General of England, and the following members of the Canadian bar: Mr. C. Robinson, K.C., Mr. F. C. Wade, K.C., Mr. L. P. Duff, K.C., Mr. A. Geoffrion, K.C., and Mr. S. A. T. Rowlatt. The Hon. Clifford Sifton, K.C., M.P. (afterwards Sir Clifford Sifton, K.C.M.G.), the Minister of the Interior of Canada, was His Majesty's Agent before the Tribunal. Mr. J. R. Carter, Second Secretary of the American Embassy, and myself were chosen Associate Secretaries.

The oral arguments began on the 15th of September and were ably presented on the part of His Majesty by Sir Robert Finlay, Mr. C. Robinson, Sir Edward Carson, and Mr. Rowlatt, and also by Mr. Dickinson and others of the American bar, and were concluded on the 9th of October. On the 20th the President announced the decision of the Tribunal, and our worst fears were realized. With the aid of the Lord Chief Justice, the three American Commissioners decided that the line of demarcation ran round the heads of the inlets, instead of crossing them, according to the British contention. At this no one could have been surprised, for Lord Alverstone had virtually announced it before he had heard a word of the oral argument, but what amazed everybody was his decision that the boundary line should run between Sitklan and Wales Island. I have heard various theories put forward to account for his

extraordinary judgement, all more or less unworthy of Lord
Alverstone's great office and himself. I prefer to disbelieve them all,
and to regard his attitude as one of those mysteries destined to
remain unsolved. Fortunately, Lord Alverstone's decision as to the
course to be taken by the boundary line along the Portland Channel
was without practical significance. Both Sitklan and Kannaghunut,
which by this decision were assigned to the United States, are small
rocky islands three and a half and three and a quarter miles long
respectively, covered with a thick growth of spruce, and valueless,
for any purposes at present known. These islands are fifteen miles
from Port Simpson, from shore to shore, and are strategically
unimportant, being commanded by Wales Island. This, however,
was not known at the time. The decision caused great dissatisfaction
in Canada, a dissatisfaction which would have been more acute had
Lord Alverstone's part in the affair been more fully known.

I desire to record here that Lord Alverstone never, at any time,
suggested to me in the most remote manner that he thought Tongass
Passage was Portland Channel, or hinted that our case for Wales
and Pearse Islands did not cover Sitklan and Kannaghunut Islands.
See our case, page 50, which he himself declared to be 'quite
convincing'. In it we say 'Great Britain contends that "la passe dite
Portland Channel" means the channel which Vancouver named Portland Canal, and which enters from the ocean between Tongass Island
and Kannaghunut Island, leaving Sitklan, Wales and Pearse Islands on
the South and East, and extending northerly 82 miles to its head.'

At no stage of the proceedings was such a claim ever put forward
by the American counsel. Nobody on either side ever suggested such
a thing as a division of these four islands. When we were awaiting
the signing of the award on the 20th of October a legal gentleman
associated with our case and one extremely well informed on the
whole question asked me if I knew where the 'Chief' got the idea
of running Portland Channel between Sitklan and Wales Islands.
I said, 'I think I should ask you that question.' He answered, 'I'm
blessed if I know. I can't see anything in Vancouver of it. I never
heard such a theory mentioned until a day or two ago.'[1]

[1] The following extract from *Theodore Roosevelt* by Lord Charnwood seems to
explain Lord Alverstone's attitude: 'In 1903 there met in London a new Commission:

We all of us felt aggrieved by the treatment we had received at his hands. We were angry and, like Job, 'we did well to be angry'. On the evening of the 19th of October I received a note from Lord Lansdowne, then Secretary of State for Foreign Affairs, whom of course I knew intimately, asking me to call upon him at Lansdowne House next morning, which I did, and we had a talk on the subject of the Alaska boundary decision, at which I expressed myself some-what plainly regarding Lord Alverstone's conduct. Lord Lansdowne, who received me cordially, expressed his regret that things had not gone better with us. He added that he knew Lord Alverstone very slightly, and had purposely refrained from any connection with the case or knowledge of the progress of the Tribunal. Though, unlike the Lord Chief Justice, he exacted no pledge of secrecy, the con-versation was undoubtedly meant to be confidential, and was so regarded by me.[2]

Our second stay in London was not so marked by gaiety as our visit earlier in the year, we being less in the mood for that sort of thing. At the same time my wife and I dined more than once with the Siftons, Robinsons, Rowlatts, Leonard Courtneys, Wades, Duffs, Sir R. Finlay, with the Lord Mayor at the Mansion House, with the Pilgrims at Claridge's Hotel, with Lord and Lady Strathcona, with the Baroness Macdonald, and at several other places.

three Americans, two Canadians, and the Lord Chief Justice of England (Alverstone), to whom it fell to give the deciding vote against the Canadian claim in the Alaskan matter. There is reason to think that the American Commissioners insisted very little upon some of their minor claims, though they believed them to be in themselves sound. When the new Commission was to meet, Roosevelt took a step characteristi-cally drastic and characteristically gentle in manner, to make a miscarriage unlikely— or in other words to prevent any influence that might make the Lord Chief Justice vote wrong. Avoiding the offensiveness of any diplomatic representation, he wrote to a valued American friend of his own and of the British statesmen concerned, and asked to have his real determination made known to them in friendly conversation. It was, he said, only his "very earnest desire to get on well with England", which had made him consent to this second Commission. If it failed, he should take measures which would make arbitration quite impossible, and use the troops (which in fact he had sent to Alaska to keep order) to "run the line as we desire it, without any further regard to the attitude of England and Canada. . . . If," he said, "I paid regard to mere abstract right, that is the position that I ought to take anyhow; I have not taken it, because I wish to exhaust every effort to have the affair settled peacefully and with due regard to England's dignity." This step of his was of course not publicly known till long afterward.'

[2] When nearly forty years ago my father wrote the foregoing, he did so with noticeable reserve. After a lapse of more than half a century it would not, perhaps, be amiss to append some extracts from his diary of that day. They are given on pages 296 to 299.

On Sunday, the 18th of October, we lunched with Lord and Lady Ilchester at Holland House, where we spent a most delightful afternoon. Lady Ilchester showed us over the historic old house personally, and was in every respect most kind.

My wife and I left London for Liverpool next morning and sailed by the s.s. *Cedric* the same day, reaching New York on the following Friday, and thence to Ottawa. We found a good deal of excitement in Canada over the Alaska boundary affair, which quieted down after a while, leaving behind it, as far as I was concerned, a sense of injustice and wrong.

On our return to Ottawa we resumed our intimacy with the Lauriers, dining or spending the evening at their house, at least once, almost every week and sometimes oftener. I found Sir Wilfrid on my return in November 1903 looking very frail, but his health subsequently improved. I took an early opportunity of telling him my story of how Lord Alverstone had treated me and received his renewed assurance that I had acted rightly, and not to worry over it. Lord Minto sent for me and we had some conversation over Alaska, at which I was very guarded after my experience with Lord Alverstone, not quite knowing *whom* to trust. I did, however, say to Lord Minto that I thought that His Majesty's Ministers, in virtually ignoring the members of our commission (I mean in the social line) during their stay in England, had made a serious mistake.

Shortly after my return to Canada the Hon. Mr. Fisher, Minister of Agriculture, spoke to me at length on the subject of the Archives, in which I had always taken a great interest. He conveyed to me the gratifying intelligence that he had submitted to his colleagues a scheme for the organization of an Archives Department, with Dr. Doughty as Archivist. This I have always regarded as the beginning of the present system, which under the capable hands of Dr. Doughty has become a credit to the Dominion.

In February 1904 I experienced the unusual incident of meeting and greeting old Senator Wark of New Brunswick, who had been born on the 19th of February 1804, and was tendered a reception in the Senate Chamber to commemorate the event by the presentation of an oil painting on the part of his colleagues. I had already sent him a telegram of congratulations wishing him many more years,

adding that he was twenty years behind Moses, the last legislator
to cross the century mark, at which the old man was much taken.

During the early part of 1904, a sensation was caused by the Earl
of Dundonald, then commanding the Canadian militia, publicly
accusing the Hon. Sydney Fisher, at the time Minister of Agriculture,
of interfering, for political purposes, with the administration of the
militia, an episode which resulted in Lord Dundonald's removal
from office. While there were probably faults on both sides, I, as
a Government official, was not required to discuss them with
anybody, and I was most careful not to do so, though more than
once afforded the opportunity. There was a good deal of excitement
over this affair. Though on personal grounds I could not help
feeling a genuine sympathy with Lord Dundonald, I considered that
his offence involved a grave act of insubordination which could not
be passed over. Whether his fault justified the extreme penalty
dealt out to him is another question upon which I was not called
to express an opinion. It suggested to my mind, however, Sir John
Macdonald's reply to an enquiry once put to him relative to a
punishment imposed upon a civil servant, in which the Prime
Minister took the merciful view. Lady Macdonald, who was present
at the discussion, remarked, 'But Sir John, don't you think ——
—— deserved it?' 'My dear,' answered he, 'if we all got what we
deserved, some of us might be in a bad way.' I note in my diary that
the farewell demonstration to Lord Dundonald of the 26th of July,
at which I was not present, was in size and enthusiasm quite unprecedented in the history of the capital.

It was announced in the course of this summer that Earl Grey
was to succeed Lord Minto as Governor-General of Canada, and
my friend Maude told me that Lord Grey had offered him the
position of Governor-General's Secretary, which however he had
to decline as he had been appointed second-in-command of his
battalion and was obliged to return home. I regretted this more
than I can say. We had been close and constant friends, much more
so than this book discloses, and I had been the recipient of many
confidences which do not admit of being recorded. Maude also
told me that his successor would be Colonel Hanbury Williams, of
whom I was destined to know more.

At about this time I attended a dinner at the Rideau Club, which I record in my diary as follows: 'I dined this evening at the Rideau Club the guest of Mr. W. L. Mackenzie King [at that time Deputy Minister of Labour] to meet Professor Goldwin Smith. A very pleasant evening. The old gentleman was reminiscent and oracular as usual, but is getting very old. He said Morley's 3rd volume of Gladstone was not history. The other two were. Gladstone, he added, has most wonderful powers of self-delusion. Chamberlain was about to betray Balfour, as he had betrayed Gladstone, and so on.'

We spoke of Imperial statesmen. Among others I happened to mention Mr. Asquith as a possible Liberal Prime Minister. This the Professor deprecated on grounds which I do not recall with any degree of precision, but the general effect produced on my mind was that Professor Goldwin Smith regarded Mr. Asquith as quite out of the running for the Premiership. Yet, like my suggestion made to Sir John Macdonald in 1888 of Mr. Abbott as his possible successor, which was fulfilled in 1891, so Mr. Asquith succeeded Sir Campbell Bannerman in the corresponding office of Prime Minister of England a few years after the date of this conversation at Mr. Mackenzie King's hospitable table

The general elections came off in November of this year, and resulted, as was generally looked for, in a large majority for the Government, which carried the whole eighteen seats in Nova Scotia. Mr. R. L. Borden, then leader of the Opposition, who was beaten in his own constituency, behaved very pluckily. To a newspaper reporter who asked him if he was going to retire, he recalled the case of the naval captain who had a leg shot off in action. As he lay on the deck, with his ship on fire about him, a summons came to surrender. 'Surrender?' he cried. 'Why, the battle has only just begun!'

On the 8th of November I attended a farewell dinner to Lord Minto given at the Rideau Club. The president (Dr. Montizambert) made a capital speech in proposing Lord Minto's health. His Excellency's reply was equally happy. This action of the Rideau Club in entertaining a departing Governor-General was without precedent, and testified to the extreme popularity of the retiring Governor, to whom and to the Maudes, a few days later, we bade an affectionate farewell. This latter occasion is especially impressed upon my memory as being the only time in my life that I can recall applauding a woman's speech in public, for I am a firm believer in St. Paul's dictum that a woman should 'be in silence'. In this case, however, Lady Minto, who was merely acknowledging the receipt of a civic address and the presentation of a parting gift in the name of the citizens of Ottawa, performed her part with such grace and sweetness as I think would have reconciled St. Paul to making an exception in her favour, as I know it did me.

Of all the Governors-General under whom I served I think perhaps I was most intimate with Lord Minto (1898–1904). This probably arose from the fact that I knew him in two capacities— first, in 1885, as Lord Melgund, when he filled the office of Governor-General's Secretary, and I was Private Secretary to Sir John Macdonald, and then thirteen years later when he came as Governor-General himself.

In both I liked him more than I can say, and well I might, for he was always most courteous and friendly to me. Lady Minto too was everything a Governor-General's wife should be, and by her grace and charm must have been of great assistance to her husband.

In the interregnum between the departure of Lord Minto and the assumption of office by Lord Grey, the administratorship of the Government was filled by Chief Justice Sir Elzéar Taschereau, who in a note to me as Under-Secretary of State, laid claim to the title of 'His Excellency', which for the past few years had been discontinued as having been employed in the past without authority. This view was taken by the Governor-General's office, as well as by my own. So keenly did the Administrator feel upon the subject that he cabled the Secretary of State for the Colonies on the point, and received a reply to the effect that the Administrator was rightly styled 'His Excellency', which settled the question. Some years after this, Lord Minto told me himself that this whole affair was the result of a misapprehension—that no such telegram as that referred to above was sent from the Colonial Office by anyone having authority to speak in the name of the Colonial Secretary, and I gathered from Lord Minto that the original position taken by the Governor-General's Secretary in 1904 was with his full approval. The conduct of the Administrator on this and subsequent occasions

on which he was called to act in that capacity struck me as childish
in the extreme, and showed that he altogether misconceived his
position. An Administrator is appointed as a matter of necessity to
do things which must be done, and he should do those things which
are necessary as quietly and unostentatiously as possible. For this
reason it is neither expected nor desired that an Administrator should
assume any social obligations in the way of entertainment, or do
anything beyond what is imperatively required of him. This is all
set forth in a Colonial Office dispatch from the Secretary of State
for the Colonies to the Earl of Dufferin dated 8 April 1875.

On the 7th of December a number of Ministers and officials,
including myself as the Custodian for the Secretary of State of the
Great Seal of Canada, left Halifax by a special train organized to
bring Their Excellencies Lord and Lady Grey to Ottawa. Everything
passed off without incident. A few days after our return, and in
obedience to a summons from the new Governor-General, I waited
upon His Excellency at Government House, who received me very
cordially, and, in his own impulsive manner at once began, 'I know
all about you from my brother-in-law Minto.' He went on to say
that what he specially wished to discuss at the moment was the
question of precedence and the need of revision of the present
Table, which he understood had been in force for a long time and
was in many respects obsolete; that at the state dinner, which was
approaching, he wanted his Prime Minister and leading members
of his Cabinet about him, and not a number of Lieutenant-Governors
and bishops interposed between him and his Ministers. I told him
that I agreed in thinking that both the Lieutenant-Governors and
bishops were too highly placed, but I added that they were there by
the royal authority exercised by the late Queen Victoria, and that
they could only be displaced by like authority; that the prerogative
of honour did not, unless specially delegated, appertain to the
Governor-General, and that the only way of meeting His Excellency's
wishes in this matter was for the Governor-in-Council to send home
a minute advising the Imperial authorities to sanction an amendment
to the Table in the direction of the Prime Minister's wishes. To this
Lord Grey replied that there was not time before the approaching
session of Parliament to carry out this plan. Observing me smile, he

added, 'Could it not be done by cable?' I told him that this question
of precedence had periodically engaged the attention of various
Governors-General and their Prime Ministers to my knowledge for
at least a quarter of a century; that at the present time the non-
episcopal churches were pressing for recognition similar to that
accorded to archbishops and bishops; that religious susceptibilities
were very easily aroused, and that this question was one to be
treated, not by telegraph, but with great circumspection. The
Governor-General then went on to say that he could not see how a
proposal to lower the bishops' status, which was what he wanted to
effect, could be ill received by the non-episcopal bodies. He repeated
that he wished to have Sir Wilfrid Laurier sit beside him at the
approaching state dinner, and that the necessary changes should be
effected at once. Upon my observing that no change such as His
Excellency had in view could be made without the direct sanction
of the Prime Minister; that in giving such sanction Sir Wilfrid
would be opening the door to difficulties which the Government
naturally desired to avoid, and that altogether I did not see how it
could possibly be done, the Governor-General vehemently exclaimed,
'Well, I am d——d if I am going to eat my dinner between two
priests.' He was as good as his word. The dinner came off, presided
over by the Governor-General, who had on his right side Sir
Wilfrid Laurier, and on his left Sir Richard Cartwright. Immediately
there ensued a commotion. Just as I had predicted, the archbishops
remonstrated against a violation of their undoubted rights, confirmed
by the custom of many years. The upshot of it all was that when the
next state dinner came off, the archbishops and bishops were back in
their old places, where they have ever since remained.

I related this incident to Sir Wilfrid for whom, however, questions
of precedence possessed little interest. I am told that when spoken to
on the subject, he has been known to say, 'Go and talk to Pope
about it. He is our great authority on such subjects,' but he took
good care that nothing was ever done. Twenty years more were
destined to pass before any changes to speak of were made in the
venerable Table, and then only after Lord Grey and Sir Wilfrid
Laurier had both passed away.

The year 1905 saw the establishment of the Provinces of Alberta and Saskatchewan. I was much interested in the retention of the historic name of Assiniboia, temporarily assigned to it as a Provisional District in 1882, and wrote to Sir Wilfrid on the subject.

Ottawa, 21st February 1905.

Dear Sir Wilfrid Laurier,

Will you pardon me if I venture to express my regret that the Government propose to discard the historic name of Assiniboia.

That sonorous designation—sounding like the rolling Greek of Homer—was, as you know, applied to the original Red River Settlement in the days of the Hudson's Bay Company. Its retention would connect the new Province with the beginning of things out there, and thus tend to preserve the continuity of the history of the North West. 'Alberta' possesses no significance save that it is the third name of the Duchess of Argyll. While it was all very well to pay a transient sojourner the passing compliment of calling the Provisional district after her, there is, I humbly submit, no sufficient reason to perpetuate a now meaningless appellation on a country which already possesses the euphonious high-sounding name of Assiniboia.

Believe me,

Yours faithfully,

JOSEPH POPE

The Rt. Honourable
  Sir Wilfrid Laurier, G.C.M.G.,
    Premier of Canada,
      Ottawa.

To which the Prime Minister replied:

PRIME MINISTER'S OFFICE
CANADA

Ottawa, 22nd February 1905

My dear Pope,

I regret as much as you do the disappearance of the word 'Assiniboia'. I struggled for it all I could, but it appears that 'Alberta' is now a matter of importance which the members of the North West could not give up. It is really too bad.

Yours very sincerely,

WILFRID LAURIER

Joseph Pope, Esq.,
  Under-Secretary of State,
    Ottawa.

On the 28th of February I was told confidentially by my Minister that the Cabinet was on the verge of disruption over the educational clauses in the North West Provinces Bill, that Mr. Sifton had resigned, and that Mr. Scott looked for a general break-up. In fact, the old gentleman was in the act of packing while speaking to me. I told him I thought he was unnecessarily alarmed—that Mr. Sifton, although a very able man, was not the whole Cabinet, and that we had better (to use Mr. Asquith's phrase of a later day) 'wait and see'. And so it turned out. After an exhibition of furious bigotry amounting to what Sir Wilfrid rightly styled 'a regular panic', such as periodically sweeps the Province of Ontario, or at any rate the city of Toronto, the whole affair fizzled out. A compromise was arrived at between the Government and its western supporters, and the occasion served but to afford one more illustration of the adroitness of Sir Wilfrid Laurier and the unskilfulness of the party calling itself Conservative. As I note in my diary of the 21st of March: 'The "Compromise" in the Educational clauses of the Autonomy Bill was published today. To my mind there is no compromise to speak of. All the essential features of the old clauses are maintained, i.e., Parliament imposes Separate Schools forever on the territories of Alberta and Saskatchewan and provides for their maintenance.'

The Opposition lamentably failed to take advantage of this occasion. Had their leader announced that in conformity with the unbroken tradition and policy of the Conservative party—the party of Macdonald and Cartier, who had opened the Northwest to Canada—he was prepared to give unhesitating support to the educational clauses of the Government as originally introduced, the Opposition would have preserved their own consistency and at the same time rent the Liberal party in twain, besides securing what is known as the 'Catholic vote', without which, as Sir John Macdonald time and again told them, it was impossible to win in Ontario. Instead of this, they took refuge in the narrow and parochial cry of Provincial Rights, which had hitherto been the watch-word of their opponents, and suffered the golden opportunity to pass.

I note in my diary on the 5th of May 1905: 'I forgot to mention that yesterday I showed Sir Charles Fitzpatrick a cypher telegram dated 5th March 1870, from Lord Granville, Colonial Secretary, to Sir J. Young, Governor-General, making the assistance of Imperial troops in the Red River difficulty, contingent upon generous treatment being accorded to the Roman Catholics of that region. Sir Charles used it in the debate. Today Tarte asked permission to have this document photographed, which I gave him. Afterwards I saw him in the Library on the subject.'

And earlier, under the date of 24 March: 'How dexterously has Sir Wilfrid played his cards in this affair. He has united his supporters, divided his opponents, consolidated the Catholic vote all over the country in his favour, and his bill will carry by a large majority.'

In March I accepted an invitation from Messrs. H. and A. Allan of Montreal to be their guest to meet their new turbine steamer *Victorian* at Halifax, and proceed in her to Saint John, New Brunswick. We travelled by special from Montreal to Halifax and a most enjoyable trip it was. Even in those days I had had many trips, but while often very enjoyable they were all more or less official. This was the first occasion on which I travelled perfectly free from responsibility of any kind, with nothing to do but enjoy myself, which I did to the full, and I retain the most pleasant recollections of Sir Montagu Allan's sumptuous hospitality on this occasion. The day after leaving we presented an address of thanks to the Messrs. Allan, which I drafted. It was well received, and was I think the proper thing to do.

1905 — 1907

Expedition to Labrador to Observe Total Solar Eclipse | The Elements Unpropitious | Canadian Minute of Council re Colonial Conferences | H.R.H. Prince Arthur of Connaught's Visit to Canada | Lady Minto | Provincial Conference | Prince Fushimi's Canadian Visit

THE year 1905 was signalized by a total eclipse of the sun visible in Labrador, to observe which the Canadian Government dispatched an expedition. The first section of the party sailed from Quebec in the s.s. *King Edward* on the 4th of August in charge of Dr. W. F. King, Chief Astronomer of the Department of the Interior, having on board Mr. E. Walter Maunder, F.R.A.S., Superintendent of the Solar Department of the Royal Observatory, Greenwich, and also the Rev. I. J. Kavanagh, S.J., of Loyola College, Montreal, and some others. A few days after her return from the first trip, the second section sailed in the *King Edward* on the 22nd of August in my charge, having on board the Rev. C. P. Choquette, President of St. Hyacinthe College, the Rev. H. Simard, Professor of Physics, Laval University, Quebec, Messrs. H. H. and Walter Lyman of Montreal, Mr. Montague Aldous, head of the Land Department of the Hudson's Bay Company, Winnipeg, Mr. A. S. Johnson, representing the Toronto *Globe*, and others—ten persons in all.

Our destination was the Hudson's Bay Post of the North West

River at its confluence with the Hamilton River, in latitude 53° 31′ 31″ North and longitude 60° 3′ West. Our trip was a very pleasant one, but unfortunately the morning of the fateful 30th of August was cloudy, and we did not see the sun, which was a great disappointment to us, as we had come a long way, and total eclipses of the sun are very rare. I think I am right in saying that no total eclipse of the sun has been seen in London for upwards of six hundred years.

I thus record in my diary an account of my experience on that memorable occasion:

MONDAY, 28 AUGUST 'Another lovely day. At 4 a.m. we departed from our anchorage near Saddle Island and proceeded to Rigolet, situated within Hamilton Inlet on the north side of the Narrows leading to Lake Melville. There is no wharf at this place, which nevertheless is the principal settlement along the coast. One can see here the house occupied by Lord Strathcona when Hudson's Bay agent, some Esquimaux, Esquimaux dogs, and that is about all.

'A Newfoundland Customs officer boarded us at Rigolet, and after breakfast I had a chat with him. He was very civil, merely asking for a list of the names of our party. I put several questions to him with the object of ascertaining to what extent Newfoundland exercised jurisdiction in Labrador. He told me he was the only stationary Customs officer on the coast. Another patrolled the coast all summer from Blanc Sablon to Nain in the Newfoundland packet, but Rigolet was the only place possessing a resident officer, and he remained at Rigolet only during the summer months—leaving about the 1st of October. The mails were left periodically during the season by the Newfoundland packet. There were no courts of justice along the coast—all prisoners being taken for trial to St. Johns. There was no administration of any kind in the interior. The sum of all being that the Newfoundland Government had no officials along the coast save the sub-collector at Rigolet, and no one inland.

'About 11 a.m. we steamed into Lake Melville which is about 20 miles wide at its inlet. At three o'clock we could discern the buildings of the North West River Hudson's Bay Post, and a few minutes later the tents of our friends. Later still we espied the flag they had raised in our honour which closer inspection showed to be a representation of the Corona.

'Our ship was gaily decorated with bunting, and as we approached the shore I, as leader of the party, sounded the syren. We found the party all fairly well, though a good deal bothered by black flies and mosquitoes. They were camped on a spot adjoining the Hudson's Bay Post—cleared, it is said, by Lord Strathcona when agent here in the fifties. In fact the encampment was almost on the very point of land formed by the confluence of the North West River with Lake Melville. At the easterly corner—directly across the mouth of the River, a distance of perhaps 200 yards—is the establishment of Révillon Frères, a French firm of fur traders; while across the Lake to the south is the milling establishment of Messrs. Gillis Bros., before alluded to. The latter have a lumber mill which they expect will shortly attain a capacity of 100,000 feet a day.

'The first contingent certainly have not been idle. Besides all the living arrangements they have built stone foundations and erected their instruments on concrete pillars thereon. They have also constructed various working huts—shelters for their instruments, etc. In fact they must have worked like trojans.

'King reports stormy unsettled weather here during the past three weeks—never two days the same. Tonight, after a beautiful day, was fairly fine though the stars shone somewhat dimly and the breeze blew from the East. Altogether the indications are none too favourable.'

WEDNESDAY, 30 AUGUST   'At 4 a.m. I awoke and looked out of my window which faced the south east. The sky was unpromising, but at 5 it was better. The gleam however was but transitory, for at 6, when Aldous, Cotter and I walked over to the camp, it was raining. We were early on the ground. A few minutes later our friends issued from their tents one by one, and we made an effort to be cheerful, but it was hard work. The sky was so completely overcast that if one had not known, it would have been impossible to have told in which quarter of the heavens the sun was situated. Notwithstanding the dismal outlook all the instruments were set up, the clock work going and each observer at his post precisely as though the sky had been without a cloud. Mr. Maunder very kindly

lent me his 4-inch telescope, the stand of which he was using in
photographic work. With the aid of Mr. Upton I succeeded in
rigging up a temporary tripod. With heavy hearts we took up our
positions, ready to take advantage of any miracle that might be
wrought. Alas! none happened. The heavens continued obdurate
and it became manifest that the eclipse was doomed.

'Precisely at 6.49 a.m. Dr. King called out, "First contact",
which meant that the eastern limb of the advancing moon had
apparently touched the western edge of the sun's disk, but both sun
and moon being completely invisible, of course nothing could be
observed. Nor was there any obvious diminution of light for nearly
an hour or until 10 minutes before totality. For myself, had I not
known of the eclipse, I should have ascribed the dullness observable,
even at 10 minutes before the beginning of the total phase, to
increasing cloudiness, though as a matter of fact the wind had
shifted to the west since the eclipse began and the clouds to the
south east had not grown any heavier.

'A few minutes later a noticeable change came on. It began to
grow dim and the gloom continued to deepen gradually until perhaps
a minute or less before totality, when by two or three irregular
throbs or pulsations, the light failed. Some seconds before the
supreme moment I turned towards the west looking for the onrush
of the shadow which I did not see, but I distinctly observed the
distant hills take on a darkness more pronounced than the gloom
which enveloped us. During the period of totality we stood motion-
less at our instruments facing the quarter of the heavens where we
knew the sun to be. It seemed a long 151 seconds. Suddenly something was, as it were, lifted off. Mr. Maunder, my right-hand neigh-
bour, broke the silence with the remark, "It is all over", and almost
immediately the light returned—the transition being very marked.
And so came and went the long-looked-for phenomenon. Another
minute all was as usual at North West River, and the moon's shadow
was speeding over the Atlantic Ocean towards the coast of Spain.

'I should estimate the darkness during totality as decidedly less
than that of a clear night with a full moon. At no time had I any
difficulty in reading the seconds on my watch, nor, had I been
engaged in working any of the instruments, should I have needed

artificial light, except to read the finely graduated circles which would have been impossible without such aid.

'I observed no colour in the clouds beyond a livid hue, which pervaded everything. Low on the western horizon could be discerned a small strip of clear sky which lay beyond the shadow line, but there was no gorgeous colouring purple and gold such as one reads of in accounts of total eclipses. Throughout the phenomenon the feeling that the effect was produced by mechanical means was to me quite marked. The minute immediately preceding totality recalled to my mind the first magic lantern I had seen as a child, and powerfully suggested artificial agency. The sensation produced by the falling darkness which I have likened to throbs or pulsations were rather *jerks*—exactly as though somebody were intercepting the light by pulling a string.

'I noticed that the light came back much more rapidly than it failed. Possibly this is to be ascribed to physiological reasons, the eye at the end of the eclipse being—owing to the darkness—more sensitive to the return than it had been to the waning of the light. I saw no shadow bands at any time.

'Far outweighing the personal disappointment which I naturally felt on the occasion, was my deep sympathy with the professional astronomers who had come so far and worked so hard—for nothing. The evidence of their labours was on every hand. The concrete foundations, the rigid pillars, the wooden buildings for the instruments, besides the numerous erections of various kinds incidental to a three weeks' encampment of 30 people, bore witness to the zeal and industry which they had displayed. And when I considered that the material for these works had been brought 1400 miles, and carried by them from the landing place to the observation site— quite a little way—that the foundations had been dug, the concrete mixed, the boards sawn and put together with their own hands, I felt proud of my association with such splendid fellows.'

Shortly after my return from Labrador I lost my dear mother who had been ailing for some time. She was in her eighty-third year, and had survived my father twenty-six years. She rests by his side in the churchyard at St. Eleanor's.

During these days I was occupied in preparing a paper for Sir Wilfrid Laurier dealing with a claim of Manitoba for an extension of its boundaries. When I submitted it to him, he read it, and said, 'It is perfect.'

I also prepared for him about the same time a memorandum which formed the basis of a reply to a dispatch from the Colonial Office to the Governor-General dated 20 April 1905, tracing the history of the various Colonial Conferences and making certain suggestions in relation to that body, which resulted in the following minute being approved on the 13th of November 1905:

The Committee of the Privy Council have under consideration a confidential despatch from the Secretary of State for the Colonies to Your Excellency, dated 20th April, 1905, tracing the history of the various Colonial Conferences and making certain suggestions in relation to that body, upon which His Majesty's Government invite the views of Your Excellency's advisers. These suggestions briefly are:

1. That the title of 'Colonial Conference' be changed to that of 'Imperial Council'.

2. That a permanent Commission be appointed to prepare subjects to be discussed by the Imperial Council, which Commission should occupy in the civil atmosphere the same relation to the Conference that the Imperial Defence Committee does in regard to military questions. It is further proposed that to such a Commission might be referred questions for examination and report on the best mode of carrying out principles laid down by the Conference.

The Committee at the outset are disposed to consider that any change in the title or status of the Colonial Conferences should rather originate with and emanate from that body itself. At the same time, being fully alive to the desire of His Majesty's Government to draw closer the ties uniting the Colonies with each other and with the Motherland, they are prepared to give the proposals referred to their respectful consideration, and having done so beg leave to offer the following observations:

Your Excellency's advisers are entirely at one with His Majesty's Government in believing that political institutions 'may often be wisely left to develop in accordance with circumstances and, as it were, of their own accord', and it is for this reason that they entertain with some doubt the proposal to change the name of the Colonial

Conference to that of the Imperial Council, which they apprehend would be interpreted as marking a step distinctly in advance of the position hitherto attained in the discussion of the relation between the mother-country and the Colonies. As the Committee understands the phrase, a Conference is a more or less unconventional gathering for informal discussion of public questions, continued, it may be, from time to time as circumstances external to itself may render expedient, but possessing no faculty of power or binding action. The assembly of Colonial ministers which met in 1887, 1897, and 1902 appear to the Committee to fulfil these conditions. The term Council on the other hand indicates, in the view of Your Excellency's Ministers, a more formal assemblage, possessing an advisory and deliberative character, and in conjunction with the word 'Imperial', suggesting a permanent institution which, endowed with a continuous life, might eventually come to be regarded as an encroachment upon the full measure of autonomous legislative and administrative power, now enjoyed by all the self-governing Colonies.

The Committee, while not wishing to be understood as advocating any such change at the present time, incline to the opinion that the title 'Imperial Conference' might be less open to the objections they have indicated than the designation proposed by His Majesty's Government.

As regards the second suggestion of His Majesty's Government, the Committee are sensible that such a Commission would greatly facilitate the work of the Conference, and at the same time enhance the dignity and importance of that assembly. They cannot, however, wholly divest themselves of the idea that such a Commission might conceivably interfere with the working of responsible Government. While for this reason the Committee would not at present be prepared to adopt the proposal for the appointment of a permanent Commission, they feel that such a proposal emanating from His Majesty's Government should be very fully enquired into, and the Canadian representatives at the next Conference, whenever it may be held, would be ready to join the representatives of the sister colonies in giving the matter their most careful consideration.

The Committee advise that a copy of this Minute, if approved, be transmitted to the Secretary of State for the Colonies, for the information of His Majesty's Government.

E. J. LEMAIRE
Clerk of the Privy Council

Sir Wilfrid was apparently pleased with my efforts, as he very kindly addressed me the following note:

PRIME MINISTER'S OFFICE

CANADA

Oct. 16, 1905.

My dear Pope,

I received on Saturday the draft of despatch which I asked you to prepare for me the other day.

I have just read it, and I hasten to offer you my thanks as well as my congratulations. It could not be in better form and style.

Yours very sincerely,

WILFRID LAURIER

J. Pope, Esq., C.M.G.

During the summer of 1905 I was asked to propose half a dozen names for the Imperial Service Order. I suggested G. L. B. Fraser, W. M. Goodeve, F. Gourdeau, S. St. Denis Lemoine, and L. D. Sutherland.

The following is from my diary:

13 SEPTEMBER   'Sir Wilfrid sent for me this morning about a Japanese treaty, and had some talk also about Newfoundland and Labrador. He said he would counsel Sir Lomer Gouin, Prime Minister of Quebec, to seize timber leased by Newfoundland to Gillis Brothers.'

21 OCTOBER   'I attended the ceremony on Parliament Hill of the centenary of Nelson's glorious victory of Trafalgar. All the school children of the town were grouped round the Queen's statue, forming a pretty sight. They were addressed by Lord Grey and Mr. Scott. Altogether the ceremony, though simple, was effective. Met Lady Morley, Sir F. Pollock and other notables. The weather was cold and raw, with fitful gleams of sunshine and a high wind.'

30 OCTOBER   'I learned today that £. s. d. was legal money in Canada up to 1871. In 1853 the currency was declared to consist of £. s. d., dollars, cents and mills, and the two systems remained side by side until 1871. Sir Allen Aylesworth, who is seeking election in North York as Postmaster General, publicly announces that he disapproves of the pension system to ex-ministers, and will seek to repeal it. The papers take up the cry and clamour for its abolition.'

8 NOVEMBER   'I attended a meeting of deputy heads this afternoon, called by Hanbury Williams at the instance of the Governor-
General to talk over a suggestion of His Excellency's that the various
deputy heads should give a series of lectures during the coming
winter upon the functions of their several departments, with the
object of causing the working of the public machinery of the State
to be better known. The idea seems a good one, if it can be carried
out without ruffling the Ministers. A sub-committee of Messrs.
Pinault, King, Pedley, and one or two others was appointed further
to consider the matter. Mr. King and I walked home together.'

15 NOVEMBER   'Another meeting of deputy heads in Hanbury's
office today. We are making progress with the scheme under which
a course of lectures will be delivered during the coming winter on
various public topics relating to the Service, the object being to
cause the departments and the deputy heads to be better known.
There is little doubt that if Lord Grey sticks to it, he can do quite
a lot to improve the positions of the deputy heads.'

9 DECEMBER   'My new telescope continues to give me great
satisfaction. With it I can see Riga's companion and divide Epsilon
Lyrae 1 and 2. The nebula in Orion is very fine.'

19 DECEMBER   'I was asked today if I could suggest a suitable
person for the honour of knighthood. I replied that if the enquiry
were confined to Toronto, I would suggest Mr. G. W. Ross, but
if it applied to Ontario, I regarded my own Minister, the Hon.
R. W. Scott, as most deserving of the honour.

'Hanbury Williams saw me today and told me with reference to
the approaching visit to Canada of Prince Arthur of Connaught,
that the Governor-General had suggested that he (Hanbury Williams)
associate himself with me in the making of the arrangements and
that Sir Wilfrid cordially assented, remarking at the time that "they
could not get a better man".'

Lord Grey intimated that he was very desirous that the Royal
party should travel on this occasion by the Canadian Northern route.
I myself much preferred the C.P.R., one reason being that the
Canadian Northern was not finished, and portions of the road were
likely to be more or less unballasted and bumpy. Lord Grey, however, was insistent, and the upshot of the matter was that we arranged

to run by Canadian Pacific from Vancouver to Strathcona, along the Canadian Northern to Winnipeg, and thence to Ottawa over the C.P.R.

The occasion of this mission, known as the Garter Mission to Japan, was the presentation of the insignia of the Order of the Garter by H.R.H. Prince Arthur of Connaught on behalf of His Majesty the King, to His Imperial Majesty the Emperor of Japan. The members of the mission consisted of His Royal Highness Prince Arthur of Connaught, K.G., &c.; the Lord Redesdale, G.C.V.O., C.B.; Admiral Sir Edward Seymour, G.C.B.; General Sir Thomas Kelly Kenny, G.C.B.; Colonel Arthur Davidson; Mr. M. W. Lampson of the Foreign Office; and Captain W. F. C. Wyndham, Equerry to His Royal Highness.

While the Garter Mission ceased to be a mission in the strict sense of the term on arrival at Victoria, the Canadian Government desired to receive H.R.H. with some measure of ceremony and to show him the hospitalities of the Dominion in a manner befitting his rank and station.

We left Ottawa on our western tour on the 19th of March 1906. Our party consisted of Captain Gerald Trotter, A.D.C., representing the Governor-General; myself, acting for the Canadian Government; Mr. W. R. Baker of the C.P.R.; Mr. Bernard Howard, a cousin of the Duke of Norfolk who accompanied us as far as Calgary where he had a ranch.

We had a pleasant run to Vancouver and thence to Victoria, where we arrived on Sunday afternoon, putting up at the old *Driard*. I immediately waited on the Lieutenant-Governor, and early next morning got news that the *Empress* was sighted and would soon be in port. This came rather as a surprise as we had not been led to expect the landing before Monday afternoon, so Trotter and I got a launch and went out to the ship, boarded her at quarantine, and found the royal party preparing to land in tweeds and bowler hats. Trotter presented me, and we both pointed out that the Lieutenant-Governor and his Ministers looked forward to a more ceremonious landing, and that preparations had been made with that end in view.

H.R.H. was very nice about it, and after a little grumbling on the part of some of the suite, they consented to don their uniforms.

Those of us who had charge of the arrangements felt that there was a time for all things, and if ever there was a suitable time for a formal display, this was the occasion. A Prince of the blood, returning from a Royal Mission to a foreign power, being greeted by the Lieutenant-Governor in the presence of assembled numbers gathered to do him honour—what could be more fitting? This was so generally recognized as the proper thing, that I think everybody was ultimately satisfied.

Prince Arthur and suite were suitably entertained by the Lieutenant-Governor, Sir Henri Joly de Lotbinière. We had some good fishing at Cowichan Lake, where the royal party killed thirty fine trout. On our return to Victoria, we left almost immediately for Vancouver where the Prince inspected the 1st British Columbia Regiment (Duke of Connaught's Own), and the Cadets, H.R.H. appearing to be much interested in the latter. We lunched at the Vancouver Hotel, to which I invited Sir Charles Tupper, Bt., and a few other gentlemen to have the honour of meeting His Royal Highness. On our way east the Prince did a little trolling on Salmon Arm at Sicamous. My diary continues:

4 APRIL   'Lovely day. Arrived at Banff. After breakfast, H.R.H. under the escort of Mr. Howard Douglas, the Superintendent of the National Park, drove to the Cave and basin, where H.R.H. took some photographs of the buffalo; visited the Bank Head Coal Mine, which H.R.H., Trotter, and I explored to its depths. H.R.H. and I each mined a piece of coal. We bathed in the sulphur springs, and returned to our car where we received the unwelcome intelligence that smallpox had broken out among the Indians at Morley, which meant that the arrangements planned for that place had to be cancelled. At Strathcona our train was taken over by the Canadian Northern Railway.'

I was far from feeling at my ease throughout this journey. The royal party had just come off a long and stormy ocean voyage, some of the suite were not in the best of humour, and all rather anxious to get home, whereas in deference to Lord Grey, I was taking them round by way of Edmonton, where I had never been myself, knew nobody, and where things bade fair to be marked by an absence of ceremony calculated to gratify the greatest democrat, though I was not quite prepared for what actually happened.

Moreover, while Prince Arthur was at all times altogether charming, I knew royal Princes never forget they are royal, and look to other people to remember it also, and further, that some of the older members of the party were a little given to expecting special consideration being shown to them individually, which could not always be managed. I rather dreaded, too, the wild and woolly western spirit, to which Sir Henri Joly formed such a distinguished exception. It was, therefore, in no very buoyant frame of mind that I descended from the train on the morning of our arrival at Edmonton, and began my enquiries as to the programme awaiting us there. There was the inevitable civic address, the usual presentations and drive, followed by a luncheon given by the Legislature of the newly constituted Province of Alberta, to which I learned incidentally that seventeen mayors of the surrounding villages had been invited. At the end of a dusty drive our carriage stopped before the door of what looked to be a large shop, hastily converted into a banquet hall for the occasion. I found a horse-shoe table in the course of being set, everybody most loyal and enthusiastic, but everywhere a complete absence of order and direction. It is only fair to emphasize here that everything was then in the rough. The Province had only been constituted a few months. There had been no time for the erection of public buildings, and consequently there were none.

On entering the room, I took Prince Arthur's hat, placed it on some coils, whence it promptly rolled off under the table. Realizing that immediate measures had to be taken, and seeing a shock-headed fellow rushing about, I asked him if luncheon was ready. 'No,' replied he, 'it isn't ready, and I don't know when it will be ready,' adding in a burst of fury, 'for two pins you'd git no ——— lunch at all.' 'Shut up,' I said in an agony, as Lord Redesdale surveyed me through his eyeglass, 'the Prince will hear you,' which was more than likely, seeing that we were only a few feet apart. The restaurant man went on, 'I don't care for no Prince. I can cook a lunch and I can serve a lunch, but I don't want no ——— ——— idiots round me when I am at my work.' Seeing that the poor fellow was goaded to the last pitch of exasperation, I smoothed him down as best I could, got from him a list of guests, and enquired who was giving the lunch. He told me the Legislature. I asked him if they had a Speaker. He replied 'Yes.' 'Well,' said I, 'place the Speaker here. Put Prince Arthur at his right hand, and the Lieutenant-Governor on his left, and seat the rest anywhere, as there is no time for anything else.' He followed my instructions. I arranged that the King's health should be appropriately drunk at the proper time, and everything passed off admirably. I particularly remarked the excellence of the viands on that occasion. I never ate anything more delicious than the prairie chicken they served us, while the wine was something long to be remembered. I could not ascertain where it came from, but have understood that the cellars of the Hudson's Bay Company could disclose something on the point. The seventeen mayors showed a slight disposition to conviviality, but under the circumstances their manifestations of loyalty were quite excusable.

We reached Winnipeg on the morning of the 9th of April where the royal party were most hospitably received and entertained by the Lieutenant-Governor of Manitoba and Lady McMillan. Two days later we ran out to Regina, and thence we proceeded on our way east. At Fort William the royal party inspected the grain elevator at that place, at which General Kelly Kenny was nearly killed by a lift which started up suddenly. The General, who was a good deal upset by this accident, had received a bouquet from some lady admirers a few minutes before, and I, with the object of further mollifying him, drew attention to this pleasing incident, but though gratified, he was not going to come round so quickly, and he almost sobbed, 'They must have meant it for my grave.'

We reached Ottawa on Saturday evening, the 14th of April, and the royal party proceeded quite informally to Government House and I to my home. On Monday Sir Wilfrid Laurier entertained Prince Arthur and his suite at luncheon, twenty-two people in all, and there was a large dinner at Government House in the evening, followed by a State Ball on the 19th.

The royal party afterwards visited Toronto, Niagara, and different places, including Niagara Falls. A few days later we took the train for Halifax, which we duly reached on Friday the 27th of April, rested on the Sabbath, and started on Monday morning for the fishing grounds. We had a pleasant outing, but no luck. Thence we returned to Quebec where we visited Montmorency, saw the Falls to advantage, and passed through Ottawa on our way to St. Germain. We reached Low Station at 9 a.m. and started for our drive to Lake St. Germain over a road worse than my imagination could portray. Our luck was moderate, the ice having only very recently disappeared, and the water being too cold. We spent a merry evening at the Club House, H.R.H. insisting on having the story of the Edmonton lunch told over again. Next morning we had a final try and were rewarded with quite a bit of luck. Altogether we killed about two hundred trout during our stay at the lodge. Poor W. A. Allan, to whom His Royal Highness as everybody else was much attached, dined with us.

From my diary:

9 MAY 'Montreal—cold wretched weather. A number of friends drove out this morning to the Hunt Club where Sir Montagu Allan gave a lunch. I sat on the host's left hand, I presume as representing the Government. Dined this evening at Ravenscrag, a beautiful dinner of fifty or so. After dinner we went to the Horse Show, stayed for an hour or so and then went out to the *Virginian* where we all had supper and where I made a little speech, proposing His Royal Highness's health, bidding him good-bye and wishing him *bon voyage*. Then we shook hands and the Royal Tour of 1906 became history.'

On the eve of his departure, H.R.H. addressed me this charming letter:

> *Ravenscrag,*
> *Montreal,*
> *May 9, 1906.*
>
> Dear Mr. Pope,
>
> *Before leaving Canada I must write and tell you how grateful I am for all the trouble you have taken from start to finish, to make my journey such a pleasant one. I shall be quite lost without you to frame the eloquent replies to addresses and shall miss the 'crack of the whip'. I am afraid you had a lot of hard work and bother on my account. But I can assure you that it has been a great pleasure to me to have*

*had you with me on the journey. I enjoyed the whole thing very much
and it has been a most interesting experience.*

*Again thanking you so much for all your kindness and invaluable
assistance, and with kind remembrances to Mrs. Pope,*

Believe me,

Yours very sincerely,

ARTHUR

To which I replied:

Sir,

*I have received with much gratification the very kind and gracious
letter of farewell with which Your Royal Highness has honoured me.*

*I fear that you place too high an estimate upon the slight services
I was able to render, and which were many times repaid in the rendering,
for I account it a great privilege and pleasure to attend your Royal
Highness.*

*I trust, Sir, you do not overlook the fact that many contributed
towards the success of the tour, especially Col. Hanbury Williams and
Captain Trotter. Nor should Captain Wyndham be omitted from the
category. Indeed, I realize very keenly how much we, on this side, are
indebted to the genial courtesy of your Equerry, whose achievements
(perhaps your Royal Highness is not aware) were not confined to the
sphere of his official duties. Indeed his Canadian successes, though won
in more peaceful fields, are not less conspicuous than his military
exploits in a more distant colony, for while in South Africa his con-
quests were over his foes, here, like Orlando, he has overthrown more
than his enemies.*

*Your Royal Highness will be glad to learn that there is not an
unfavourable word here in any quarter about the Tour or anyone
connected with it. The newspapers (when not discussing the curse under
which this country still languishes) have nothing but nice things to
say of the way it went off.*

*My wife was charmed to receive your Royal Highness' 'wireless'
from sea.*

*She much regrets that in singing the French-Canadian songs we
should have forgotten the most appropriate of all called 'A la Claire
Fontaine', each verse ending with 'Jamais je ne t'oublierai', but
we venture to hope that the sentiment was conveyed in other words.*

It only remains for me to thank your Royal Highness once more for

the great kindness you have shown both to my wife and myself, which
will remain to us a pleasant and enduring memory.

> *I am,*
>> *Sir,*
>>> *With great respect,*
>>>> *Your Royal Highness' faithful servant,*
>>>>> JOSEPH POPE

His Royal Highness,
Prince Arthur of Connaught, K.G.

At about this time Lady Minto also addressed me the following
from India:

VICEREGAL LODGE

> *Simla,*
> *23rd June,* 1906.

Dear Mr. Pope,

It was a great pleasure to me to receive your letter and I intended
answering it many weeks ago but our life here is very full indeed and
every day brings me some unexpected duty which interferes sadly with
my correspondence.

I am writing to you in type as I have sprained my finger and find it
difficult to hold a pen.

I have received several newspaper cuttings of Prince Arthur's tour
in Canada which I have followed with great interest. It seems to have
been a great success, as I am sure it was bound to be if you had the
management of it. I always look back to the Prince of Wales' tour
throughout Canada as a most masterly piece of organization. I think
everything was adhered to with the most wonderful punctuality
throughout and it must always be a satisfaction to you to look back
to that most successful programme.

Our life here is entirely different to what it was in Canada. I think
we have even more social duties than we had there, but I have fewer
charities although at this moment I am immensely busy in trying to
organize a nursing scheme for Northern India which is sadly needed.
It requires an immense amount of thought as one has to deal with so
many different provinces, all needing a variety of management.

I think everything so far has run very smoothly. One could not help
feeling great anxiety at first as to the Army question and the dis-
satisfaction caused by the Partition of Bengal, but it is wonderful how

things have quieted down and I think the sympathy with which His Excellency has treated all parties has been thoroughly appreciated.

We are just expecting the rains to begin. We have had perfect weather here for two months and I am hard at work improving the garden and grounds and also in decorating and furnishing the house. I have no Mr. Tarte to propitiate here; the Viceroy is allowed a very considerable fund for furnishing and I fancy if I exceed it it does not much signify. I am so glad my brother has taken such interest in the skating club. I delight in getting news of our many friends in Ottawa, and I am glad to know that we have not yet been forgotten. Will you give many messages to Mrs. Pope from me. I heard on very good authority that she has had a very great succès with Prince Arthur.

Please remember that it always gives me a great deal of pleasure getting letters from Ottawa.

Always yours sincerely,

MARY MINTO

P.S. *His Excellency begs me to give you both many warm messages.*

Another missive:

PRIME MINISTER'S OFFICE
CANADA

Oct. 8, 1906.

My dear Pope,

As I told you last night, I desire that you should act as secretary to the Conference. Will you be in attendance at 11 this morning in my office.

Yours very sincerely,

W.L.

This refers to a Conference of the Provincial Governments which met in Ottawa in October 1906 on the invitation of Sir Wilfrid Laurier to discuss certain financial questions between the Dominion and the Provinces.[1] It was attended by the Prime Minister, Messrs. Fielding, Aylesworth, and Lemieux, as well as by a number of provincial Ministers. I did not know at the outset whether the Canadian Premier and his colleagues considered themselves part of the Conference or not, but this may have been the result of my

[1] The report of the proceedings of this Conference will be found in Sessional Paper 29a, Vol. XLI, No. 12, 1906–7.

want of acquaintance with the subject. During its first session they withdrew at an early stage of the proceedings, and I naturally followed them. At the meeting held on the following day, on motion of Sir Wilfrid Laurier, Mr. Charles Lanctot, K.C., Deputy Attorney-General of Quebec, and myself were appointed Secretaries of the Joint Conference. When the time came for the drawing up of the proceedings, Mr. Lanctot signed before me. Unwilling that there should be any difficulty over this, I raised no question, though at the same time it seemed to me odd that Mr. Lanctot, a Provincial officer, should take seniority over me as Under-Secretary of State of Canada. Indeed, I never could see why I should have been asked to be present at the Conference or to sign at all, but on this point nothing could be clearer than Sir Wilfrid Laurier's wishes, which in all cases were my guide.

Regarding this conference, I felt most of the time as if I were standing on my head. The Provincial Premiers sat together, and when they were ready, they sent for Sir Wilfrid and his colleagues, who were assembled in an adjoining room. When the Ministers entered and took their seats, forthwith the Provincial Conference became a joint Conference. One difficulty I remember in the way of unanimity was the attitude of the representative of the provincial government of British Columbia—the Hon. Richard McBride— who argued, it seemed to me with much force, that when British Columbia entered the Union it made its bargain with Canada; it had made no arrangement with Nova Scotia or New Brunswick, and that they had nothing to do with any alteration of the terms of the bargain. The upshot of the whole negotiation was that the Senate and House of Commons of Canada passed an Address to the Crown which resulted in an amendment to the British North America Act readjusting the financial terms of union between Canada and the Provinces. This address will be found in the beginning of Volume I–II of the Statutes of the Tenth Parliament of Canada, 1907–08, under which the better terms to the Provinces became effective at the Dominion's cost.

I note in my diary:

21 JUNE   'Hanbury Williams told me today that Lord Grey had recommended me to the King for an I.S.O. I replied that I was

very grateful to His Excellency, and at all times felt honoured to receive any mark of my Sovereign's approbation.'

Some months later the Governor-General's A.D.C. wrote:

Dear Mr. Pope,

I am desired by His Excellency to say that he wishes personally to invest you with the decoration of the Imperial Service Order, and would therefore be pleased if you could lunch at Government House tomorrow (Wednesday the 24th of October) at 1.30 p.m.

With kind regards, I am,

Yours sincerely,

DENZIL C. NEWTON, *Capt.,*

A.D.C.

The investiture was held on the 24th of October preceded by a luncheon, in the course of which His Excellency became so greatly absorbed in the conversation regarding questions then interesting the public men of Canada and the United States that he quite forgot about the investiture and had to be reminded by his secretary, which was so like Lord Grey. In giving me the decoration His Excellency said he felt he was conferring an honour upon the Order, which, though I thought rather strong, was still very nice to hear. I, not to be outdone, replied that the honour was much enhanced in coming to me on His Excellency's recommendation.

Sir Wilfrid sent for me a few days after these events and gave me Mr. Root's confidential proposals looking towards a settlement of outstanding questions between Canada and the United States. He asked me to study them and prepare a draft reply, which I did. These questions related principally to (1) pelagic sealing, (2) the North Atlantic fisheries, (3) the inland fisheries, (4) United States pecuniary claims, and (5) boundary waters. They will be found in a confidential dispatch from the Hon. Elihu Root, Secretary of State of the United States to His Majesty's Ambassador at Washington, dated 3 May 1906. Most of these questions were settled during Mr. Bryce's tenure of office as His Majesty's Ambassador at Washington (1907–13), which was highly successful in allaying differences between the two countries.

The year 1907 opened with rumours of my going to England on

business connected with the Imperial Conference. Lord Grey especially was full of the idea, and pressed it on the Prime Minister with all his characteristic energy. Sir Wilfrid, however, evidently had other plans in view, and perhaps Lord Grey urged the matter a little too insistently for my advantage. At any rate, I was not chosen to accompany the Prime Minister to England, at which I was not disappointed, for I felt that I had been getting more than my share. Sir Wilfrid and party left for Europe on the 4th of April.

On the 8th of May, Sir Richard Cartwright, acting as Prime Minister, sent for me and asked me on behalf of the Government to undertake the task of looking after General His Imperial Highness Prince Sadanaru Fushimi, G.C.B., who was visiting this country on a special mission from the Emperor of Japan and sailing from England on the 31st of May by the s.s. *Empress of Ireland*. Their Excellencies Lord and Lady Grey, who were paying a flying visit home at the time, came out by the same ship, which docked at Quebec on the morning of the 7th of June. At 10 a.m. I went on board and was presented to His Imperial Highness and suite.

The Imperial party left almost immediately for Montreal, where they were the guests of Sir Montagu Allan at Ravenscrag, whom before dinner H.I.H. invested with the third class of the Order of the Rising Sun. Sir Montagu's hospitality was of the most splendid order, and I was quite struck by it. On the following day at Ottawa His Excellency the Governor-General gave a state dinner in honour of His Imperial Highness, immediately before which the Prince invested me with the insignia of the second class of the Order of the Sacred Treasure. We then paid a visit to the Royal Military College, which H.I.H. had expressed a desire to see, and after including Niagara in our itinerary, we bore away for the West.

Throughout this whole tour the Prince insisted on my lunching and dining with him every day in his car and on attending him wherever he went in public. We spoke together of many things connected with the discovery and early history of the country, of its system of government and its constitutional development, in all of which I found him to take a sympathetic and intelligent interest, ever manifesting a desire to acquaint himself with a civilization so different from his own.

Prince Sadanaru Fushimi was described as an elder member of the Imperial family of Japan, being a second cousin to the Emperor. He appeared to be from fifty to fifty-five years of age, above the average height of a Japanese, of compact figure, well set up, somewhat reserved, extremely courteous in manner towards those about him, and evidently desired to respond to the cordial welcome extended to him by the Canadian Government.

I devoted a good deal of pains to this trip—Sir Wilfrid Laurier's absence from Canada, and the wholehearted manner in which Sir Richard Cartwright confided the matter to my hands, alike moving me to a special effort to have everything down to the smallest detail as it should be, in which I was most ably seconded by Mr. W. R. Baker, c.v.o. I had ordered, in advance, copies of music of the Japanese national hymn, and had them distributed along the route the Prince was to travel, so that at every stopping place H.I.H. was greeted on arrival—it might be in the recesses of the Rocky Mountains—with the strains of his national anthem. Now, while everybody likes this sort of thing, perhaps the Japanese are peculiarly susceptible to such little attentions, and I am sure that we greatly pleased them by our forethought.

On arrival at Victoria, the Japanese Imperial party became the guests of the Lieutenant-Governor and Mrs. Dunsmuir at Government House, at whose residence a state dinner was given on the evening of the 24th of June, in honour of the royal visitor. On this occasion I spoke as follows:

> May it please your Imperial Highness: as the official who has had the honour of attending your Imperial Highness throughout this country it has seemed to me not out of place that on the eve of your departure I should express to you in the name of the Canadian Government the deep gratification and pleasure they have experienced in extending to your Imperial Highness the hospitalities of the Dominion.
>
> We have welcomed you, Sir, as the representative of the friend and ally of our King, and of that dear land to which we owe loving allegiance, whose enemies are our enemies, and whose friends we delight to honour.
>
> We have welcomed you as the representative of your gallant race whose deeds of valour, constancy, endurance, whose high sense of

*public duty, and above all whose pure and exalted patriotism have
won our warmest admiration.*

*We, a young community, have derived a special gratification in
being permitted to greet in the person of your Imperial Highness the
most ancient civilization in the world. May I venture to add that we
have welcomed you also, Sir, by reason of your own gracious and
winning personality.*

*We bid you farewell with regret. We cherish the hope that you may
revisit us some day. In the meantime we wish your Imperial Highness
a safe and prosperous voyage to your native land, and we trust that
you will bear from these shores a kindly feeling towards Canada and
its people.*

His Imperial Highness thus replied:

*Your Honour, Mr. Pope, Ladies and Gentlemen: I am deeply
gratified by the kindly sentiments towards my country and myself to
which you have so eloquently given expression. I can assure you that
it gives me the very greatest pleasure to have had this further proof
of the friendship towards Japan on the part of the Government of this
vast Dominion.*

*I shall ever consider it a great privilege to have had extended to me
on this historic occasion the generous hospitality of the Canadian
Government, and to thus have been afforded such a splendid opportunity
of making the personal acquaintance of so many prominent men in this
country.*

*The journey across Canada has been full of interest to me, and I
am very glad to have been thereby enabled to study at first hand the
great natural resources of the country of which I had heard so much.
I bear away with me the pleasantest of recollections of my brief sojourn
in your midst.*

*I consider it a piece of good fortune to have had attached to my
suite so able and trusted an official as Mr. Pope, and I am fully aware
that the smoothness with which all the arrangements for my visit
have worked throughout were largely due to his untiring energy and
forethought.*

*I thank you for your good wishes at my departure, and with you
I hope that on some future occasion I may be able to revisit these
hospitable shores. The English adage that 'the best of friends must
part' is no doubt a very true one; but it is my earnest hope that the*

P.S.—I2

*many friendships which I have established in this country may ere
long be renewed.*

*Before resuming my seat I wish to thank you, ladies and gentlemen,
for the kind way in which you have responded to the toast of my health,
which Mr. Dunsmuir was so good to propose. I give in turn the toast
of the people of Canada to whom I wish every success and prosperity.*

Prince Fushimi and suite sailed from Esquimalt for home on the
morning of the 25th of June, taking with them, if words count for
anything, a pleasant impression of their Canadian visit.

On my return to Ottawa I was much gratified to receive the
following letter from Sir Richard Cartwright:

Ottawa, June 27th, 1907.

My dear Pope,

*I am very much pleased at the way in which Prince Fushimi's visit
has been arranged, and not least at the reception he met with in B.
Columbia. On the whole I do not think with the time and income at
your disposal you could possibly have done any better.*

*If you can get hold of any Japanese papers with a description of
his visit, it may be well to publish them here.*

Yours faithfully,

R. J. CARTWRIGHT

This was followed by a gracious letter of appreciation from His
Excellency:

CITADEL

QUEBEC

July 21/07.

Dear Mr. Pope,

*I have just read the report of your speech at the Lt.-Governor's
dinner at Victoria, and gladly avail myself of the opportunity which
its perusal has given me to congratulate you both on the sentiments
expressed and on the form of their expression.*

*Your speech is a fitting and admirable conclusion of a political and
international incident of no small importance.*

*The visit of Prince Fushimi as the guest of the Dominion will, I
trust, prove historical in its effect, by reason of the goodwill it has*

generated, for all time I hope between the two peoples of Canada and Japan.

I have read with the greatest satisfaction the reports of the spontaneous demonstration in honour of our Japanese guests by the Canadian people, and I realize that the influence of your example and of your efforts to secure a proper appreciation by the people of Canada of what the occasion required, has contributed largely to the creation of what, I trust, may prove to be a permanent friendship between Canada and Japan.

I remain,

Yours very sincerely,

GREY

The following month I was honoured with this personal letter from His Imperial Highness:

Tokyo, Sept. 25th, 1907.

Dear Mr. Pope,

I am very glad to write you that the trip on my way home was accomplished throughout under the British flag in the most comfortable manner in consequence of your thoughtful arrangements.

I think that I could never repeat it again and be received with such enthusiastic welcome on every side.

I regret that I was not able to write you sooner my sincere gratitude for your attendance owing to H.M. *the Emperor's command to inspect the various Regimental districts since my return.*

Thanking you sincerely for all the courtesy and trouble you have taken and wishing you good health and prosperity.

Sincerely yours,

SADANARU

Part Two: Biographical

1907 — 1908

Lemieux Mission to Japan / Object / Causes
of Anti-Asiatic Agitation in British Columbia /
Sir Claude Macdonald / First Meeting with
Count Hyashi / Sight-Seeing in Tokyo / Imperial
Garden Party / Progress of Negotiations with
Japanese Foreign Office / Received in Audience
by H.M. The Empress of Japan / Further
Negotiations / Conclusion of Satisfactory
Arrangement / Visit to Nikko / Return to Canada

A FEW months after the departure of Prince Fushimi from Canada, the Government decided to send the Hon. Mr. Rodolphe Lemieux on a special mission to Japan, to inquire into and discuss with His Majesty's ambassador at Tokyo, and the Japanese Government, the causes of the anti-Japanese agitation then prevailing on the Pacific coast. Mr. Lemieux was also enjoined to endeavour, by friendly means, to make some arrangement with the Japanese so as to prevent a recurrence of such causes which might disturb the happy relations which had hitherto existed between the two countries. Mr. Lemieux was good enough to ask Mr. Pope to accompany him on his mission as counsellor and friend, and the party consisting of Mr. and Madame Lemieux, Mr. Pope, and Mr. Verret, Mr. Lemieux's private secretary, sailed from Vancouver by the s.s. *Empress of China* on the 31st of October 1907.

The importation of Oriental labour to British Columbia began with the opening of the Cariboo gold mines. Later, more was brought in to assist in the construction of the Canadian Pacific

Railway. Originally these Orientals consisted entirely of Chinese coolies, and during the construction of the railway their presence was not objected to owing to the general scarcity of labour. However, when the railway was completed, the coolies scattered to the more settled parts, and to some extent entered into competition with the whites. It was then that a strong prejudice became manifest.

As far back as 1884 a commission had been appointed by the Dominion Government to investigate and report on the question of Chinese immigration, and the following year the government of the day introduced a measure imposing a head tax of fifty dollars on each Chinese immigrant. Time went on, and as the Chinese continued to come in such large numbers, the head tax was raised to $100, and then to $500. This action so effectually restricted the inflow from China that it ceased to be a cause for alarm.

The anti-Asiatic feeling which existed at this time was directed more against the Japanese and Hindus than against the Chinese, for the reason that the latter were more content with menial occupations, and so did not come into such direct conflict with the whites. The Japanese, however, were then coming to British Columbia in limited numbers, and the commissioners being cognizant of the instructions of the Japanese Department of Foreign Affairs, prohibiting entirely for the time being the emigration of labourers for the Dominion of Canada, expressed the opinion that the imposition of a head tax on the Japanese might be deferred. There was, further, a tacit understanding between the Government and the Japanese authorities that the flow of immigration from Japan would be so regulated as not to exceed some four or five hundred annually.

In 1894 Japan concluded a treaty with Great Britain revising a previous treaty between the two countries which did away with certain extra-territorial rights, tariff rates, and so on, which were humiliating to the Japanese. Article 1 of this treaty read as follows: 'The subjects of each of the two High Contracting Parties shall have full liberty to enter, travel or reside in any part of the dominions and possessions of the other Contracting Party, and shall enjoy full and perfect protection for their persons and property.' But this treaty excluded the Dominion of Canada, as well as a number of other British possessions, from participation therein. For various reasons Canada expressed her desire to become a party to the treaty in 1905, and a special convention giving effect to the stipulation of the treaty was signed at Tokyo on the 31st of January 1906.

The real cause of the agitation which culminated in the anti-Japanese riots in Vancouver in September 1907 was the unreserved interpretation of Article 1 of the treaty by some enterprising emigration companies. With the passing of the treaty a wave of Japanese immigration surged across the Pacific both from Japan and Hawaii, but more particularly from the latter place. During the period from 1 July 1904 to 30 June 1905, 354 Japanese immigrants arrived in Canada. From 1 July 1905 to 30 June 1906 the number was 1,922; from 1 July to 31 December 1906, a six-month period, the numbers rose to 2,233; and during the first ten months of 1907 the number of Japanese immigrants to Canada rose to the impressive total of 8,125. This was an exceptionally large and progressive increase.

Now this sharp rise was due, not to any desire or action of the Japanese Government, but, as has been said, to the activities of emigration companies operating at Vancouver, Tokyo, and Honolulu. These immigrants were not content to confine themselves to menial tasks. They filtered into the fisheries and lumbering industries and occupations incidental thereto. They engaged in mining, were employed on the railways, in sealing, in farming, as tailors, and as hotel servants. And the feeling which grew up against them was based not only on prejudice but on the instinct of self-preservation. In 1907 there were some 25,000 Asiatics in British Columbia, nearly all of whom were male adults. There were at the same time in that province not more than 75,000 male adults of the white race. It followed then that every fourth man competing for a living was an Asiatic, and in consequence the white population feared that the very foundations of its social structure were in danger of being undermined. Such, briefly, was the situation when the Lemieux Mission proceeded to Japan.

Mr. Pope's diary records an unusually rough passage. While the ship behaved well, the fact that she had sunk at her moorings at Vancouver several days prior to sailing, by reason of some seacocks having unaccountably been left open, was not conducive to the passengers' peace of mind. The ship, however, arrived at Yokohama without further incident on the 13th of November, and the party proceeded to Tokyo by train the following day. On the afternoon of their arrival, Mr. Lemieux and Mr. Pope drove to the British Embassy to pay their respects to Sir Claude Macdonald. It was found that he knew nothing of the Canadian case, and the diary goes on to say that this defect was soon remedied, whereupon Sir Claude expressed himself as much impressed by its strength as well as by its reasonableness. That same afternoon he brought his visitors to call on Count Hyashi, the Minister of Foreign Affairs, who, thought Mr. Pope, received them in a rather off-hand sort of way. When Sir Claude asked him when it would suit his convenience to receive Mr. Lemieux, he replied that he was extremely busy, and that he was afraid that he could not give him much time, but that his Vice-Minister would represent him at their meetings. Mr. Pope thought that Count Hyashi, with more courtesy, might have received them in the first instance, and subsequently handed them over to his subordinate.

The mission found, however, a good friend in Sir Claude Macdonald. His original instructions required him to bring Mr. Lemieux and the Japanese together, but such was his enthusiasm and so sympathetic was his interest in the question at issue that he cabled to England for authority to present it as that of the Imperial Government. Sir Claude Macdonald's aid proved to be invaluable in the meetings that followed, and so impressed was Mr. Pope in the efficacy of the 'full support' of His Majesty's Government that during these days, when writing to one of his sons in Canada, he concluded his letter with the words, 'And remember, my boy, always to keep both hands on the Union Jack,' a phrase made somewhat famous in Ottawa by Lord Dundonald a few years previously.

The next meeting at the Japanese Foreign Office was fixed for Monday the 25th of November. The intervening period was filled with the work of adding the final touches to the Canadian case, which included a number of meetings and discussions at the British Embassy. Count Terashima, Count Hyashi's private secretary, arranged a number of visits, and the time appears to have passed quite pleasantly.

On Sunday the 17th Mr. Pope with Mr. and Madame Lemieux

attended mass at the Cathedral, after which they called on the
archbishop, Mgr. Mugaburé, a Basque, who spoke English fairly
well, and to whom Mr. Lemieux had letters of introduction from
the Archbishop of Montreal. In the course of the conversation it
was learned that the Catholic population numbered about 65,000,
served by approximately one hundred and thirty mission priests.
The archbishop also informed his visitors that after a lapse of some
two hundred and fifty years, Christians were found in Nagasaki;
that a man in each village baptized the children and that they had
preserved, since the time of the Jesuit martyrs, more than a trace
of the ancient faith.

During these days a hint was received to the effect that the
United States desired Canada to make common cause with them in
the matter of Japanese emigration to the two countries. But the
hint fell on deaf ears. At the time the Canadian mission was not
without hope of achieving at least partial success; there was current
in Japan a certain amount of feeling against the Americans on
account of their alleged lack of regard for the susceptibilities of the
Japanese, and the mission was of the opinion that it could not more
effectually ruin its prospects of a satisfactory solution than by identi-
fying itself with the Americans.

The next morning, under the guidance of Count Terashima, an
interesting visit was paid to the University of Tokyo. After being
presented in due form to the Rector, the Dean, and certain Pro-
fessors, the usual rounds were made. In the first class-room there
were upwards of three hundred students, while in the second there
were seven hundred or more. In both classes the visitors were
impressed by the absolute silence and close attention which prevailed.
Among the many interesting things seen were a number of documents
dating back to the eighth and ninth centuries, one of which was by
a man unable to write, whose signature consisted of the measurement
of the first two joints of his fore-finger laid laterally across the
paper. It was then learned that in those days documents were
occasionally subscribed to by illiterates by an impression of the
hand. The Bertillon system of identification was just then coming into
vogue, yet here was evidence of the same principle being known
and practised some eleven hundred years ago—a circumstance which

moved Mr. Pope to write; 'Truly, as Solomon says, "There is nothing new under the sun." ' The party then enjoyed an uncommonly good lunch at the University, afterwards repairing to the Embassy where the afternoon was spent at work.

A few days later a visit was paid to the house of a wealthy Japanese in order to view his art gallery. The party was received in the first instance by the old gentleman's son, who spoke English quite well, having lived for nine years in Europe, two of which had been spent at Cambridge. Then the father appeared, and the inevitable tea followed. Afterwards, inspection was made of the art gallery, which was a marvellous collection of heathen gods and warriors—Buddhist, Chinese, Korean, Tibetan, and Indian. A part had belonged to the old shoguns, while the remainder had been purchased during the older man's travels. The diary notes an old lacquer cabinet as being 'beautiful beyond words'.

Then followed luncheon *à la Japonnaise*, in an attempt to describe which, Mr. Pope again states that words fail him. They were first served some form of stew, which he promptly upset by awkward and possibly fortunate mis-manipulation of his chopsticks. Then followed raw fish in various forms, and later a series of dishes which Mr. Pope, never an expert in these matters, is unable to describe. To add to his discomfiture, he records that immediately opposite sat a member of the party *visibly turning white*. This guest later told him that the only thing he touched was rice, which he feared he was not going to keep—*and he didn't.*

In due season came the 25th of November, the day fixed for the first meeting at the Japanese Foreign Office, at which negotiations were to be opened. It had previously been arranged that both sides would be represented as follows: JAPAN by His Excellency Count Hyashi, Minister of Foreign Affairs; Baron Chinda, Vice-Minister of Foreign Affairs; and Mr. Ishii, Director of the Bureau of Commerce. CANADA by His Excellency Sir Claude Macdonald, the British Ambassador; the Hon. Rodolphe Lemieux, Special Envoy of the Canadian Government; the Hon. F. O. Lindley, Secretary of the British Embassy; and Mr. Joseph Pope, Under-Secretary of State of Canada.

The proceedings were opened by a statement of the Canadian

case by Mr. Lemieux, who began by referring to a recent increased influx of Japanese immigrants to British Columbia and to the regrettable disturbances in Vancouver which had been occasioned thereby. He explained that the Canadian Government greatly regretted these unfortunate occurrences, and that settlement had been made of all just claims for damages incurred by Japanese residents. Canada's attitude towards Japan had ever been one of amity and good will, as was instanced by the fact that the Dominion Government had disallowed no less than nine statutes of the Legislature of British Columbia prohibiting the immigration of Japanese into that province. Mr. Lemieux then emphasized the uneasiness of the people of British Columbia at the fact that in that province one man in every four was of foreign race, and that the disparity was rapidly growing less. Thus the Dominion Government found itself faced with an awkward situation. On the one hand, as British subjects they were gratified at their participation in an alliance with such a great nation as Japan, as well as not being insensible to the advantages of the commercial treaty recently entered into by them, while on the other hand, in view of the recent disturbances that had taken place in British Columbia, they fully realized the responsibilities resting upon them for the peace, order, and good government of Canada. Mr. Lemieux concluded by inviting the serious consideration of the Japanese Government to the necessity of restricting the immigration of artisans and labourers to British Columbia to a number which could be absorbed without unduly disturbing the proportion of the races in that province. It was considered that a total of some three hundred per annum would satisfy this requirement. The Canadian Envoy then laid before the Minister of Foreign Affairs a memorandum fully stating the case in detail.

Count Hyashi replied that the views of the Canadian Government would receive careful consideration, and that a written answer would be given in due course. He appreciated the kindly feeling of the Government of Canada towards the Japanese Government, and he assured Mr. Lemieux that the sentiments he had expressed were fully reciprocated. He understood the difficulties of the Canadian Government arising out of this question, but it must be remembered that Japan also had troubles of her own. The Japanese were a high-spirited and sensitive people, and would not brook any fresh treaty or convention imposing restrictions upon them in respect of immigration, nor could they tolerate being regarded as inferior to other races against whom there were no restrictions.

The foregoing sentence appears to express the principle which guided the Japanese in the conduct of the negotiations. The Japanese did not desire that their nationals should emigrate to British Columbia. From an economic point of view such a movement was a distinct loss to Japan, in consequence of which it was her policy to discourage such emigration and to divert it towards Korea and Manchuria. Therefore, while Japan was prepared to meet Canada's wishes in this matter, it must be voluntary on their part, and any binding treaty in this respect would be unacceptable to public opinion, and, therefore, out of the question. Count Hyashi concluded his remarks by stating that he would draw up certain regulations which would restrict emigration to British Columbia which he undertook to explain more fully at their next meeting. He informed Mr. Lemieux that he had already taken effective measures to curb the activities of certain emigration companies which, relying on the letter of the treaty, had acted injudiciously in the matter. It was arranged that the next meeting should be held on the 2nd of December.

That evening Mr. Pope dined with Prince Fushimi, whom he had escorted across Canada earlier during the same year. The diary records: 'Dined this evening with Prince Fushimi who was most gracious. 32 people. Took Countess Hyashi in to dinner. Superb entertainment.'

On the morning of the 28th of November the Canadian mission was received in audience by the Empress. To quote from the diary: 'At 11 a.m. we four left the hotel for the Embassy *en grande tenue*, i.e., the men. At a few minutes to twelve, we drove to the Palace, and after meeting many officials we were led into the presence of the Empress. The Presence Chamber is a small room—I should think not more than 15 feet square. Lady Macdonald first presented Madame Lemieux and then we followed in due order. The prescribed ceremonial required one profound bow to be made on the threshold, one in the middle of the room and one just before the

Empress. Her Majesty is a small and rather weary-looking woman of about sixty. She speaks neither English nor French but an interpreter stands beside her. She shook hands with me and then spoke a few words in Japanese to the effect that she thanked me for my attention to Prince Fushimi in Canada. I replied: "Please say to Her Majesty that I considered it a great honour and pleasure to attend H.I.H." She then displayed some little solicitude about the state of my health, in respect of which I reassured her, whereupon she shook hands again and I backed away making three bows as in entering.

'We then assembled in a large and extremely handsome room of State and shortly after proceeded to another equally magnificent hall where tiffin was laid out. The table was, I think, the finest I have ever seen and the appointments, waiting, etc., on a par with the rest. After luncheon we went back to the other large room and after a while were summoned to say goodbye to H.M. who stood in the middle of the room. After she had said a few words to each one, she shook hands with us and the same ceremony followed with the Crown Prince and Princess and two Princesses who were present at tiffin though not at the presentation.

'We were then shown the Throne Room which was particularly interesting to me as it was here that the investiture of the Emperor with the Order of the Garter by Prince Arthur took place. These rooms all remind me of the Banquet Halls and Ball Rooms of Versailles. We then left the Palace, put off our finery, and I went for a walk on the Ginza.'

On the 2nd of December was held the second meeting at the Foreign Office, at which Count Hyashi informed Mr. Lemieux that his Government was unable to agree to the Canadian proposal that the treaty be amended so as to limit the number of emigrants to Canada, as it would be resented as a national humiliation. He could, however, by a series of voluntary restrictions, which he had the power to enforce, arrive at the object which Canada had in view. He then handed Mr. Lemieux a draft copy of the instructions he intended to issue prohibiting all emigration to Canada, excepting as regards certain classes, such as emigrants who had previously had their residence in Canada together with their wives and children, emigrants specially invited by the Japanese residents or other nationals in Canada, and contract labourers, the details of whose contracts were satisfactorily specified.

Mr. Lemieux immediately stated that he could not agree to any such terms; that far from being restrictive they were lax and that instead of removing the cause of the agitation they would accentuate it. A long discussion followed, in which each clause was gone over in detail, and during the course of which several important concessions were made by Count Hyashi. Before adjourning, Count Hyashi, at Mr. Lemieux's request, stated that in addition to the regulations the Japanese Government would give him an assurance which might be laid before Parliament that Japan would effectually restrict emigration to Canada.

A number of informal meetings took place at the British Embassy and at the Foreign Office the first week of December, at which the Japanese regulations to guide the governors of the 'préfectures' and consuls were recast. At the meeting on the 5th of December Count Hyashi stated that on the afternoon of Monday the 9th he would formally present the counter-proposals of the Japanese Government. Generally these were to be that the Japanese Government would prohibit all emigration to Canada save resident Japanese returning to Canada for the second time, domestics for Japanese residents, emigrants brought in under contracts approved by the Dominion Government, and agricultural labourers for work on farms owned by Japanese, the number in each case being in proportion to the acreage of the farms. Mr. Lemieux then stated that much as he appreciated the spirit in which these counter-proposals were made, he felt that before expressing unreserved agreement thereto he was obliged to submit them to the Canadian Government.

The meeting arranged for the 9th of December was postponed, and for the remainder of the time during which Mr. Lemieux was able to remain in Tokyo nothing but informal interviews were held, at which a number of minor points were settled. During this period there appears to have been considerable cabling back and forth between the Canadian Envoy at Tokyo and the Dominion Government in Ottawa which would lead one to infer that the Government did not altogether appreciate that, in view of Clause 1 of the treaty referred to above, Canada was not in a position to restrict the immigration of the Japanese into Canada, but that its representative was obliged to do whatever lay in his power to induce the Japanese Government to limit the annual emigration from Japan to Canada to the desired extent. Mr. Pope records this quite plainly on the 6th of December: 'Lindley called this morning and we had a long talk over the difficulty arising out of the fact that we have no protection against Japanese with passports for elsewhere changing their minds en route and demanding admission to Canada. Nothing is clearer than that the Japanese Government will not allow *us* to restrict the immigration of their people into Canada. They are ready enough to restrict at their own end but they won't allow us to demand passports from their people and not from other nationals.'

By the 23rd of December matters had been concluded, save an exchange of letters which was to be made between Count Hyashi and Mr. Lemieux. On this day Messrs. Ishii, Lindley, and Pope met at the Foreign Office to agree on the drafts of these letters which were in the course of preparation. Of the meeting, the diary states: 'This morning Ishii, Lindley, and I met at the F.O. and went over the drafts of letters to be written. In that of Count Hyashi to Mr. Lemieux, Ishii proposed to say the Japanese Government would exercise "due and adequate discretion". I told him I could not accept these words and pressed for "effectively restrict". This he shied at but finally agreed to "to take efficient means to restrict", which amounts to pretty much the same thing.'

But it was becoming clearer and clearer that nothing short of a detailed explanation of the negotiations by Mr. Lemieux to his colleagues in Ottawa would bring them round to the point of view held by their Envoy at Tokyo. It was obvious that the necessarily brief telegraphic summaries which were being transmitted to Ottawa during the course of the negotiations did not completely portray the situation as it really existed. So, in consequence of a communication received from Sir Wilfrid Laurier on the 24th of December, Mr. Lemieux decided to sail for Canada on Boxing Day in order to lay the result of his mission before the Cabinet with the least possible delay.

The negotiations had practically been completed. Mr. Lemieux was satisfied that in the conduct of his delicate mission he had obtained every possible concession from the Japanese Government. He had every confidence that the restrictions which that Government voluntarily proposed to put upon the emigration of its own people to Canada would be honourably enforced and that they should be accepted. Accordingly he sailed for Canada on the 26th of December, leaving Mr. Pope to complete the few remaining formalities.

While the diary for the month of December records many conferences and rather trying meetings, Mr. Pope was able to do a certain amount of sight-seeing. It is quite obvious from the diary that Mr. Pope was disappointed in the show-places of Japan. There was much to be seen that he really admired, but he felt that many of the descriptions of the country which he had read and listened to had been marred by extravagant praise. He had, undoubtedly, a profound admiration for the people of that country and for their extraordinary development in the course of a comparatively few years. But then he was of another civilization, and the remark of one of his cronies at the Rideau Club that 'according to Joe Pope the only thing in Japan really worth seeing is the British Embassy', while a palpable exaggeration, nevertheless contained a germ of truth.

On the 17th Mr. Lemieux gave a dinner at the Imperial Hotel which the diary describes as follows: 'The dinner came off tonight and was a great success. 62 persons in all sat down. The menu, wine, music and all were excellent, and Lady Macdonald told Madame Lemieux that it was the finest hotel dinner they had been at in Tokyo. I took Mrs. Lindley in to dinner. Went to bed tired, but much pleased at the success of the dinner.'

On the last day of the year Mr. Pope called for the last time at the Foreign Office, where he had a conversation with Mr. Ishii. Later he proceeded to the Embassy and delivered Mr. Lemieux's original signed letters of the 23rd of December to Count Hyashi to be used if occasion required. At about this time Mr. Pope had several meetings with the Canadian Trade Commissioner, Mr. W. T. R. Preston, the British Consul-General, and Sir Claude Macdonald

with regard to a project to advertise Canadian flour in Japan, a
question in which Lord Grey displayed much interest. At that time
the obstacle in the way of the increased use of Canadian flour
appears to have been high freight charges, which it would seem has
been largely, if not altogether, overcome in recent years.

Having said goodbye to the friends he had made at Tokyo, Mr.
Pope sailed for San Francisco by the s.s. *Mongolia* on the 3rd of
January 1908. The voyage across the Pacific, while exceedingly
pleasant, was uneventful. Honolulu was reached on the 12th, and
the passengers were able to make a short visit ashore. Mr. Pope
landed at San Francisco on Sunday the 19th, and owing to the inevitable bother regarding luggage, he was unable to proceed eastwards
until the following day. Just prior to landing, Mr. Pope was delighted
to receive a wire from Mr. Lemieux informing him that the cabinet
had accepted their arrangement with the Japanese Government, and
that they thought it a good one—news which prompted Mr. Pope
to write: 'So thank God for all his goodness.'

On his arrival at San Francisco Mr. Pope was met by a number of
newspaper reporters who were eager for news, particularly as some
days previously a report was current that the mission had ended in
failure. Mr. Pope received the reporters hospitably but gave them
no information, telling them merely that he had been in the Government service for thirty years, and that he had held his job by holding
his tongue, which caused one of the disappointed scribes to write:
'He held it by both ends yesterday.'

Ottawa was reached on the 27th of January, and the last entry
in the special diary reads as follows: 'I find that our work in Japan
has been recognized more quickly than I had hoped for. The Government has accepted our arrangements and Mr. Lemieux has been
congratulated on all sides for the success of the mission.'

1908 — 1910

On his return to his department Mr. Pope found things much as usual and he was content, after his long absence, to settle down to the customary routine. For some months there was a fair amount of correspondence in connection with the mission to Japan in order to clear up several small misunderstandings that arose after his departure from that country. A letter from Sir Claude Macdonald to Lord Grey, which the Governor-General kindly sent him, caused him no little gratification for it contained a most flattering allusion to the part he had played during the negotiations.

On the 20th of February he lunched at Government House, where he met Mr. Bryce, the British Ambassador to Washington. With him he had a long talk on Japanese affairs. That same day Lord Grey informed him that Sir Wilfrid Laurier had quite resolved upon the establishment of a Department of External Affairs in accordance with his (Pope's) recommendations and suggestions, and that the Prime Minister's only regret in the matter was that he had not done so ten years previously. Lord Grey further told Mr. Pope that he was

most anxious to see him appointed Secretary to the Quebec Tercentenary Celebration Commission—which Mr. Pope, then in his
fifty-fourth year, refers to as 'A position I am not anxious to fill.'
However, the diary records that some ten days later, in company
with Col. J. Hanbury Williams, the Governor-General's secretary,
he paid his first visit to Quebec in connection with the celebration.

The diary for the 6th of March records a conversation with Lord
Grey as follows: 'Lord Grey stopped me on my way to lunch and
told me that he had been at Sir Wilfrid again about the Quebec affair
and that Sir Wilfrid Laurier said Hanbury Williams and I were to
act as interim secretaries to the Battlefields Commission—and he
didn't envy us our job. An impression is everywhere abroad that
Lord Grey wishes to subordinate the Champlain end of this affair
to the Battlefields Park, turning what was originally a local celebration of the founding of Quebec into a great imperial demonstration.
No doubt there is something in this.'

And on the 12th of March: 'The Battlefields Commission held its
first meeting this morning at 10.30 a.m. at Government House.
Present: His Excellency, Garneau, Byron Walker, Col. Denison,
and Turgeon. Sir George Drummond came in later. Doughty was
also present. Garneau wanted Doughty appointed as secretary (there
are already 3; Hanbury, Chouinard of Quebec, and I). It was also
decided to appoint J. M. Courtney as Treasurer. Too many officials,
in my judgement, and I am going to get out.' However, he appears
to have overcome this disinclination, and several weeks later, on
the 5th of April, he again went down to Quebec to inspect the
quarters at the Citadel, to which he refers as follows: 'Hanbury
Williams, Leveson Gower, the Comptroller, and I went over the
Citadel, officers' quarters, etc. They are in a bad state and much
will have to be done to render them fit for the Prince of Wales.'

Early in April Mr. Pope published a monograph, entitled *The
Flag of Canada*, partly as a rejoinder to those who advocated a
distinctive Canadian flag, and, in addition, to refute the statement
that such a step was in accordance with the views held by Sir John
Macdonald. Mr. Pope argued that a national flag is the symbol of
supreme authority; that Canada formed a portion of the dominions
of the King of England, as much so, as His Majesty had declared, as

do the counties of Surrey and Kent; and he asked, in consequence, how it was possible for us to fly any other flag than that which denotes British sovereignty? In a review of Sir John Macdonald's public statements selected during the whole of the statesman's long career, he appears to have proved conclusively 'that far from entertaining any sympathy with a propaganda having for its object the lowering of the Union Jack on this continent at any time, Sir John Macdonald held the very idea in detestation.'

Mr. Pope venerated the memory of his late chief, and he never failed to make reply to any criticisms directed thereat which he felt to be unjustified. Moreover, as he himself has written earlier in this volume, 'loyalty to his Sovereign was the dominating impulse of his life', and he felt moved to do whatever lay in his power to counteract the activities of those to whom he refers 'as those, happily very few, whose allegiance sits lightly on them'. So conservative was he by nature that were he alive today he would undoubtedly maintain with vehemence that the successive changes in inter-imperial relations of the last twenty years culminating in the pronouncement of the Imperial Conference of 1926 that the Dominions are free and independent nations, have wrought no change in the question of the desirability of a distinctive emblem for the Dominion of Canada.

Meanwhile the frequent trips to Quebec continued. With Col. Hanbury Williams he was specially deputed by Order-in-Council dated 5 May 'to make the necessary arrangements in connection with the visit of H.R.H. the Prince of Wales, and the Representatives of France and the United States of America, at the forthcoming Tercentenary celebration at Quebec.'

These arrangements involved an immense amount of hard work. To judge from the diary and the voluminous files of correspondence that Mr. Pope preserved, it is obvious that from mid-May until the celebration was over he had not a moment to spare for the administration of his department. While he and Col. Hanbury Williams had no responsibility with regard to the pageant, which formed an important part of the programme, there seems to have been little else which was not directly in their hands.

He was well aware of the importance of creating a favourable impression at the outset and, in consequence, he did not spare himself in his efforts to ensure that the ceremony incidental to the Prince of Wales's landing at the King's Wharf should be as nearly perfect as possible. Many were the arrangements which had to be made for the reception and accommodation of the score or more guests of the Government, in addition to the Prince of Wales and his suite. There was much to be done with regard to the selection of an adequate number of motor cars and carriages required during the celebration, and it is noted that on the 6th of June he travelled to Montreal for the special purpose of trying several motor cars, not so dependable in 1908 as they are today, that he had specially selected for the use of His Royal Highness. There were innumerable requests for information from people from all parts of Canada to which it was necessary to make reply while he was required to advise as to the selection of suitable inscriptions to be used in connection with the decorations of the city's streets and public places. The preparation of the official programme was no small task in view of the scope of the celebration, and it was necessary to ensure that this programme was printed in a manner in keeping with the importance of the occasion. Morocco cases had to be obtained to contain sets of the special issue of postage stamps which was made in connection with the Tercentenary for presentation to the guests of the Dominion Government, and in his zeal that Canada's flag should fly from every public building, Mr. Pope generously supplied Union Jacks to those officials who did not appear to have one in their possession. And lastly, it is to be inferred that when the Prince of Wales eventually landed at Quebec, the addresses of welcome which were read and even the replies thereto did not in every case fall upon entirely unfamiliar ears.

These multifarious duties must have been somewhat trying, for the entry in the diary for the 2nd of June reads as follows: 'Learned today to my indignant surprise that during my absence last week the *Great Seal* was put to an authentication of a document for use in a u.s. Court. They would not take the Privy Seal. This is the first occasion on which such a thing has happened and I hope it will be the last. If the Yankees would not take the Governor-General's signature with the Privy Seal I'd see them d——d before I would give them anything else. The Great Seal should be reserved for executive acts, such as appointments, conveyances, pardons, etc., and never derogated by being employed merely to authenticate a document for use in a Yankee Court.'

In view of his long experience and of his extensive knowledge of public affairs, Mr. Pope's advice was often sought with regard to the bestowal of honours. Early in June there is record of Lord Grey's speaking to him in connection with the honours to be given on the occasion of the Tercentenary celebration. The diary for the 19th of that month refers to a conversation that he had with Sir Wilfrid Laurier on this same subject. Apparently Sir Wilfrid sent for Mr. Pope, and asked him if the Governor-General had spoken to him on the subject of honours. Mr. Pope replied that Lord Grey had made some casual references thereto. Sir Wilfrid then read a list of the Governor-General's suggestions, to which Mr. Pope gave certain advice. Thereafter the diary reads: 'Lord Grey (at my suggestion) proposed that Sir Wilfrid Laurier should be made a G.C.B. He demurred, but I urged his acceptance of this great honour. Why should he decline, said I, to be numbered with Pitt, Canning, Peel, Palmerston and the great statesmen of England? He told me that he had twice refused "a greater honour than that" by which I understood a Peerage. I said I could quite understand that, but the G.C.B. was for those distinguished men who preferred to remain Commoners. Just his case. He said it would hurt him. I don't think so, seeing that he has already accepted honour.'

The Tercentenary celebration lasted a full week from Wednesday, the 22nd of July, until the following Wednesday. Briefly, the programme was as follows: The Prince of Wales arrived in Quebec on Wednesday afternoon and on landing at the King's Wharf was presented with an address of welcome read by the Prime Minister. On Thursday morning His Royal Highness returned naval visits, and in the afternoon he was presented with an address by the Mayor of Quebec, following which speeches were made by the representatives of France, United States, and Canada. In the evening there was a state dinner at the Citadel and later a display of fireworks. On the morning of the 24th there was a military review on the Plains of Abraham, and on this occasion the Prince of Wales presented Lord Grey with the title deeds of the Plains of Abraham and Ste. Foy.

Then followed a luncheon given by the mayor in honour of His Royal Highness at the Garrison Club, and in the evening a ball was given by the Provincial Government at the Legislative Building. On Saturday the Prince of Wales passed down the line of assembled warships, and in the afternoon was held the pageant on the Plains of Abraham. That evening there was a dinner at the Citadel given by the Governor-General. On the Sunday the programme called only for attendance at divine service. On Monday the 27th the Prince of Wales visited the village of St. Joachim and lunched with the prelates of the Quebec Seminary at the Château Bellevue, Petit Cap. On Tuesday there was a tree-planting ceremony at Victoria Park, which was followed by a garden party at Spencerwood in the after-noon. Late in the afternoon His Royal Highness boarded his ship, gave a dinner party on board, and sailed for home early next morning. Thus the diary for this period:

WEDNESDAY, 22 JULY   'Pouring rain this morning. Up at 6 a.m. and over in the rain to Levis to meet Vice-President Fairbanks. Drove with the Fairbanks party to Spencerwood. Then to the wharf. H.R.H. in the *Indomitable* arrived about 3 p.m. Went on board and called on the Prince of Wales with Sir W. Laurier. H.R.H. landed at 4 and this reception was a great success. Not a hitch in any respect. The weather cleared off at noon and was beautifully fine. The sight was long to be remembered—and the whole ceremony exceeded my expectations to my very great relief. Sladen told me this evening I was to have a c.v.o.'

THURSDAY THE 23RD   'Up to the Citadel this morning. At 3 p.m. there was an investiture at which I received the honour of a c.v.o.— Hanbury getting promotion to a K.C.V.O. Many people were dis-appointed that I did not receive a knighthood, but in this feeling I do not share. The ceremony went off very nicely. Lord Lovat and General Pole Carew were my sponsors, and General Lake and I were sponsors to Mr. H. J. J. B. Chouinard who received a c.m.g. After this ceremony we proceeded into town to the foot of the Champlain statue where the civic address took place followed by speeches by Turgeon, Fairbanks, Jaureguibery,[1] etc. Then the actors of the Pageant filed past. State dinner tonight at the Citadel. After

[1] Admiral Jaureguibery, Commanding the French warships in port.

dinner a lot of people were invited to view the illuminations from the King's Bastion. They were more or less of a failure, by no means worth the $9000 paid for them. It is understood that Sir W. Laurier declined a G.C.B.!'

FRIDAY THE 24TH 'Went out to the Review this morning which was highly successful, though having missed breakfast, owing to numerous calls upon me, I did not enjoy it particularly as I had no seat and so left early. Lunched with the Mayor at the Garrison Club—95 guests—very good affair. Then for a drive. The Provincial Ball came off in the evening. . . . I spent the evening in the hotel chatting with Lady Falmouth. . . . Fine weather continues and the whole Celebration is a great success.'

SATURDAY THE 25TH 'This morning we were invited to accompany H.R.H. on board H.M.S. *Arrogant* and sail down the line of assembled battleships of France, U.S. and our own. The spectacle was very fine and the saluting almost deafening. In the afternoon to the Pageant which was splendid. No other word for it. I enjoyed it immensely. In the evening I dined at the Citadel—the Empire dinner—and a notable assemblage it was. I told Lord Grey on leaving that it must be a proud moment for him. All the speeches were good and the tone excellent.'

At this point it is deemed expedient to interrupt the diary to quote in part a speech made at this dinner on behalf of the South African colonies by Sir Henry de Villiers, the Chief Justice of Cape Colony. In 1908 the only bond of union between the four separate South African colonies was their common allegiance to the one Crown. The confederation of these colonies into the Union of South Africa was not carried out until a year later. In the circumstances it was natural that Sir Henry de Villiers should have desired to ascertain at first hand how the Canadian scheme of 1867 had worked in practice. In later years Mr. Pope frequently referred to the several long conversations he had had with the South African representative on Canadian Confederation matters, and how he had impressed upon his visitor the importance of a strong central government.

On this occasion Sir Henry spoke as follows: 'Unfortunately I cannot speak for a constitutionally united South Africa. We have four separate self-governing Colonies, each independent of the other; the only bond of union being that they all now form part of the great British Empire and the problem now before us is how to unite upon terms that shall be fair and fit to each Colony and to every section of its population.

'The first and most important step has been taken in the appointment of the different parliaments of delegates to a convention which is to meet in Natal in October next. . . . They will have before them the great example of Canada, which has flourished by the union of the provinces, in a manner exceeding the wildest dreams of the fathers of your confederation. They will profit by your experience, but they will, of course, have to suit their constitution to the needs of their own country.'

The diary continues:

SUNDAY THE 26TH   'To High Mass on the Plains of Abraham. A most solemn and affecting ceremony. We were in the tribune with the Duke of Norfolk, Lord Lovat, and all the dignitaries. The day was perfect. Nothing could have been better.'

MONDAY THE 27TH   'This morning—the first cool day—we proceeded by special train for St. Joachim where Mgr. Mathieu gave a luncheon to H.R.H. at the Petit Cap. We lunched under the trees and though a little cool was very pleasant and successful. Returned about 4.30 p.m. and dined at the Citadel.'

TUESDAY THE 28TH   'This morning we attended the tree-planting ceremony at Victoria Park, and very pretty it was. In the afternoon to the Garden Party at Spencerwood and then to the King's Wharf to see the Prince of Wales off. Dined on board the *Exmouth* the guest of H.R.H.—about 70 were present. A most distinguished company. Perfect dinner. Thus ends the visit of the Prince of Wales to Quebec, an unqualified and unhoped-for success.'

WEDNESDAY THE 29TH   'At 3 a.m. this morning the British Fleet weighed anchor and departed. Dined this evening at the Citadel. Big dinner in honour of the Representatives of France and the U.S. The latter were not there, having sailed at dawn. It is said that Fairbanks was huffed at the dinner being given after the departure of the Prince of Wales.'

THURSDAY THE 30TH   'Excessively hot. Felt quite unwell today, being in fact quite played out.'

On the 1st of August Mr. Pope left for Murray Bay. After spending a pleasant holiday, he returned to Ottawa much refreshed some three weeks later.

Shortly after his return from the Lower St. Lawrence, the diary again refers to the new department of External Affairs in which he was so interested. Under date of 9 September there occurs the following entry: '— sent for me this morning and with reference to the recent appointment of the Civil Service Commissioners told me that Sir Wilfrid Laurier had informed the Cabinet of his resolve, immediately after the elections, to erect a Department of External Affairs such as I have long advocated and to place me in charge of it. This the Cabinet unanimously agreed to. If they really mean this, it is a welcome piece of news. To tell the truth I have been feeling discouraged and disheartened over the apathy with which my suggestions have been received. The present state of our external affairs can only be described by the one word "chaotic". One dispatch is referred to one minister—the next one on the same subject to another—the next perhaps to nobody, the fourth somewhere else, so that nobody has any connected knowledge of any of the questions and the dispatches remain undealt with.'

The elections referred to were held on the 26th of October. A few weeks previously, Mr. Pope learned with considerable regret that his Minister, Mr. R. W. Scott (afterwards Sir Richard Scott) had resigned from the Cabinet, and was to be succeeded by Mr. Charles Murphy, an Ottawa barrister whom he did not even know. However, his apprehensions on this score were soon set at rest, and thereafter he frequently makes mention of the cordial relations which grew up between himself and the new Secretary of State.

While it may be said that Mr. Pope's conduct as a civil servant, particularly with reference to his loyalty and sense of duty towards the Government he served, was never anything less than exemplary, yet it may also be said with equal truth that he never forgot his early political associations. The political instinct was strong within him. And so, as the October days wear on, the diary makes occasional references which indicate that the approaching contest was quickening his pulse. In common with many people experienced in politics, he could not refrain from an attempt to prophesy its result, even though he was wont to quote one of Sir John Macdonald's favourite maxims: 'An election is much like a horse race—you can tell much more about it the following day.' Thus the 26th of October: 'Pouring rain. Warm. Election day. Much uncertainty. I myself do not look for the return of the Government with a small majority. I rather think that one of two things will happen: either the Government will be sustained or they will be swept out by a wave of popular indignation which would operate equally in all the constituencies. I predict it will be either Laurier with 40 majority or so or Borden with 15 or 20.'

And this in spite of the fact that the entry for the 3rd of November 1904 had read as follows: 'Election day. To office. Went to the club at about half past five o'clock and found people gathering awaiting the returns. The prevailing impression was that the Government would have a majority of 30 in the whole country and that the opposition would carry both seats in Ottawa. Instead of which the Government won both Ottawa seats by 1200 and 1500 majority and the whole country by something like 75. The result in Nova Scotia is marvellous, Fielding carrying the whole 18 seats including that of the leader of the opposition. My estimate was very close as regards Ontario and Quebec, *nevertheless I think I will go out of the prediction business.*'

Meanwhile the plans for the erection of the new department of External Affairs appear to have matured slowly. On the evening of the 12th of January 1909, Mr. Pope called on Sir Wilfrid Laurier and had a long talk with him in this connection. At this meeting Sir Wilfrid was very friendly, as usual, and told Mr. Pope that he meant to go on with his plan; that he intended to place him at the head of the department, and that he would give him all the assistance that he required. The Prime Minister apparently instructed him to prepare the necessary bill, for on the 6th of February the diary states: 'I sent Sir W. L. a draft of the External Affairs Bill today.'

A few days later, on the 11th of February. Mr. Pope was informed by his Minister that the Prime Minister had given up the idea of creating a separate department, and that he had resolved to make it a branch of the State department. To Mr. Pope this was a great disappointment, for he had always contended that such a department should be placed under the Prime Minister.

On the 16th of February Mr. Murphy gave notice of the new bill, and on the 4th of March following it was introduced in the House of Commons. 'It places the new department under the Secretary of State, which is a *great* mistake,' observes the diary. 'It should be under the Prime Minister. I fear that Ministers will resent having their reports presented to His Excellency by the s.s., whereas that would be natural enough were the First Minister the s.s. for External Affairs.'

In speaking in favour of the bill in the House of Commons, the Prime Minister said in part: 'When I came into office, now twelve years ago, and when dispatches began to come in relating to foreign affairs, I had not in the Department of the Privy Council any official who could inform me, or on whom I could rely; I had to go to another officer, who is fortunately well qualified for that position— I have no hesitation in giving his name, Mr. Pope, the Under-Secretary—and get from him all the information I needed relating to those foreign affairs before I could come to a decision and advise my colleagues, or His Excellency the Governor-General in relation thereto.'[2]

To those interested in the development of Canada's status, the entry for the 12th of March may be of interest: '—— told me today that His Excellency is much worked-up over the wording of the External Affairs Bill as brought down, particularly Sect. 3 which provides that the Secretary of State shall have "the conduct of official communications between the Government of Canada and the Government of any other country." I merely said that in the circumstances I could not do anything, and that His Excellency ought to see his Ministers on the point. I added that the meaning conveyed by these words was quite contrary to Mr. Murphy's speech and that I was sure that the intention of the Government was not to interfere in any way with His Excellency.'

[2] *Debates of the House of Commons*, 4 March 1909, p. 2066.

The bill was duly passed by Parliament, and on the 3rd of June Mr. Pope took the oath as Under-Secretary of State for External Affairs. But apparently little had been done in the way of organization, for on the following day he wrote in his diary: 'I am in the most extraordinary position—a deputy head without an office or a staff.' There were many vexatious delays before he was provided with more or less suitable accommodation. During the month of June he appears to have shared his old office with his successor Mr. Mulvey. For the summer he sought temporary shelter in some rooms in the House of Commons, and early in October his department found quarters in the Trafalgar Building on Bank Street. Here it remained for several years.

It was soon realized by the Prime Minister that the Department of External Affairs was inconveniently located, but Mr. Pope, still in the throes of moving, and, it must be said, somewhat disheartened by the lack of interest that had been shown his department during the course of the summer, begged Sir Wilfrid to be allowed to stay where he was. Shortly afterwards Lord Grey, with that enthusiasm that characterized many of his actions, arranged with the Prime Minister that certain rooms in the East Block belonging to the Indian Affairs should be handed over to the Department of External Affairs, for he too desired to have the new department close to his hand. But Mr. Pope, at the risk of incurring the Governor-General's displeasure, as will subsequently be noticed, requested Sir Wilfrid Laurier not to order any change, as he did not desire to offend, even indirectly, or inconvenience, a brother Deputy-Minister.

But if for a time Mr. Pope felt somewhat hurt at the Government's failure to provide him with suitable and conveniently situated quarters, as the diary leads one to believe, the Prime Minister soon made amends therefor by a renewal of interest in the work of establishing the new department on a sound basis. Thus the diary for the 15th of January 1910: 'Sir Wilfrid sent for me this morning and spoke to me of the desirability of my visiting England to look into the Foreign Office system and to collect back records on the subjects with which I am called upon to deal. He told me he was much interested in the development and success of this Dept. of External Affairs and he wished the foundations well and truly laid.' In due course the trip was authorized, and Mr. Pope sailed for England on the 2nd of April following.

Several days before his departure for New York to board his ship, Mr. Pope lunched with Lord Grey, who had displayed much interest in the creation of the new department. Of the meeting the diary states: 'Lunched with Lord Grey in his private car at the station today. His Excy. was most cordial. Is writing Sir Edward Grey about me suggesting that he consult with me with regard to any possible scheme he may have in mind touching the federation of England, Scotland, Ireland and Wales, i.e., of applying the federal principle to them.[3]

'At the Quebec Tercentenary Sir Henry de Villiers had several long chats with me on the subject of a constitution for South Africa. I exposed my views, laying particular emphasis on the danger of allowing the Provincial Legislatures too much power. I was most gratified to find when the s.a. Confederation scheme was announced my representations appear not to have been wholly ignored.'

On this question of the subjection of the provinces to the Federal Government Mr. Pope held decided views. He much preferred the system laid down by the British North America Act of 1867 and the Union of South Africa Act of 1909—whereby only definite and express powers are conferred on the provinces of Canada and South Africa respectively, thus, by implication, leaving all other powers of self-government in the hands of the Dominion Parliaments —to that of the Australian Commonwealth Act of 1900, which

[3] While the foregoing may occasion some surprise, it will be remembered that at this time a proposal (popularly known as 'Home Rule all round') had been much discussed in England (see p. lxxiv of Introduction to A. V. Dicey, *Law of the Constitution*, Eighth Edition, 1920). Professor Dicey quite definitely was against the proposal and so, it should be said, was Mr. Pope. Later in the year he thus wrote to Lord Grey: 'I am much obliged to Your Excellency for allowing me to read your letter to Mr. Prothero which I now return. While it is beginning to look as if some such step might be necessary, I cannot say I am enthusiastic over the proposal, which involves the disruption of the ancient constitution of England. Rather do I sympathize with your Excellency's ancestors when they brandished their spears and shouted "*Nolumus leges Angliae mutari*". But if it has to come, and I am no judge of the necessity, I am prepared sorrowfully to acquiesce. I quite agree with what your Excellency says about the Federation of the Empire. There is no necessary connection between the two schemes, though one may prepare the way for the other. The larger proposal is yet far in the future. Union for Defence, with a system of Preferential Trade—our political relations remaining as they are—is an ideal more easy of realization and, I cannot help thinking, the more excellent way.'

reverses this process by conferring only definite and express powers on the Federal Government, and leaves the residuum of legislative power with the different states. These views, in part, are clearly set forth in some correspondence he had in May 1909 with Sir John Hanbury Williams on the subject of the status of Lieutenant-Governors of the Canadian provinces, views which in Canada may occasion surprise measured only by the degree in which they are contrary to present popular opinion:

GOVERNMENT HOUSE

OTTAWA

4.5.09.

My dear Joe,

A friend of mine, Mr. Clark, K.C., of Toronto, sent me the enclosed in which you will find an article by him which mentions that a Lieutenant-Governor represents the crown—for provincial purposes.

I wrote him and enclose his answer.

J. HANBURY WILLIAMS

Ottawa,

5th May 1909.

Dear Hanbury Williams,

Thanks for the Canadian Law Times, *which I return, together with Mr. Clark's letter. I was aware of these unfortunate rulings of the Judicial Committee of the Privy Council, which, however, I do not think are quite so absolute as Mr. Clark makes them out to be. Without going deeply into the matter, I think the decisions were to the effect that Lieutenant-Governors,* when opening and closing their legislatures and when assenting to bills, *do so in the Sovereign's name, which is bad enough.*[4] *The Judicial Committee have acquired a very undesirable reputation for some of their decisions have done great harm to Canadian unity. The reason for this perpetual sacrifice of the Dominion to the Provinces is generally ascribed to Lord Watson, who when dealing with the Canadian questions in the early days of Confederation, could not get out of his head the Civil*

---

[4] Actually, the essential part of Lord Watson's judgement, given in 1892, read as follows: 'A Lieutenant-Governor, when appointed, is as much the representative of Her Majesty for all purposes of Provincial Government as the Governor-General himself is for all purposes of Dominion Government' (Appeal Cases, 1892, p. 437). In a judgement rendered in 1919, Lord Haldane practically repeats the above words (Appeal Cases, 1919, p. 938).

War in the United States, and fearing that something of the same kind might happen in Canada, he took the line of conciliating the Provinces by giving them every mortal thing they asked for, arguing that if he pleased the Provinces individually, it should not matter what the Dominion—which was the aggregation of all—suffered. It was an unworthy position for so able a man to take. Recent decisions seem to indicate that the Judicial Committee at last see this, and are going on the other tack, but I fear it is too late. Much mischief has already been done by sanctioning the pretensions of the Provinces—pretensions which were undreamt of when the Union was formed.

Yours very truly,

J. POPE

Colonel Sir John Hanbury Williams,
     K.C.V.O., C.M.G.,
Governor-General's Secretary,
     Ottawa.

But while Mr. Pope in 1909 definitely expresses his dissatisfaction with the trend of developments with regard to the position of the provinces, he was not devoid of a philosophical point of view. Sometime in 1919 or 1920, when Canada's status within the Empire had become to all practical purposes that which it is today, he was heard to say reflectively that it was probably well that a spirit of provincialism here and there had made itself manifest. For, he observed, while the aims of the Fathers of Confederation had been as far as possible to weld British North America into a unified whole, he feared that had they been completely successful it was not improbable that the country might have been led to seek complete independence, even perhaps outside the orbit of the British Empire. And so to him a certain provincialism, in a degree natural enough in view of the commercial, racial, and geographical differences which exist, tended to retard an eventuality to which he was unalterably opposed.

As has been said, Mr. Pope sailed for England on the 2nd of April. He arrived in London some eight days later, and on the 11th he called at the High Commissioner's office, where he found a telegram from Sir Arthur Davidson inviting him to dine with the Prince of Wales the following evening at the Naval and Military Club. Of that evening Mr. Pope retained the pleasantest recollec-

tions. It was a small dinner, there being present only ten persons:
His Royal Highness, Sir Arthur Davidson, Sir Arthur Bigge, Sir C.
Hardinge, Sir Ronald Lane, Sir E. Henry, Commander Fawcett,
and one or two more. The diary records that the Prince of Wales
was particularly cordial to the Canadian visitor, and that His Royal
Highness engaged him in conversation on various subjects until a
comparatively late hour.

Mr. Pope remained in London until the latter part of May, during
which time he paid frequent visits to the Foreign Office and to
official friends, elsewhere employed, in order to gather the information he required for his new department. On the 3rd of May
he had a short but cordial interview with Sir Edward Grey, but the
latter made no allusion to the federation question respecting which
Lord Grey had written him.

On the night of the 5th of May, when coming out from the
theatre, Mr. Pope was startled to hear the newsboys selling extra
editions of the evening papers, and crying out 'Serious illness of the
King!' King Edward died that same night at a quarter before twelve.
The following day being Sunday, Mr. Pope went to High Mass at
the Jesuits' Church, Farm Street, where he records that the noted
preacher of the day, Father Bernard Vaughan, s.j., made a touching
allusion to the late King. Through the kindness of the Duke of
Norfolk, whom he had met at the Quebec Tercentenary Celebration,
Mr. and Mrs. Pope were privileged on the Monday following, the
9th of May, to witness the ceremony of the proclamation of the
accession of King George the Fifth. This ceremony is described in
the diary as follows: 'At 20 minutes to 9 we drove to the Friary
Court, St. James's Palace, where we were ushered to a gallery in which
a few privileged people like ourselves were admitted to see the
quaint old ceremony of the publication by the Garter King of Arms
of the Proclamation announcing the accession of George v. With us
were Mr. Churchill (Winston), Lloyd George, Pierrepont Morgan
and other prominent persons, most of whom I did not know.
Punctually at nine o'clock the Earl Marshal (The Duke of Norfolk)
and with him the Garter King of Arms, heralds in their tabards,
trumpeters, etc. After a fanfare by the latter, the Proclamation was
read. Then followed God Save the King. A most impressive and

beautiful ceremony which was repeated three times at Charing Cross, Temple Bar, and the Mansion House.'

20 MAY   'Today, through the kindness of Lord and Lady Mount Stephen, we saw the Royal Funeral from the vantage ground of Carlton House Terrace. We had a splendid view of the most imposing spectacle I ever beheld. It was truly wonderful.'

But interesting journeys must end, and Mr. Pope had soon to prepare for the return to Canada. He paid several more visits of an official nature to the Foreign Office and then bade goodbye to his many friends, not least among whom was Col. Maude, for whom he entertained such a warm regard. Mr. and Mrs. Pope sailed from Liverpool on the 28th of May and duly arrived in Ottawa some ten days later.

1911

*International Pelagic Sealing Conference at
Washington | Negotiations Subsequent to Paris
Award of 1893 | Sealing Treaty Between Great
Britain and United States, February 1911 |
Four-Power Conference Meets at Washington,
May 1911 | The Canadian View-point |
Rejection Thereof by United States and Russia |
The Botkine Incident | Canada Ignored in
Conference | British Delegates Hold Divergent Views |
Inability of United States to Settle with Japan
Makes Canada Mistress of Situation | The Treaty*

IT will be remembered that the award of the Bering Sea Arbitration Tribunal, which sat in Paris in 1893, declared that the United States possessed no right of property in the fur-seals found outside the ordinary three-mile limit, and that the regulations made pursuant to this award, in addition to the establishment of a close season extending from the 1st of May to the 31st of July in all the waters of the north-eastern Pacific Ocean, forbade pelagic sealing within sixty miles of the Pribylof Islands. These regulations obviously applied only to British and American subjects, and they were to remain in force until abolished or modified by the mutual consent of the two powers.

For the next eighteen years, during which time the seal herds that resorted to the rookeries of the northern Pacific Ocean constantly diminished in numbers, the question of pelagic sealing was destined, in varying degree, to occupy the attention of the Governments of those countries whose nationals were engaged in the industry, namely, Great Britain and Canada, the United States,

Japan, and Russia. The three last named were also rookery-owning powers, and they desired to restrict, if not to prohibit, the capture of seals in the open sea, while on at least one occasion Her Majesty's Government stated its opinion that the danger of the extermination of the seals was due to indiscriminate slaughter on land rather than to pelagic sealing. During this long succession of abortive negotiations subsequent to the Bering Sea Arbitration of 1893, both the British and Canadian Governments maintained the principle that Canada could not surrender her right to pursue wild animals in the open sea without some equivalent compensation.

On the 7th of February 1911 a treaty was signed at Washington between Great Britain and the United States respecting measures for the preservation and protection of the fur seals. This treaty laid down that the subjects of both countries were to be prohibited from engaging in pelagic sealing in that part of the Bering Sea and the Pacific Ocean north of the thirty-fifth degree of north latitude and east of the one hundred and eightieth meridian. In return for her cessation of pelagic sealing Great Britain was to receive from the United States one-fifth, in number and in value, of the seal-skins taken annually upon the Pribylof Islands, subject to the proviso that the United States reserved the right to impose such regulations and restrictions as might seem necessary to protect and preserve the seal herd habitually resorting to these islands. The two countries agreed to maintain such patrols as might be necessary to enforce the aforesaid prohibitions. It was further agreed that the articles of the treaty were to go into effect as soon as, but not before, an international agreement was concluded and ratified by the Governments of Great Britain, the United States, Japan, and Russia, whereby each of these powers undertook to prohibit its subjects from engaging in pelagic sealing for a period of fifteen years in the waters of the area defined above. The treaty was signed by Mr. Bryce, His Majesty's Ambassador to Washington, and Mr. Philander C. Knox, the American Secretary of State. Ratifications were duly exchanged at Washington on the 7th of July 1911, the Governor-General of Canada having previously informed Mr. Harcourt, the Secretary of State for the Colonies, that his Ministers had no objection to its immediate ratification.

In March 1911, a few weeks subsequent to the conclusion of the treaty between the two countries, the Canadian Government was informed by Mr. Bryce that His Majesty's Government had received a note from the United States Government inviting them to be represented at a conference to be held in Washington at an early date, at which Great Britain, the United States, Russia, and Japan should concert measures for the preservation of the fur seals. This communication states that the British Ambassador had been selected to act as first British delegate, and the intimation was expressed that the Government of the United Kingdom would invite the Canadian Government to appoint a second delegate. In due course the Canadian Government nominated Mr. Pope to act with Mr. Bryce as the second British delegate. Messrs. W. A. Found and James M. Macoun of the Departments of Marine and Fisheries and Mines respectively were appointed to act as experts to the British delegation.

The International Sealing Conference held its first meeting at Washington on the 11th of May, the plenipotentiaries of the various countries being as follows: for the United States, Mr. Charles Nagel, Secretary of Commerce and Labour, and Mr. Chandler P. Anderson, Counsellor of the State Department; for Great Britain, Mr. Bryce, the British Ambassador to Washington, and Mr. Joseph Pope, Under-Secretary of State for External Affairs of Canada; for Japan, Baron Yasuya Uchida, Jusammi, the Japanese Ambassador to Washington, and the Hon. Hitoshi Dauké, Shoshii, Director of the Bureau of Fisheries, Department of Agriculture and Fisheries; for Russia, M. Pierre Botkine, Minister to Morocco, and Baron Boris Nolde of the Russian Foreign Office.

Prior to Mr. Pope's departure for Washington, Sir Wilfrid Laurier addressed to him certain instructions. Briefly, these were to the effect that Canada, having, by the separate treaty recently entered into with the United States, accepted the principle involved in assenting to a temporary cessation of pelagic sealing within a circumscribed area in return for a pecuniary consideration, the attitude of the Canadian delegate towards proposals for an extension of this arrangement to cover the Asiatic side of the North Pacific Ocean was to be that taken in the prior negotiations, namely that

Canada was prepared to abstain from the exercise of her undoubted right only in return for an adequate consideration. The Prime Minister further enjoined Mr. Pope to impress upon the members of the conference that Canada's relation towards this question differed essentially from that of rookery-owning powers, which naturally desired to suppress sealing at sea in order to enhance the value of their property on land, whereas Canada's interests lay wholly in the ocean. In consequence, any general agreement between the powers for the suppression of pelagic sealing should provide for the admission of Canada to a share in the land take on the Russian and Japanese islands. Mr. Pope was also to keep Sir Wilfrid fully informed of the course of the discussions and of the progress of events.

Mr. Pope arrived in Washington on the afternoon of the 10th of May. Without loss of time he called upon Mr. Bryce. The conversation which ensued filled Mr. Pope with foreboding, for he notes in the diary: 'Called upon Mr. Bryce. Fear we are going to have trouble to get him to sustain our view, i.e., that we should receive compensation from Russia and Japan in return for our abstention from pelagic sealing in the western half of the Pacific Ocean.'

The first meeting of the conference was held on the afternoon of the 11th of May. The delegates were first introduced to Mr. Knox, the Secretary of State, who made a short address. Then Mr. Bryce proposed Mr. Nagel as chairman of the conference. This proposal was seconded by both the leading Russian and Japanese delegates. The conference was now ready to proceed, but the Japanese were not prepared to engage in any serious work owing to the non-arrival of one of their representatives. In consequence the conference adjourned until the following week.

In accordance with his instructions, Mr. Pope kept his Minister in touch with the situation as it developed. While little had as yet been accomplished, he had learned enough from his conversations with Mr. Bryce to be able to report that it was probable that the United States proposed to take the attitude that, as Canada now possessed an interest in the Pribylof Islands herd, she had become a rookery-owning power, an opinion he emphatically declined to entertain. He writes as follows: 'All I can do at present is to watch

the progress of events and, at the proper time, state our opinion
in the conference. My position is a rather difficult one, the more so
as it does not appear strongly to commend itself to our Ambassador.
However I must hope for the best. I feel satisfied that it is sound in
itself, and in full accord with the traditional policy of our Government from the beginning. I should much like to have the opinion
of the Minister of Justice as to the soundness of the view that
one-fifth interest in the land take on the Pribylof Islands constitutes
us a rookery-owning power. We are not partners, nor shareholders
in the ordinary sense, nor even lessees, for we have absolutely no
voice in the regulation of the seals on the islands.'

The conference met again on the 16th of May. The proceedings
were begun by the Japanese, who made large demands for compensation, both as pelagic sealers and as rookery-owners, from the
United States and Russia. These two countries naturally enough
asked for time to consider the Japanese proposals, and the next
meeting was fixed for the 19th of May. Mr. Pope's impression was
that the Japanese had allowed themselves a good bargaining margin.
He also notes that in the meantime Japan in a sense was fighting
Canada's battle, and that she would have difficulty later in refusing
Canada's request for compensation.

Before the delegates separated, Mr. Pope, with Mr. Bryce's
approval, took occasion to state Canada's position. He informed the
conference that, as a country interested in pelagic sealing, the
question possessed for Canada a special concern. Her right to
pursue and capture wild animals in the open sea, which she had
exercised for many years, and in which a number of her citizens
were engaged, was one she could agree to surrender only in return
for compensation. There was hardly any need to dwell on this
position, the reasonableness of which was acknowledged by the
United States when it undertook to give Canada a share in the land
catch on the Pribylof Islands, and by Russia when this latter power
made an offer of compensation to Canada in 1904. This view, he
stated, must necessarily commend itself to Japan. Mr. Pope further
desired to press for recognition of the fact that, in entering into a
conference with rookery-owning powers assembled to concert
measures for the protection and improvement of their property,

Great Britain as a non-rookery-owning power, but largely and for many years interested in sea rights, occupied an exceptional position which called for special recognition.

The following evening the delegates to the conference dined with General Foster. After dinner, M. Botkine, the Russian delegate, remarked to Mr. Pope that, if he had not contradicted Mr. Pope's statement that Russia had offered Canada compensation in 1904, it was because he was unwilling that there should be any differences between their respective countries. To this remark Mr. Pope smilingly dissented, whereupon M. Botkine beckoned Mr. Chandler Anderson and repeated his denial with some vehemence, and threatened, should Mr. Pope not withdraw his statement, that he, M. Botkine, would bring up the question in conference. To this Mr. Pope, who was quite sure of his ground, made reply that M. Botkine might act as he thought fit. Later that evening, however, he decided that it would be politic to spare the Russian the humiliation his proposal would have entailed, for the evidence in Mr. Pope's possession, which admitted of no dispute, showed that the Russian offer of compensation to Canada had been made by *M. Botkine himself* to a Canadian delegate in London in 1904, when he and Mr. Henry Little of Woodstock, Ontario, had conferred with regard to the seizure of Canadian sealing schooners by Russia. Accordingly, Mr. Pope privately communicated his evidence to M. Botkine, who, it is to be said, expressed his appreciation of Mr. Pope's considerateness.

On the 18th of May Mr. Pope had a private conversation with Mr. Chandler Anderson at which he showed him the minutes containing M. Botkine's statement in 1904. This Mr. Anderson explained by saying that M. Botkine had evidently referred to a private understanding in force at that time, whereby Russia was to handle Japan while they (the United States) were to handle Canada. Mr. Pope made no reply. It may be said, however, that he did not attach any great importance to this explanation; for in the 1904 statement M. Botkine had made no mention of Japan, and in addition, for the reason that at that period Japan and Russia were at war.

Mr. Anderson went on to say that he did not think Canada's attitude was very helpful to the United States, as Mr. Bryce had thought it would be, and he asked Mr. Pope if he would consent to the omission of his statement from the protocol of the second meeting of the conference. This Mr. Pope declined to do. Mr. Anderson then professed his fear that Canadian insistence on compensation from Russia and Japan might break up the conference. 'That the conference may collapse', notes Mr. Pope, 'is quite possible, but if it does it will primarily be because the United States cannot come to an arrangement with Japan.'

The meeting fixed for the 19th of May was postponed until the 22nd in order to afford the United States further time to consider the Japanese proposals. On this later date Mr. Anderson opened the proceedings by giving a long, though interesting, historical account of the question at issue. Then, referring to Canada's claim, which Mr. Pope had advanced at the last meeting, Mr. Anderson declared, in an almost threatening tone, that the questions it raised were so serious that in his opinion it should be discussed and settled before proceeding further with the matter before the conference. Mr. Pope inferred that Mr. Anderson's design was to induce him to make a premature statement which might later cause him some embarrassment. But he was not to be drawn. Mr. Bryce, however, intervened by pointing out that Canada had already declared her position in general terms, and that before saying anything further the British delegation desired to know how the United States meant to deal with Japan's proposals, as the British attitude might be influenced thereby.

Then followed the Russian delegate, who stated that whatever Russia's position with regard to compensation to Canada might have been in 1904, the situation had now completely changed, and who added, by way of clinching his argument, that Canadian sealers had not taken a seal in Russian waters during the last ten years. Mr. Pope induced M. Botkine to say that his refusal to entertain the Canadian claim was contingent upon the correctness of this statement. The Canadian delegate then informed M. Botkine that he was in error, for it was a fact, for which proof would be adduced at the next meeting, that during the last ten years Canadian sealers had taken upwards of 10,000 seals belonging to the Russian herd.

The apparent determination on the part of both the United States and Russia to ignore Canada in the conference caused Mr. Pope to review the situation with concern. He appreciated that he might soon be confronted with the choice of adhering to the traditional British contention at the cost of the treaty with the United States, or of sacrificing the principle and temporarily giving up something of little value in order to secure the satisfactory treaty previously entered into with the Americans. As yet, however, he made no move in conference.

The diary says little of the meeting of the 23rd of May beyond the fact that he produced a statement taken from departmental returns showing that within the previous ten years Canadian sealers had taken no less than 12,802 Commander seals—that is, of the Russian herd. The diary goes on to say that M. Botkine was unabashed by this statement, and simply repeated that Russia was not bound by the offer made in 1904.

The crisis was reached at the meeting held on the 25th. At this meeting much familiar ground was gone over yet once more. The United States again repeated that they had given Canada a share in the Pribylof herd in order that she might qualify at this conference as a rookery proprietor. Russia again denied having acknowledged the principle of compensation to Canada, in spite of the fact that at the previous meeting they had repudiated the 1904 offer on the ground that Canada had not taken it up at the time and secondly because Canadian sealers did no damage to their seals. Both of these reasons, to Mr. Pope's mind, inferentially admitted the principle the Russians now denied.

Japan as yet had made no answer to the Canadian demand for compensation, and Mr. Pope was in no hurry to press her. The Canadian case with regard to Japan was not so strong as it was in the case of Russia, for Japan possessed a pelagic sealing fleet whereas Russia had none. And it was not to Canada's advantage to force Japan at the present time, as in some respects that country was in the same position as Canada. It was stated that Russia and Japan's private negotiations had not sufficiently advanced to make any arrangement, and the conference adjourned until the 29th.

At this juncture it appeared to Mr. Pope that the United States and Russia had agreed to a division of labour. He felt that the United States had arranged to take charge of Canada, while Russia, probably also with the secret assistance of the United States, would endeavour to settle with Japan. Mr. Pope did not see how the plan could succeed, for he felt that Japan must ask for compensation from the United States. However, he feared that, should such a compact be made, Canada might find herself in the position of having to bear the odium should the conference end in failure.

He felt, therefore, that the time had come for him tentatively to put forward some constructive proposal. He stated that before the conference adjourned he would like to say, with reference to an enquiry recently raised by Mr. Anderson as to whether Canada would be prepared to contribute a portion of her interest in the Pribylof Islands' seals towards effecting an arrangement with Japan, that this suggestion had received his serious consideration; that while at the moment he was not prepared to make a definite statement on the subject, he was disposed to view it as a possible basis of a proposal which he might receive authority from his Government to submit at the next meeting of the conference; that any such proposal would involve as a necessary condition a recognition by Russia and Japan of a Canadian interest in their land catch analogous to that which would be surrendered by Canada, as he had just indicated.

This offer was received almost with contempt; in fact, an American delegate left the room while Mr. Pope was in the act of addressing the conference. The chairman made it plain that the United States would not consider any proposal which included compensation to Canada. M. Botkine enquired, almost indignantly, if Canada actually proposed a scheme which would offer something to Japan which she withheld from Russia. 'In vain', writes Mr. Pope, 'I urged that Japan had sealers to compensate, while Russia had none.' 'Oh, then,' observed the chairman, 'it's the bad boy who gets the plums.' Both countries declined to entertain his proposals.

It must be said that Mr. Pope felt the responsibility that rested on him. From day to day he kept his Minister informed as to the course of events. On the 23rd he asked for instructions as to whether he was to maintain the Canadian contention that she could give up her right to hunt seals in the open sea only on the condition that she receive adequate compensation, at the risk of losing the satisfactory treaty previously entered into with the United States; and he ends his letter with the words, 'I await instructions with anxiety.'

Two days earlier he had dispatched Mr. Found to Ottawa bearing a private letter to Mr. Murphy in which he expressed himself more freely than he could in a communication to be transmitted through the post. In this letter he reported that the United States now bitterly regretted having allowed Canada, by the previous treaty, freedom to seek advantages from Russia and Japan similar to those which the United States had granted her. The Americans had given Canada a good treaty hoping thereby to bind her to them so that when they went into conference they would find in Canada their echo. 'The Americans hint privately at sharp practice on our part. The humour of such a charge coming from such a quarter', he observes, 'goes far to make one forgive the imputation.'

But it was Mr. Bryce's views that occasioned Mr. Pope most concern. The Ambassador privately shared the American point of view. He was opposed root and branch to pelagic sealing; he believed in the partnership theory; he considered that Canada should join hands with the United States in bringing matters to a successful issue. He stated that he had no idea that Canada seriously intended to advance such a claim. In vain Mr. Pope had urged upon him that there was no reason why Canada should not apply the principle of compensation recognized by the United States in respect of Pribylof seals to the Russian and the Japanese herds. The fact that Canada had spent a considerable sum to vindicate, by the Paris Award, the principle of the freedom of the seas, that for the past twenty years Great Britain and Canada had on all occasions stood by that principle, did not appear to appeal to Mr. Bryce. Mr. Pope, further, had little doubt that the United States were aware of the divergence of the views held by the two British delegates.

Mr. Pope undoubtedly found himself in a difficult position, even though the British Ambassador had supported him officially in conference. He felt personally that the Americans were 'bluffing' when they threatened to allow the destruction of their herds should the conference fail, and he felt that Mr. Bryce had tried to frighten him by threatening collapse. Yet Mr. Bryce had told him that he would ask the Canadian delegate later to authorize him to assure the United States that Canada would not adhere to its stand to the extent of wrecking the treaty, a statement which Mr. Pope confessed he did not much like.[1]

It occurred to him, however, that the counter to the *bluff* is the *call*, and in consequence he suggested that he be officially informed that he should continue to press the Canadian claim; that it was by no means certain that the Government would consent to sacrifice consistency in order to secure a treaty which did not affect more than two hundred persons in Canada, many of whom were Indians; and that it was a question of grave consideration whether for such trifling benefit it was worth while to abdicate rights vindicated to Canada by an international arbitration, which the Government had consistently upheld for twenty-five years.

The suggestion fell upon sympathetic ears. On the 27th of May Mr. Pope received instructions by wire from the Canadian Government which were practically a transcription of the proposals he had submitted, followed by the words, 'Adhere to the above whatever the consequences.' This telegram was followed by a letter of the same date which repeated the Government's instructions in greater detail. These communications from Canada Mr. Pope did not delay in transmitting to Mr. Bryce, at the same time expressing his regret 'to be obliged to take a course which I fear will not commend itself to Your Excellency, but my instructions leave me no option.'

This resolute attitude does not appear to have been without effect. The next meeting of the conference had been fixed for the 29th. At 11 o'clock that morning both the British and Japanese were on hand, but the Russian and United States delegates had not arrived. They were sent for. Soon two Russians appeared explaining that they had not understood that the meeting was for that day, and that M. Botkine had gone to Baltimore. Shortly afterwards Messrs. Anderson

[1] It is quite definitely not the intention to create the impression that, in the slightest degree, Mr. Bryce was indifferent to Canada's interests. Such was not the case. At the beginning of the conference the British ambassador in all sincerity held the views outlined above. On the day following his return to Ottawa, Mr. Pope, in a private letter to Lord Grey, thus referred to the part Mr. Bryce had played in the negotiations: 'While, at first, the Ambassador did not regard the matter quite from Canada's point of view, as soon as he seized the position, he brought to its support the whole influence of his high office with each nation in turn—I am glad to say successfully in each case.'

and Lansing, the latter the American legal expert, arrived, but without Mr. Nagel, the chairman. With the chairman and the principal Russian delegate absent no conference could be held, and adjournment was made until the 1st of June.

Before leaving the room Mr. Lansing asked Mr. Pope if he had had any reply from Ottawa regarding the proposal he (Mr. Pope) had outlined at the previous meeting. Mr. Pope replied that, from the manner in which the United States and Russia had treated his suggestion, he regarded the proposal as a dead issue. Mr. Lansing then said that there was some misunderstanding in the matter—that the United States could propose no arrangement with Japan until they knew what Canada was prepared to do by way of assisting them, and that matters were absolutely held up in the meantime. Mr. Lansing added that, if Canada would consent to some such arrangement, the Americans, on their part, would undertake to obtain for Canada a share in the Russian and Japanese rookeries, and otherwise make things pleasant for her.

This sudden change in the attitude on the part of the United States was not lost upon the Canadian delegate. He realized that the Americans had come to the conclusion that they could not reach an agreement with Japan without Canada's help, and that the situation had completely changed. He felt that it was the part of wisdom to take advantage of this *volte-face* of the United States and he concludes: 'From being regarded as almost a negligible quantity, this kaleidoscopic change of attitude on the part of the United States has made Canada the mistress of the situation. I cannot doubt it is to be ascribed to our Government's resolute attitude as embodied in your telegram of the 27th, an inkling of which may have in some way reached the powers.'

With this abrupt acceptance of the Canadian point of view the conference set to work to come to an agreement with regard to the proportions to be allotted to the various countries, a laborious and exacting business which took over five weeks to accomplish. The demands originally made by certain powers, as is usual in such circumstances, allowed a considerable margin over the minimum requirements. As the days wore on hopes rose and fell alternately. On the 25th of June the British and Japanese delegates met privately, but the diary records: 'They are hard bargainers and nothing was done.' A week later, 'at the close of a hard day's fruitless efforts to effect a much-desired compromise, it became evident that their demands are impossible and that our conference must come to nothing.' But the delegates applied themselves assiduously and the much-desired treaty between the four powers was duly signed on the 7th of July.

By the terms of the treaty the High Contracting Parties mutually and reciprocally agreed to prohibit their citizens from engaging in pelagic sealing in the waters of the Pacific Ocean north of the thirtieth parallel of north latitude and including the seas of Bering, Kamchatka, Okhotsk, and Japan. This prohibition was not to apply to Indians and other aborigines employing primitive methods and appliances. The United States, Japan, and Russia agreed to maintain a guard or patrol so far as might be necessary. The United States agreed that of the total number of sealskins taken annually under its authority at the Pribylof Islands, fifteen per cent. were to be handed to each of the authorized agents of the Canadian and Japanese Governments. Russia agreed to hand over an equal percentage of the land catch on the Commander Islands to each of the representatives of Japan and Canada. In her turn Japan bound herself to give ten per cent. of her takings on the Robben Islands to the Governments of the other three powers. The Convention was to supersede, where inconsistent, that entered into by the United States and British Governments on the 7th of February 1911. And lastly the treaty was to come into force as from the 15th of December 1911, for a period of fifteen years, with the provision that it could be terminated on twelve months' notice after fourteen years had elapsed.

On his return to Ottawa Mr. Pope was warmly congratulated by his Minister on the part he had played in bringing the conference to a successful issue. On the 9th of July Lord Grey wrote:

My dear Pope,
    I was sorry not to see you before I left Ottawa. I should have been glad to be able to congratulate you personally on your diplomatic triumph. I realize the difficulty of the position in which you found yourself at Washington sufficiently to know that it was no easy one and I should like to take this opportunity of saying how much I

appreciate and admire the strength and dignity and the nerve with which you fought for Canadian interests.

I feel sure that the way in which you handled a very difficult and delicate situation has secured for Canada an increased measure of respect from all concerned.

Yours very truly,

GREY

In an official dispatch to the Governor-General, Mr. Bryce referred to the part he had played in the following words:

It is not for me, as Mr. Pope's colleague in the privilege of representing His Majesty at the late conference, to offer any observations on the discharge of that duty. But I hope that I may be permitted, speaking in my personal capacity, to convey to Your Excellency my sense of the satisfaction which it gave me to have as an associate in this responsible post such a representative of Canada as Mr. Pope, whose thorough knowledge of the matters in hand was equalled only by the frankness, courtesy, and practical good sense which made his co-operation a constant source of pleasure.

And in March of the following year Sir Wilfrid Laurier, who had been absent in England during the conduct of the negotiations, wrote:

My dear Pope,

Accept my thanks for a copy of the negotiations at Washington on the suspension of pelagic sealing. I have commenced to read it, but I am not yet near the end. I have seen enough, however, to fully endorse the high appreciation often expressed to me by Aylesworth upon the efficiency and thoroughness of your work.

Apart from your other claims, this alone would have well warranted the honor bestowed on you by the Imperial Government.

Yours very sincerely,

WILFRID LAURIER

1911 – 1913

*General Elections of 1911 | Resignation of
the Laurier Government | H.R.H. The Duke of
Connaught Becomes Governor-General | Sir
Wilfrid Laurier in Opposition | Receives
Knighthood | Lord Grey's Congratulations |
Accompanies Mr. Borden to England | Social
Festivities | Conversations with Mr. Walter Long |
Sir Richard Cartwright's Reminiscences |
Visit to Italy*

SHORTLY after Mr. Pope's return to Ottawa, the Government decided to appeal to the country in view of the continued obstruction which the Opposition had offered to the bill respecting reciprocity of trade with the United States. On the 27th of July he was sent for by Lord Grey. In the course of the conversation, the Governor-General intimated that dissolution was a question of hours, and he asked if he could dissolve Parliament without first proroguing. Mr. Pope replied that he thought the rule was first to prorogue and then to issue a proclamation dissolving Parliament, but that he would look up the point at once. Early next morning he received a telegram from Sir Wilfrid Laurier asking the same question and, thanks to Lord Grey, Mr. Pope was able immediately to advise the Prime Minister to prorogue by proclamation, and then to dissolve Parliament by a second proclamation. The date of the general elections which followed was fixed for the 21st of September.

It is remarkable that the diary makes no mention of the strenuous campaign which was waged by both parties during the next few weeks. Rather does Mr. Pope's mind seem to have been concerned with the outcome of the political struggle in England, where Mr. Asquith was forcing the Lords to pass the Veto Bill. That the House of Lords should be shorn of its power so filled him with dismay that on the 11th of August he was moved to write: 'The House of Lords yesterday extinguished themselves in passing the Veto Bill . . . the humiliating end of this ancient and venerable institution is a grief to me.'

The entry for the 21st of September is terse: 'The Laurier Government was overthrown and completely destroyed today; no fewer than 7 Cabinet Ministers and the Solicitor-General being defeated. It is a wonderful revulsion of feeling brought on, no doubt, by the loyalty cry.'

22 SEPTEMBER 'To office. Nothing is talked of but the General Elections. I called on Lady Laurier this afternoon. She is feeling the blow but bears up bravely. Lord Grey called at my house this evening to ask me to breakfast with him tomorrow morning.'

23 SEPTEMBER 'Breakfasted with Lord Grey. After which we had a long talk over things. I pressed him not to follow the Aberdeen precedent—not to hurry Sir Wilfrid—but to allow him plenty of time to close up matters *and to fill all vacancies*. This, I pointed out, was, *pace* Lord Aberdeen, in accordance with the best British traditions.'

24 SEPTEMBER 'To High Mass. Met Sir Wilfrid. Shook hands with him and accompanied him to his house. I am pleased to hear that he is going to retain the leadership of his party in opposition.'

27 SEPTEMBER 'Sir Wilfrid Laurier and his colleagues, by accepting responsibility for Lord Aberdeen's action fifteen years ago, when the latter refused Sir Charles Tupper the courtesy, always accorded in England to a retiring Premier, of filling vacancies, have put themselves to the greatest possible inconvenience. I fear the practice of summarily turning out a defeated Government will become the rule in Canada which is greatly to be regretted, as there are few enough amenities in public life as it is.'

4 OCTOBER   'To office. Saw Sir Wilfrid Laurier today in his office for the last time. I understand he resigns tomorrow. Personally I am much attached to him. Like Joe in Bleak House, I say: "He wos wery good to me, he wos".'

6 OCTOBER   'Sir Wilfrid Laurier resigned the Premiership today—and his Government has passed into history.'

On the occasion of Mr. Pope's last interview with the Prime Minister, Sir Wilfrid Laurier kindly promised that he would suggest to Mr. Borden that he would do well to take over the Department of External Affairs from the Secretary of State. In this connection the diary for the 7th of October states in part: 'Met George Perley at the Rideau Club this evening. He said: "I understand your Dept. (or you, I am not quite sure) are coming over to the Privy Council." I said I knew nothing of it, but it probably means that Lord Grey and Sir Wilfrid have been as good as their word. They both told me that they were going to recommend Mr. Borden to take External Affairs to himself.'

The new ministry was sworn in on the morning of the 12th of October. Later the same day, the members of the Government, together with the people of Ottawa, assembled at the Union Station to bid goodbye to Lord Grey and his family who were returning to England on completion of the former's term of office as Governor-General. Mr. Pope records that the Greys were given a truly splendid send-off, there being present hundreds of people all genuinely sorry to see them go. It was at this gathering that Mr. Pope met Mr. Roche, his new Minister, whom, as in the case of Mr. Murphy in 1908, he met for the first time.

The new Governor-General, H.R.H. The Duke of Connaught, and the Duchess of Connaught, landed at Quebec on the 13th of October and made their state entry into Ottawa the following day.

Mr. Pope soon established friendly relations with the Governor-General's staff. On the 16th of October he called on Col. Lowther, the Duke of Connaught's secretary, and by him was presented to His Royal Highness. His advice was soon desired. Two days later Colonel Lowther called on Mr. Pope, and had a long talk with him with regard to the state dinner list, which it was considered was somewhat large. Thus the diary for the 22nd of October: 'Lowther called this afternoon and told me privately that the Duke had approved the revision of the state dinner list exactly as I had suggested. If it were known *I* had such a say in these matters, what a row there would be. All that I can say is that I did not seek it. When asked to help them curtail the list (which had been a necessity owing to 14 new Cabinet ministers who were not Privy Councillors being added), I could not refuse, and did the best I could, ruthlessly sacrificing personal friendships.'

The new régime was now firmly in the saddle, but Mr. Pope did not forget the Leader of the Opposition, who, although he was of the other party, had shown him such marked favour during his long term of office. And so on the 20th of November he called on Sir Wilfrid Laurier. Of this visit the diary relates: 'Sir Wilfrid Laurier's birthday. Called on him this morning to offer my congratulations and we had a long chat. Although well, he seemed dull—said he would much rather be out of the leadership of the Opposition but that he could not leave his shattered followers. He saw no hope for them for 15 years (bar accidents). The Tories had the capitalists behind them, and the extremists of both parties in Ontario and Quebec. He added, paradoxical as it might appear, his presence helped to keep the Government ranks together—that were he to disappear they would be much more likely to fly apart, but the Nationalists and the Orangemen hate him so they will stand together to keep him down.'

On the 20th of December Mr. Pope received a note from Colonel Lowther to the effect that the Governor-General had recommended him for a K.C.M.G. This intimation must have caused him no little gratification, for he was of that number who greatly value honours bestowed by the Sovereign. He was further moved to wonder: 'Who have I to thank for this—Grey, Bryce, Laurier, Borden, or the Governor-General himself?' Some ten days later, at the close of the year, he was handed a letter from Lord Grey which made it apparent to whom he owed his promotion in the Order of St. Michael and St. George.

Howick,
Northumberland,
Dec. 11th, 1911.

My dear Sir Joseph,

I have only one regret, and that is that it will not be my privilege officially to convey to you the announcement of the King's pleasure with regard to the Knighthood he is about to confer upon you.

I am glad, however, to think that I have had some little connection with the bestowal of this well merited honour, having left to my Royal successor the inheritance of a recommendation that your great services to the Crown in connection with the pelagic sealing negotiations should be recognized in a manner that will be, I hope, as pleasing to yourself and Lady Pope as it will be welcome to your many friends and admirers.

When you have time please write me a letter giving me a confidential résumé of the present official position at Ottawa—and remember you owe it to me to secure the installation of the Department of External Affairs in the rooms previously occupied by Sir John Macdonald and during my term most improperly held by the Indian Department.

Looking back over my seven years at Ottawa, the greatest humiliation I had to endure, was the rebuff to my efforts to place you in Mr. Pedley's chair—and for that rebuff my dear Sir Joseph you were responsible. Sir Wilfrid was ready to order the change and with his knowledge and approval I saw Mr. Cory and Mr. Pedley sending for them to Govt. House to explain to them that the interests of the Crown required Mr. Pedley's office for the Department of External Affairs and then after taking all this trouble to prevent any possibility of your being held even indirectly responsible for a change which would put a brother Deputy-Minister to inconvenience, for I explained to Mr. Cory and to Mr. Pedley, that you had protested and that this change had been ordered by the Prime Minister and the Governor-General, you felt yourself obliged to beg Sir Wilfrid to stop the change which had been decided as you feared you might become the defenceless victim of Liberal hostility on the disappearance of Sir Wilfrid and myself from the scene. Could you have foreseen the change in Government last October you would not have robbed me of the pleasure I would have enjoyed during the last part of my term of having your office under the same roof as mine—It is because you are as brave as a lion when the interests of your country are concerned, that I forgave you for the humiliation which I had to endure in silence and which I should

*not now have referred to if it was not possible to wash away all
memory of it in the flood of my delight at the recognition of the Crown
of the value, loyalty and devotion of your splendid services.*

*Long may the influence of your high character and the dignity with
which you invest every act of service to the Crown remain a standard at
Ottawa which I hope it will be the ambition of others to attain.*

With my best wishes,

I am,

Ever sincerely yours,

GREY

The spring of 1912 appears to have passed quietly, there being
little or no mention in the diary of matters of public interest. A
pleasant trip, however, was in store for Sir Joseph. On the 19th of
June he was informed that the Prime Minister desired that he should
accompany him to England towards the end of the mo nth. The party
—Mr. Borden, Mr. Hazen, Mr. Pelletier, Admiral Kingsmill, and
Sir Joseph Pope—sailed from Montreal on the 26th of June and
arrived at Avonmouth on the 4th of July after an uneventful voyage.

The diary makes no mention of the actual purpose of Mr. Borden's
mission to England, and the papers relating to the visit are vague in
nature. It is to be remembered, however, that Mr. Borden had but
recently come into power, and it was natural that, at the first opportunity, he should visit England in order to confer with the Prime
Minister of the United Kingdom on subjects of imperial interest.[1]
This is clearly set forth in Mr. Asquith's speech in Parliament on the
25th of July 1912, on the occasion of the vote in connection with
the expenses of the Committee of Imperial Defence, when he spoke
as follows:

> *This year again we have had the privilege of having with us, not
> indeed the representatives of all Dominions, but a considerable repre-
> sentation from the Canadian Cabinet, including its distinguished
> Prime Minister, Mr. Borden. At my invitation they attended a meeting
> of the Imperial Defence Committee more than a week ago, and again
> my right hon. friend, the Secretary of State for Foreign Affairs, spoke
> to them and to us all on our foreign policy, and the First Lord of the
> Admiralty on our naval situation, and I am glad to say that, at the*

[1] See Sir R. Borden's *Canada in the Commonwealth*, p. 90.

adjourned meeting which we propose to have next week, Mr. Borden
and his colleagues will again attend, and I hope we shall be able to
arrive at conclusions satisfactory to them and to us. I do not think it is
possible to exaggerate, in the necessarily loose and informal develop-
ment of our Constitutional arrangements as an Imperial Power, the
value of a body like this, which, from time to time—these are two
illustrations only—gives statesmen of the Dominions and statesmen
of the Mother Country a meeting ground on which they can interchange
with the fullest confidence their respective views, experiences, and
knowledge in regard to those matters which, we growingly feel, affect
not only the Mother Country but the Dominions as much as ourselves.[2]

Needless to say, Mr. Borden was received with great hospitality,
and those who accompanied him were privileged to assist at many
functions which were given in his honour. Thus the diary:

4 JULY   'Arrived at Avonmouth about noon. The Lord Mayor
of Bristol came aboard and welcomed Mr. Borden who made an
appropriate reply. Then we took the train for London, lunching
on board. The weather was fine. We were met at the station by
Lord Strathcona and many others.'

5 JULY   'Invitations are pouring in. Called on Sir John Anderson,
Just, etc. Wrote my name in the King's book at Buckingham
Palace this afternoon. Spent the evening assisting Mr. Borden with
his correspondence which is overwhelming.'

6 JULY   'Called on Lord Strathcona and discussed invitations
with Griffith.'

7 JULY   'Sir Thomas Skinner very kindly motored me out to
Donald MacMaster's place at Charters, near Windsor, where we
had lunch. Mr. and Mrs. Borden were there for the week-end. The
luncheon party comprised Mr. Bonar Law, Burdett-Coutts, Lord
Balcarres, etc., and our Ministers and their wives.'

8 JULY   'Dined this evening with Bonar Law at the Carlton
Hotel. The most distinguished assemblage that I ever saw. There
were present the Dukes of Devonshire and Marlborough, Marquesses
of Lansdowne, Londonderry, Lord Roberts, Kipling, and a number
of others including Balfour, Austen Chamberlain, Walter Long, etc.
Had a long talk with Austen Chamberlain who agreed with me

[2] *The Times*, 26 July 1912.

about the undesirability of the referendum[3] and told me privately that the Party would drop it.'

9 JULY   'To Spithead this morning by special train with Admiral Kingsmill, the guests of the Government to the Naval Review, which is the finest thing of the kind ever witnessed. The full strength of the British Fleet was present, 223 ships of all sorts and classes. On arriving at Southampton we embarked on a Cape liner, the *Armadale Castle*, on which we lunched and then sailed through the lines of these great ships to Portsmouth. I went on board the *Lion*, the newest and best super-Dreadnought, and witnessed the aeroplanes, submarine attacks, etc. Returned to London about 10 p.m.'

10 JULY   'Dined at the Royal Colonial Institute. Mr. Borden made a good speech on the Navy question which, though it contained nothing really new, delighted the audience.'

12 JULY   'Went up to Lord Lansdowne's this morning to arrange an interview for Mr. Borden. L.L. was charming. Lunched with Mr. Lowther, Speaker of the House of Commons.'

13 JULY   'Lunched with Their Majesties, The King and Queen, at Buckingham Palace. A large and splendid assembly—about 50 in all. I sat between Lord Stamfordham (Sir Arthur Bigge) and Sir Charles Frederick. Before luncheon we were presented to the King and Queen who shook hands with us and were most gracious. Afterwards the King spoke to me for a few minutes about the Duke of Connaught's administration. Nothing could have been kinder.'

18 JULY   'Garden Party at Windsor. Over 7,000 people present.'

19 JULY   'To the Court Ball this evening which was a most stately and impressive affair—the colour of the uniforms, the wonderful display of jewels, the gold plate, and the magnificence of the rooms all contributed to a wonderfully effective display.'

23 JULY   'Lunched with Father Hugh Pope at the Constitutional and had a pleasant conversation with him. Called on several F.O. officials and put my name down in the King's book (after the Ball). Dined with Charlie Russell at Claridges to meet the Lord Chancellor. Met there Mr. H. F. Dickens, K.C., son of the novelist.'

24 JULY   'Dined this evening at the Admiralty, the guest of

---

[3] Here the diary refers to the movement in favour of introducing the referendum or 'The People's Veto' into the constitution of England.

H.M. Govt. Mr. Harcourt presided. There were present The Prime Minister, Lord Lansdowne, etc. Sat between Lord Milner and Col. Seeley.'

25 JULY   'Lunched this afternoon at the Junior Constitutional Club which gave a luncheon to Mr. Hazen who made a good speech.'

31 JULY   'Went to the Leathersellers' dinner in their beautiful hall in St. Helen's Palace. This is one of the oldest City Companies. The whole ceremony was very fine.'

1 AUGUST   'Dined at the National Liberal Club. Big dinner to Mr. Borden who made an excellent speech.'

8 AUGUST   'Left Euston at 1.40 p.m. for Liverpool. Arrived at 5.40 p.m. and at once went aboard the *Adriatic* which sailed at 6.30.'

9 AUGUST   'Arrived at Queenstown about 7.20 a.m. Had long walk and talk with Mr. Walter Long this morning. I hinted that he would do well to be discreet in his utterances in Toronto re Home Rule, making it clear that he was in no way attacking the Catholic Church. He seemed quite alive to the reasonableness of my view.'

12 AUGUST   'Smooth sea. Run 445 miles. Delightful weather. Had another long talk with Walter Long. Speaking of the formation of the Canadian Constitution, we were led to the distribution of powers in the various Dominions. I asked him what share De Villiers had in the framing of the South African Union. He replied that De Villiers had a very great, a predominating share in drawing up the act and that it was remarkable for the strength of the federal power. I told him of my conversations with De Villiers at Quebec in 1908, and how I had impressed upon him the extreme desirability of having a strong central government and of allowing the provinces no power not specially delegated, that the residuum should in all cases remain with the central government.'

Sir Joseph Pope arrived at New York on the 16th of August and proceeded to Ste. Irénée, near Murray Bay, for a short holiday by the shores of the Lower St. Lawrence. Returning to Ottawa early in September, he records in his diary that at his office all was as usual. During the month of October he had several conversations with Sir George Murray, who had come out to Ottawa at the invitation of the Canadian Government to investigate and report on its civil service. At that time Sir Joseph had just completed a monograph on the organization and working of the machinery of government at Ottawa, and he was happy to be able to furnish his visitor with an advance copy. In his acknowledgement Sir George Murray stated that from the moment of his arrival in Canada he had felt the need of a *vade mecum* of this kind, and that Sir Joseph Pope's paper had supplied the deficiency exactly.

Towards the latter part of November there were published in Toronto some reminiscences of Sir Richard Cartwright, who had died in September of the same year. This book aroused much comment. The unquestionable value it possessed for students of Canadian history was to a considerable extent marred by the bitterness of many of its passages, as well as by the number of inaccurate statements it contained. To such an extent was this the case that some of the author's former political associates desired that steps be taken to correct the erroneous impressions that it might have caused. In view of his intimate connection with Sir John Macdonald, against whom the *Reminiscences* had shown some animosity, it would seem that the choice fell upon Sir Joseph. The diary for the 2nd of December makes this clear:

'Sir Wilfrid Laurier sent for me this afternoon and we discussed Cartwright's book at length. Sir Wilfrid furnished me with several instances of Sir R.C.'s carelessness. The book really abounds in errors of fact. He told me many stories of Sir R. and how they once very nearly came to the breaking point over the increases to the provincial subsidies. I told him of Sir R.C.'s remark "that the men who built the G.T.P. through New Brunswick ought to be in gaol", which he said sounded very like him and that no doubt he said it. He further gave me to understand that Sir Richard's public career was far from being wholly unselfish, but I did not press him for particulars. Sir W.L. wants me to publish a criticism of these "Reminiscences" in a kindly spirit but pointing out what a mistake a writer makes when he trusts to his memory which is often very dangerous.'

Sir Joseph's review appeared in the *Montreal Star* of December the 14th. It met with the approval of those who were familiar with the period of Canadian history with which the *Reminiscences* deal, and by none more than that of Mr. Martin Griffin, the Parliamentary Librarian, as the following letter testifies:

> *Ottawa,*
> *December 18th, 1912.*
>
> *My dear Sir Joseph,*
> *I have just finished reading your 'critique' of Cartwright's book. It is admirably done in every particular—accuracy, temper and self-restraint. No one can object to a single sentence. Now, if I had written it, there would probably be gnashing of teeth.*
>
> *If as you have completed it you propose to publish it in pamphlet form, let me know so that I may procure copies for the Library.*
> *Believe me to be,*
> *Very faithfully yours,*
> MARTIN J. GRIFFIN
>
> *Sir Joseph Pope,* K.C.M.G.

1914 – 1918

THE first indication in the diary of the advent of the Great War which was to disturb the world for the next four years and more appears under the date of 12 January 1914:

'This morning I presided over a conference of Deputy Ministers summoned to consider and decide upon concerted action to be taken by the various departments primarily concerned on the outbreak of war, and to compile what is called a *War Book* wherein such action shall be laid down. There were present myself (Chairman), Col. Farquhar, Governor-General's Secretary, McDougald (Customs), Coulter (P.O.), Desbarats (Navy), Campbell (Railways), Stanton (for Marine and Fisheries), Sherwood (Justice). Our meeting was held in the Ante-Chamber of the Privy Council and was quite successful.'

An outline of the work of this conference was given to Parliament on the 19th of August 1914 by the Prime Minister, Sir Robert Borden, who in the debate on the address in reply to the Speech from the Throne spoke, in part, as follows:

It is proper that I should state to the House some matters which have to do with the precautions which the Government was obliged to take on the outbreak of war. I need not say that in the United Kingdom among those most closely in touch with these matters, especially among the military and naval authorities in the United Kingdom, there has been for many years a conviction that some effective organization in the dominions of the Empire should be provided so that an emergency such as that which arose as suddenly would not find them altogether in confusion.

The work[1] went on during the winter months, and, if the House will permit me to do so, I can describe what has been accomplished more conveniently by reading a memorandum which has been prepared by the Chairman, and which is as follows:

'Memorandum relating to a conference of deputy heads of certain departments of the public service, which met in Ottawa in the early part of 1914 to concert measures for the drawing up of a general Defence Scheme or War Book, embodying a record of the action to be taken in time of emergency by every responsible official at the seat of Government.

'In 1913 the Secretary of State for the Colonies communicated to this Government certain memoranda of the Oversea Defence Committee outlining the action to be taken by the naval and military authorities when relations with any foreign power became strained, and on the outbreak of war. The suggestion was conveyed that the governments of the various self-governing dominions might advantageously prepare a similar record in each case to meet such contingencies.

'By direction of the Government these recommendations were considered by the local Inter-departmental Committee (which is composed of the expert officers of the Naval and Militia Departments sitting together). The committee reported that a conference of those deputy-ministers whose departments would primarily be affected by an outbreak of war, should be held to consider how best to give effect to the proposals of the Oversea Committee.

'This suggestion was submitted to the Prime Minister and received the approval of the Government. Thereupon, a meeting of the undermentioned deputy heads, together with the Governor-General's Military Secretary, was held under the chairmanship of Sir Joseph Pope, Under-Secretary of State for External Affairs on the 12th of January 1914:

[1] That is, of the conference of deputy ministers referred to in the diary for the 12th of January.

The Deputy Minister of Militia and Defence,
The Deputy Minister of the Naval Service,
The Deputy Minister of Justice,
The Deputy Minister of Customs,
The Deputy Postmaster General,
The Deputy Minister of Railways and Canals,
The Deputy Minister of Marine and Fisheries,

with Major Gordon Hall, Director of Military Operations (representing the Department of Militia and Defence) and Lieutenant R. M. Stephens, Director of Gunnery (representing the Department of the Naval Service) as Joint Secretaries.

'At this meeting it was decided that the secretaries should acquaint each member of the conference of the various contingencies which might arise in the event of which the co-operation of his department would be required, thus enabling him to decide what steps would be necessary to give effect to the decisions of the conference, and to detail an officer of his department to confer with the secretaries in the actual compilation of the War Book.

'Meetings of sub-committees were subsequently held from time to time, at which the necessary action to be taken by the various departments in the event of certain contingencies arising was carefully considered and determined. Each department then proceeded to develop its own line of action in detail, the whole thing being subsequently co-ordinated and incorporated in one scheme, indicating the course to be followed by the Government as a whole on an emergency arising. The scheme was then submitted to and approved by the Prime Minister.

'The taking of the precautionary measures proved most fortunate as on the receipt of intelligence during the last few weeks of the serious situation in Europe, this Government found itself in a position to take, without the slightest delay, such action as the exigencies of the moment demanded concurrently with His Majesty's Government and with the sister dominions of the Empire.'

I cannot overestimate the great advantage to the country which resulted from having these matters considered, determined and arranged in advance in conjunction with the Imperial Government. The arrangements which were necessary, and to which I shall allude more in detail in a moment, were made without the slightest confusion. All communications from the Imperial Authorities were acted upon promptly and with, as I say, an entire absence of confusion. Every detail had been previously worked out with precision and I am informed by the

Chairman of the conference that especially are the thanks of the people of the country due to Major Gordon Hall and Mr. Stephens, upon whom a very large part of the work in making these arrangements necessarily devolved.

The diary for the days immediately preceding the declaration of war is not without interest:

29 JULY   'Sir Hartmann Just[2] of the Colonial Office arrived in town on his way home from Australia. This afternoon the "Warning" telegram arrived from the c.o. I immediately notified the Premier who is out of town, Mr. Hazen as acting Premier or rather the senior Cabinet Minister in town, the Deputy-Ministers of Militia, Naval Service, Customs, Marine and Fisheries, the Clerk of the Privy Council and the Chief Commissioner of Dominion Police.'

30 JULY   'Things grow more and more serious. Sir Robert Borden arrived post haste from Muskoka today.'

1 AUGUST   'H.R.H. the Governor-General left Banff by special train today. Germany has declared war against Russia.'

2 AUGUST   'At 2.40 a.m. I was awakened by telephone and received from Sladen a cypher telegram from London directing the calling out of the Royal Naval Reserve. I at once called Desbarats and Kingsmill. At 8 a.m. I informed Sir R. Borden and Mr. Hazen. At 10 a.m. a Council was held and the necessary steps taken. Took a hurried dinner at the Chateau Laurier with the Hazens; and then to the Council Chamber where I remained with Gwatkin, Gordon Hall, Farquhar till after 10 o'clock. The necessary steps re censorship were taken.'

3 AUGUST   'Germany has invaded France, while abstaining from actually declaring war which is extraordinary, the more so that her Ambassador is still in Paris. Great excitement here today and all sorts of rumours but England's participation in a great European conflict is looked upon as inevitable. Met Sir Louis Davies at the Rideau Club and had a singular conversation with him. He as Deputy-Governor was very much concerned about assenting to some Orders in Council which lacked statutory authorization. I told

[2] Sir Hartmann Just, K.C.M.G., C.B., Asst. Under-Secretary of State, the Colonial Office. Retired 1916; died 1929.

him that the emergency abundantly justified this exceptional course and that in any case he was not the Administrator but only Deputy-Governor. Later he telephoned me that he had followed my advice —merely stipulating for an early session of Parliament which it has been resolved to hold.'

4 AUGUST   'A day of waiting. At 9.15 p.m. the news came. "War has broken out with Germany." A Cabinet was immediately held and Parliament was called for the 18th of August. We are in for it now and all I hope is that the "German War Lord" will get a d——d good licking.'

While the diary says little for the next few days, it is evident that Sir Joseph worked at high pressure in common with the whole civil service. He was called upon to some extent to deal with the departing consuls of the enemy countries, as well as with those of our allies. He was keenly gratified with the expeditious manner in which Parliament transacted the important business which was placed before it, and he notes with pleasure that 'the opposition supported the Government throughout and played up exceedingly well.'[3] On the 21st of August His Royal Highness the Governor-General sent for him and thanked him warmly for his work in connection with the War Conference, which he was good enough to say had been of the greatest possible advantage in the emergency.

Sir Joseph Pope had never been connected with military activity of any nature. To him the profession of arms was a closed book. He could never perceive the object of any drill movement and at times members of his family had vainly endeavoured to explain to him the difference between a regiment and a battalion. Nevertheless, when in his sixty-first year, he joined the Ottawa Home Guard, and for many months thereafter he regularly attended drill in company with a number of his contemporaries.

The diary for the 30th of September reads as follows: 'Went to drill this evening at the Drill Hall for the first time in my life. I do this for the sake of example. Did not get on so badly.' This last sentence may appear to be at variance with the foregoing statement but it seems only to be a case of the wish being father to the thought,

[3] Parliament sat from the 18th to the 22nd of August.

for just a week later he records: 'I took private lessons in drill from Sergeant Baker this evening.' And a month later: 'To drill this evening during which I floundered things. I find it difficult.'

On the 5th of October 1914 he must have experienced a deep sense of gratification, for on this day he wrote as follows: 'Moved from my quarters on Bank Street to the East Block and I now occupy Sir John's old room—the room in which he was so ill 44 years ago, and in which I began work with him as his Private Secretary on the 27th of September 1882. My first act was to write a letter to Lord Grey acquainting him of the fact.'

Lord Grey replied as follows:

Oct. 26th, 1914.

My dear Pope,

I am indeed glad to hear that you have made the belated installation of your department in Pedley's rooms, and am glad to think that the first letter written from your new table has been addressed to me.

I really think I must cross the Atlantic for the express purpose of seeing you where I have long wished you to be. There is hardly anything I worked harder for in Canada than to effect the change which has at last taken place, to no effective purpose in my time, but everything comes to him who waits, which reminds me that Asquith's 'wait and see' policy has been wonderfully successful. We are all of one party now, and shall so remain until the end of the war. . . .

You talk of this terrible war and how shocking it is, so do not be shocked if I say—as an Australian said to me the other day—that the war is the grandest thing that ever happened. Reports from all parts of the Empire tell me the same thing, that men and women are for-getting their usual little mean selves, and that they feel not a bit of self, but a bit of their country and of the great and sacred cause which is uniting us all more closely. I have no hesitation in saying that the average man and woman in the United Kingdom is keyed to a level ten to fifteen per cent. higher than usual, and I regard it as a great privilege to be alive at such a time. Germany thought that a hundred years of peace had made us rotten through and through, and that our chief idea of liberty was not to serve the state, but to gratify our beastly, miserable, petty interests.

I need hardly tell you that we have all been thrilled at the splendid spirit existing in Canada. I was going down to meet the Canadian army at Southampton last week, but the suspected presence of German

*submarines in Southampton Water made it necessary to send a wireless
to despatch them to Plymouth where no arrangements had been made
for disembarkation—had they landed as previously arranged, all
would have been disembarked in one day. I hope to see the Canadian
Camp at Salisbury Plain on Tuesday next.*

*Next time you write please write me a long letter, and ask Lady
Pope to let me have a line also, letting me know how my friends at
Ottawa are, and any gossip at the moment. I delight in receiving letters
from, and about Canada.*

*Lady Grey has turned my house in the country into a hospital, and
twenty-five wounded Belgians are arriving today. My daughter Sybil
has been working as a nurse at Newcastle where she has won golden
opinions, and has had the happiest time of her life. She has apparently
found her true vocation.*

*Believe me, with devoted regards to Lady Pope and kindest regards
to yourself.*

Very sincerely yours,
GREY

Sir J. Pope, K.C.M.G.,
Office of the Under-Secretary
of State for External Affairs, Canada,
Ottawa.

Early in November, Sir Joseph, at the Prime Minister's request,
paid the first of the not inconsiderable number of visits he made to
Washington during the period of the war in connection with which
it was his habit to call 'Public Business'.

It will be remembered that the appointment of a Canadian
Minister to Washington was not made until 1927, so that during the
entire period of the war, when so many questions with regard to
munitions, supplies, and shipping, as well as those of a general
diplomatic nature, had constantly to be dealt with, Canadian affairs
had perforce to be transacted through the British Embassy. Matters
which concerned the Dominion and another dominion or a third
country were referred to the Foreign Office, and no action was
taken by the British Embassy until the Foreign Office had sent out its
instructions. This procedure not infrequently led to delay.

In matters concerning only Canada and the United States the
general procedure appears to have been as follows: the papers

relating to each subject were kept in separate files; action was taken in conformity with the wishes of the Canadian Government expressed in writing through the Governor-General. When some question arose involving oral explanations, such conversations were conducted by the Embassy with the State Department and, with the permission of the State Department, with the competent Department of the United States Government. When the question at issue was brought to a critical stage, the Canadian Government, on its own suggestion, or by the suggestion of the Embassy or of the United States, sent a competent official from Ottawa to Washington, a journey of under twenty-four hours. This official was presented by the Embassy to the State Department and, when that Department's permission had been obtained, to the competent Department of the United States Government. The Canadian official communicated direct with the United States official, and he embodied the result of his verbal communication in a memorandum which was communicated to the Canadian Government and to the Embassy, where it was kept on file.

To judge from the diary, the Canadian official in a considerable number of instances was Sir Joseph Pope. On this occasion his object was to discuss with Sir Cecil Spring-Rice, the British Ambassador, the question of disseminating war literature to the Americans. The result of his meeting with the Ambassador, at which was present a Mr. Willert of *The Times*, was that they doubted the wisdom of the proposal that the Canadian Government associate itself with the formation and operation of a publicity bureau in New York, though both strongly advocated the conduct of unofficial missionary work or propaganda through private individuals.

Sir Joseph Pope's long experience in the public service and the confidence reposed in him by the members of the governments he had served was such that his advice was frequently sought when unusually difficult problems, constitutional and otherwise, presented themselves for solution. During the autumn of 1914 a certain provincial government found itself confronted by a constitutional question of some delicacy, and in an endeavour to find a solution recourse was had to Sir Joseph. His views thereon were given as follows:

Ottawa, 15th November, 1914.

Agreeably to your request I will try and put down on paper my views on the present crisis.

As I understand the matter, the Premier of the Province was accused last session of improper conduct in office, and the Legislature authorized by statute an enquiry into the charges, by a Commission to be appointed under the Great Seal of the Province. The Commission so appointed duly held an enquiry, and made a report exonerating the Premier on some of the charges, but finding others proved. That the Lieutenant-Governor, personally concurring in the justice of this finding, desires that the Premier should resign forthwith, which Mr. —— declines to do, but advises a dissolution. This the Lieutenant-Governor does not feel he can properly grant. I further understand that both the Lieutenant-Governor and the Premier's colleagues, while desirous to treat Mr. —— with all possible consideration in the difficult position in which he finds himself, consider his conduct too grave for condonation. The problem is to find a way out of the difficulty.

My opinion is that in the circumstances as above set forth the Lieutenant-Governor would not be warranted in granting a dissolution at the present time. The Legislature is not a year old. No question of public policy has arisen to justify an appeal to the people. A dissolution would be regarded as a lending of the prerogative to extricate an individual politician from a difficulty of a personal nature. The Lieutenant-Governor should in my judgement refuse to do this.

The Premier should thereupon resign. If he will not do this, the Lieutenant-Governor can of course dismiss him, but that is an extreme step, and one that should not be taken except in the last resort. For the Lieutenant-Governor is constitutionally bound to extend to his chief adviser consideration in circumstances of stress and difficulty, with a view to giving him every chance. Moreover, there is at best some risk in dismissing a Premier presumably possessing in an unusual degree the confidence of the Legislature elected to support him. I am disposed to consider that should the Premier so desire, he has a right to meet his Legislature, and to receive his sentence from their hands. I think the report of the Commission should be laid before the House, either at the regular time, or if the Lieutenant-Governor feels he cannot allow the present state of affairs to continue so long, then at a special session to be convened immediately for the purpose. A motion would no doubt be offered adopting or approving the report, which if carried, would entail the Premier's retirement. It might, however, be possible for the Government to propose a qualified amendment to the main motion which without absolving him, might fall short of actual condemnation, and as it were soften the blow almost to any extent desired, short of actual rehabilitation which, I understand, the Ministry are not prepared to support.

On the passage of such an amendment, the Premier might very well resign, and if he did not, the Lieutenant-Governor, supported by the Legislature, would be abundantly justified in removing him from office. But to dismiss him in advance of any expression of opinion on the part of the Legislature which put him in power, and whose ascertained will the Lieutenant-Governor is bound to carry out, would be a harsh and somewhat dangerous course, because if by any chance the House (in which I understand Mr. ——— has many friends) were to sympathize with the Minister, or a subsequent appeal to the people result in his favour, the Lieutenant-Governor would find himself in a difficult position.

One other point: I do not consider that in this enquiry the Lieutenant-Governor can separate himself from his advisers. It is true the Lieutenant-Governor is empowered by the Statute to issue the commission, receive the report, etc., but that surely is a figure of speech, meaning 'The Lieutenant-Governor-in-Council'. The Commission was issued under the Great Seal of the Province, and the affixing of the Great Seal to an instrument is an act for which some Minister must take the responsibility. Such an act on the part of the Lieutenant-Governor personally might be legal, but not constitutional. It is a maxim of our system of Government that for every act of the Crown there must be a Responsible Minister possessing the confidence of Parliament. It is quite true that, in matters of Dominion concern the Lieutenant-Governor might be directed by the Governor-General (meaning the Governor-General-in-Council) whose officer he is, to act without the advice or, it might be, without the knowledge of his Advisers. But the matter in hand is one of purely Provincial concern, with which no outside authority has anything to do, and in respect thereof the Lieutenant-Governor, it seems to me, can act only on the advice of his responsible Advisers. In my opinion the Lieutenant-Governor should lay the report of the Commission before his Cabinet and be guided by their advice.

I think their course should be—presuming that they feel they cannot carry the Premier through:

1. To bring all possible pressure on their colleague to induce him to resign quietly.

2. If he will not do this, to recommend that the report of the Commission be laid before the Legislature at its next session.

3. If the Lieutenant-Governor is not disposed to allow the present situation to continue so long, advise an immediate summoning of the Legislature for this specific purpose.

4. If that be not convenient, publish the report in advance of the meeting of the House as we do (within comparatively recent years) with our Departmental reports. I do not like this practice myself, but it is the fashion of the times. You can probably ascertain the feelings of the members of your Legislature unofficially in regard to this, and if they do not object, no one can raise any question. If the report is condemnatory as a whole, its early publication would probably create an adverse public opinion which the Premier could not withstand. All the same, I think that if he would prefer to meet the Legislature, he is entitled to be judged direct by them and to receive his sentence at their hands.

You will of course understand that what I have written above embodies my own personal views and nothing more. I have not discussed the matter with anyone.

In conclusion it seems to me you are all bound to stand by your leader as long as you can, and if possible let the responsibility of dealing with him fall on the House. For any other course you and your colleagues (so long as you continue to be Advisers of the Crown) and not the Lieutenant-Governor, must be prepared to assume the responsibility.

Believe me,
Yours faithfully,
JOSEPH POPE

The following day he reiterated his opinion that the Lieutenant-Governor should be guided by the voice of the Legislature:

Ottawa, 16th November, 1914.

Here is an extract from a celebrated speech made by Lord Dufferin at Halifax, when Governor-General, at the time of the Pacific

Scandal. He was being urged by the Grits to dismiss his Ministers:
    '*My only guiding star in the conduct and maintenance of my
official relations with your public men is the Parliament of Canada,
in fact, I suppose I am the only person in the Dominion whose faith in
the wisdom and in the infallibility of Parliament is never shaken.
Each of you, gentlemen, only believe in Parliament so long as Parliament votes according to your wishes and convictions. I, gentlemen,
believe in Parliament, no matter which way it votes, and to those men
alone whom the absolute will of the Confederated Parliament of the
Dominion may assign to me as my responsible advisers, can I give
my confidence.*' (*From George Stewart's* Canada under the Administration of the Earl of Dufferin, *p.* 195.)
                    Yours very truly,
                    JOSEPH POPE

As the year 1914 was drawing to its close there occurred an
unfortunate incident on the border at Fort Erie which, had it not
been skilfully handled, might have aroused a feeling of resentment
on the part of the American people whom it was of paramount
importance, during the early days of the war, to conciliate in every
possible way. On the 27th of December a provincial constable, in
order to effect the arrest of two Americans who were shooting
duck out of season in Canadian waters, called upon a nearby militia
unit to come to his aid. Three armed militiamen were provided.
The soldiers were requested by the constable to fire several volleys
over the heads of the duck hunters in order to cause them to row
ashore and to submit to arrest. By some unhappy mischance the last
volley took effect with the result that one man was killed and the
other wounded.

As soon as facts had been reported, Sir Robert Borden caused a
conciliatory telegram to be sent to the American Government, and
several weeks later he instructed Sir Joseph Pope to proceed to
Washington to settle the amount which should be paid by way of
compensation to the representatives of the injured parties. Before
he left Ottawa the Canadian Government had been informed by the
British Ambassador that settlement could be effected by a payment
of $20,000 to the relatives of the dead man and of $15,000 to the
man who had been wounded. The payment of these amounts was

authorized by Sir Robert Borden. Commenting on this the diary states: 'The figures seem absurdly large.'

Sir Joseph Pope arrived in Washington on the 26th of January and as a result of several meetings with a Mr. Smith, Member of Congress for Detroit, and Mr. Lansing, the Secretary of State, and Sir Cecil Spring-Rice, he induced the Americans to accept his offer of $10,000 to the mother of the dead man, $5,000 to the wounded man, and $1,000 for the lawyers. Later Mr. Smith visited Sir Joseph with two lawyers, who argued their case for an extra $1,000 and $250 for expenses, which he finally agreed to pay, being moved, as he states in his diary, 'by the fact that this is less than one-half of the amount the Government authorized me to pay in compensation.'

The diary records that both Mr. Lansing and Mr. Smith were extremely pleasant to him during these negotiations, but that Sir Joseph performed his task with ability and discretion is apparent from the following letter from the British Ambassador to the Prime Minister, which Sir Robert Borden kindly sent him, together with a note expressing the Government's appreciation of the successful result of his mission.

PRIME MINISTER'S OFFICE
CANADA

Ottawa, Ont., February 4th, 1915.

Dear Sir Joseph,

I have much pleasure in sending you the enclosed letter from His Excellency, Sir Cecil Spring Rice, His Majesty's Ambassador at Washington. At the same time I desire to convey to you the Government's appreciation of the ability and discretion with which you performed your recent mission to Washington.

Believe me, dear Sir Joseph Pope,
Yours faithfully,

R. L. BORDEN

Sir Joseph Pope,
Under-Secretary of State
for External Affairs,
Ottawa, Ont.

[*Enclosure*]

BRITISH EMBASSY
WASHINGTON

February 2nd, 1915.

Dear Sir Robert,

I congratulate you heartily on the success of Sir Joseph Pope's mission here, as he has settled in what I hope is a thoroughly satisfactory manner the question of compensation to the sufferers from the Fort Erie shooting. I cannot speak too highly of the way in which he has handled the matter, which was one of extreme delicacy, and I think you can be entirely satisfied with the result. He will make a full report which I presume will in case of necessity be presented to Parliament. The sum of money paid is a good deal more than what could have been exacted on behalf of Canadian subjects had they been the sufferers. According to the doctrine of international law contained in the decision of M. Fromageot on the Cadenhead case no Government can require more from another Government on behalf of its own citizens than that Government would have given to its own citizens, under similar circumstances. It was of course impossible to fix with certainty what the Canadian Courts would have given to Canadian subjects. We made a rough estimate and offered to the American sufferers a sum in excess of that estimate. We added the proviso that the whole sum without any drawback or servitude should be paid in its entirety to the persons concerned, and also that the legal expenses of the lawyers who had interested themselves in the matter should be paid separately. The arrangement was come to after a good deal of negotiation by Sir Joseph Pope with the Member of Congress for the District, the Counsellor of the State Department and the lawyers themselves.

Of course the sum paid is excessive and in view of the fact that the United States Government has taken no steps in order to give compensation in the somewhat similar case mentioned above, it might be argued that we have paid too much. On the other hand, the circumstances are peculiar and in the excited state of public opinion on the frontier it is evident that it is in the interests of peace to put an immediate end to the chief grievance by the payment of compensation to the victims. I can only add that there has been practically no diplomatic correspondence on the subject, and there has been no demand, no formal complaint and that the negotiations have been conducted in the most friendly manner in a mutual spirit of give and take.

I attribute the success of these negotiations to your having sent a high official of your Government here to conduct the negotiations in person as well as to the very able manner in which he has carried this affair to a conclusion.

I am, dear Sir Robert,
Yours sincerely,
CECIL SPRING-RICE

During the month of April 1915 there were persistent rumours that Parliament was about to be dissolved, and that the Government intended an appeal to the country. The propriety of holding general elections at a time when the existence of the country was at stake became a subject of general discussion. During one of these days Sir Joseph received a visitor who desired his views on this question, and the interview is thus recorded in the diary: 'I was questioned today with regard to the general elections which, it seems to be taken for granted, are not far off. I replied that, in my opinion, the Prime Minister had a right to a dissolution on at least two grounds:

1. In consequence of the re-adjustment of the constituencies and the increased representation to the West, and
2. The fact that the Government was hampered by the Upper House.

'On either of these grounds, I said, there seemed to me no doubt he could ask for and obtain a dissolution at any time. I added moreover that four years, nearly, had elapsed since the last elections, and that it was not the custom in Canada any more than in England to run the full term.

'In reply to a question I said the Governor-General would have no justification to consult the Colonial Office; that the question was purely a Canadian one, and that the Colonial Office would not think of interfering but would refer the question back to the Governor-General who would then be in an awkward position. I added that the Governor-General could, of course, write anything he liked to the c.o. *after* he had accepted and acted upon the advice tendered him by his Ministers. If he did not like this advice it was open to him to state his objections thereto; to remonstrate, etc., but if they persisted he had no course but to yield. That the war in Europe was no factor in the case, and that questions of propriety, opportuneness, good taste, etc., had no bearing on the constitutionality of the course it was understood the Ministry were about to advise and for which they were wholly responsible.'

While in this interview he restricted himself to a discussion of the constitutional aspects of the question, he freely expressed his personal thoughts in his diary on the 30th of April as follows:

'It is looking more and more like a General Election, which while constitutional is in my judgement not merely inopportune, but a grave tactical error. For the very thought of an election (and what is even worse, the sending of ballots to the soldiers at the front) at a time when our boys are undergoing the stress and anguish of these days is repellent to me. Strong friend of the Govt. as I am, what must it be to the average man, who doesn't care much about politics at any time. The whole thing is *disgusting*. At this time, when the fate of the Empire and our national existence hang in the balance, there should be only one thought—to beat Germany—and all occasions of difference—political, social, religious—should be relegated to after the close of the war.'

On the 17th of April a member of the Government discussed with Sir Joseph Pope the advisability of his (the Minister's) accepting a seat in the Senate. Sir Joseph welcomed this discussion, for it gave him an opportunity to state his views as to one way whereby the Upper House could regain, at least in part, the influence it had wielded in the early days of Confederation.

To his mind it was patent that the Senate had not fulfilled the expectation of its founders. The Fathers of Confederation who had framed the British North America Act had proposed to themselves an independent body which would exercise a moderating and restraining effect upon the legislation of the country. But as time went on, more and more the Commons had absorbed all rule and authority and power, in consequence of which the Senate had lost greatly in prestige. There were some who held the view that the Senate would become more influential if its members were elected rather than being nominated by the Prime Minister. Sir Joseph Pope was not of that number. Rather did he believe that the remedy lay with the executive. In 1912 the ministry numbered eighteen, of whom but one was in the Senate, whereas the remainder were of the House of Commons. Of late years rarely had a Government measure been introduced in the Upper House, and it followed that during the early part of the session the Senate had little, if anything, to do. Sir Joseph was definitely of the opinion that if two or three members of the Cabinet had seats in the Senate, and if a reasonable proportion of Government measures (not money bills) were initiated therein, the Second Chamber would recover much of its old-time importance and take that place in the administration of the country's affairs which it was originally intended it should fill.

On Sunday, the 1st of August, it fell to Sir Joseph on behalf of the Ottawa Home Guard to present Colours to the 38th Battalion, Canadian Expeditionary Force, on its departure on active service. The ceremony, which was very effective, took place on Parliament Hill before an enormous crowd of the people of Ottawa who had assembled to bid Godspeed to their own battalion. In making the presentation Sir Joseph addressed the unit in words that completely express the feelings which ever dominated his mind during the whole course of the war. He spoke as follows:

Lt.-Col. Edwards, officers, non-commissioned officers and men of the 38th Battalion, Canadian Expeditionary Force:

It has fallen to me, as a member of the 2nd Company of the Ottawa Home Guard, to make this presentation.

I need not say that I esteem it an honour and a privilege thus to be associated with such a gallant body of men as I see before me. For you translate into action that which is the desire of each of us who, by reason of one disability or another, are debarred from taking our places by your side.

I am persuaded that you have not embarked on this enterprise from any mere love of excitement and adventure. You realize what so many Canadians apparently fail to grasp—you realize, as Lord Kitchener said a few days ago, that for each one of us, the supreme and solemn hour of life has struck; you realize that this country is at war; you realize that the dear land of England is in grave peril, and you are going to do your part to deliver her.

You know too, full well, that Canada's fate is indissolubly bound up with that of the mother country; that if—which may God avert— any disaster were to befall the United Kingdom, Canada—and that right speedily—would be involved in the common doom.

We commit these Colours to your charge, being well assured that you will uphold their glorious traditions.

We commend you to the favour and protection of Almighty God, and we look forward to another meeting on this hill when you shall have returned in triumph from having done your part in securing a just and lasting peace.

Although the war had considerably increased the pressure of the public business, Sir Joseph yet found time to devote to his literary pursuits. He was Sir John Macdonald's literary executor, and as such he had inherited some seventy thousand of his former chief's letters. Earlier in this volume he stated that he would ever hold Macdonald's memory in grateful and affectionate remembrance. Actuated by these sentiments, it is hardly an exaggeration to say that the paramount self-imposed obligation of his life was to do whatever lay in his power to make the position of Canada's first Prime Minister clear and, in consequence, secure in history. Acting upon his belief 'that life would be tolerable were it not for its amusements', practically his sole diversion from the daily grind in his office was that labour of love he had set himself while yet in early life—the meticulous classification of this appalling mass of correspondence, in order that all possible information relating to the period following Confederation, with which Macdonald had played such a predominating part, would be readily accessible to the historian who was to write its history with some degree of finality.

The *Memoirs of Sir John Macdonald* treated of Confederation days and thence up to the defeat of the Conservative Government in 1873; *Confederation Documents* was written in order to make clear the aims of the Fathers of Confederation. The *Day of Sir John Macdonald*, which was published in 1915, retold in shorter form than did the *Memoirs* the story of Macdonald's life, and, in addition, carried on the broad outline of that life until its close in 1891. The *Correspondence of Sir John Macdonald*, the preparation of which was begun about this time (1915), and published in 1921, was brought out in consequence of the reflection that the time was opportune to make available to the public generally a selection of the Macdonald letters which have such an intimate bearing on the history of the period with which they deal.

The value of his labours to historians of the period is thus generously acknowledged by Dr. Colquhoun, Deputy Minister of the
Ontario Department of Education, in the following correspondence:

> Toronto, .
> 27th April, 1915.

Dear Sir Joseph,

*When you found yourself unable to write 'The Fathers of Con-
federation' for the Chronicles of Canada series, the publisher, Mr.
Glasgow, asked me to undertake it. This, with many misgivings,
I am trying to do. In drafting out the rough outline of the story I find
myself drawing copiously upon your two books, the* Memoirs of Sir
John Macdonald *and the* Confederation Documents. *My effort
is to show how deeply we are indebted to you both for the material and
the manner of its elucidation. Whether I do this adequately or not,
both in the text and the note on bibliography, remains to be seen.
But I scarcely feel comfortable at times, because there are many
citations, and the framework of certain parts of the narrative is only
made substantial by your previous labours. I take this opportunity of
acknowledging the debt all writers of Canadian history owe to
you. . . .*

> *Yours sincerely,*
> A. H. U. COLQUHOUN

Sir Joseph Pope, K.C.M.G.

And a few days later Dr. Colquhoun again wrote:

> Toronto, 2 May, 1915.

Dear Sir Joseph Pope,

*. . . But the insight into the Confederation movement is derived
so largely from your books—a hint here, a phrase there, a fact
somewhere else—that it seemed uncandid to refrain from telling you
how deeply a writer on this period is indebted to you.*

> *Yours sincerely,*
> A. H. U. COLQUHOUN

Sir Joseph Pope, K.C.M.G.

'I have done my duty by old Sir John,' observed Sir Joseph
shortly after he had handed over Macdonald's letters to the Dominion
Archives—after which he added, 'What a pity it is that there was
nobody to do the same for Sir Wilfrid Laurier.'

A year or two later the diary makes a final reference to the Macdonald correspondence.

2 FEBRUARY 1917   'Today I burned all the Macdonald Papers that I had reserved when I was going through the collection. There were very few. It is indeed surprising that such an enormous collection of a public man's correspondence extending over a period of sixty years (1832–91) should contain so little that could not stand the light of day. Further, in the case of those destroyed, the great majority were burned, not because their publication would do Sir John's memory any harm, but solely out of consideration for other people.'

By midwinter of 1916 the bilingual dispute which so inflamed Canadian public opinion for the remainder of the war had become acute, and to Sir Joseph Pope the situation was fraught with danger. It is no exaggeration to say that not only did he consider the question one of considerable moment, he even felt that it might shake the Dominion to its very foundations. It may be said immediately that his sympathies lay on the side of the French. He thought it but natural and praiseworthy that they should desire to teach their children in their mother tongue. It could hurt nobody. They had done so in Ontario for upwards of sixty years.

To his mind it was of paramount importance that there should be no dissension in the country during those dark days. He felt it hideously inopportune on the part of the Ontario Government to begin to enforce the famous Regulation No. 17, which restricted, where it did not prohibit, the teaching of French in the separate schools at a time when it was incumbent on all Canadians to put by internal controversies and to unite in the defence of the country. It distressed him to observe how the harsh treatment of the French to the West of the Ottawa River seriously hampered recruiting in the Province of Quebec. And that such things could be at a time when English and French Canadians were standing together, fighting together, and dying together for the Empire in France, was to his mind inexplicable.

He was well aware that when passions are aroused reasonable counsels are of little avail, yet he did whatever lay in his power to plead the cause of his French compatriots. On the 24th of March he published a letter in the Ottawa *Citizen* exposing the French side of this deplorable controversy. A month prior to this he journeyed privately to Toronto with the object of inducing the Deputy Minister of Education to use his influence with the Provincial Government to suspend action in the enforcement of Regulation No. 17. The diary thus speaks of this visit: 'I am not hopeful, but it is worth trying.' In March he wrote a second letter to the editor of the *Citizen* appealing for better treatment of the French.

The situation rapidly became most serious. The diary for March 20 reads as follows: 'Mr. Casgrain told me on Saturday that he and his colleagues would have to resign on account of the bilingual issue. I called on him at his office today and begged him to go slow which he said he would do. I pointed out that in my opinion there were not sufficient grounds to justify their resignation and I reminded him that when Langevin, Caron and Chapleau were attacked over the Riel issue, they stuck to their guns and came through all right. There is no question that the present situation is exceedingly grave and may even threaten the disruption of Confederation, and what makes the matter more serious is the fact that the country is at war.'

In this grave situation Sir Joseph Pope's old-time political instinct did not lie dormant, as the following entry in the diary makes clear:

10 APRIL 1916   'Suggested to Sir George Foster the idea of heading off the Grits in the bilingual affair which I understand they are going to bring up, by a substantive motion, supplemented by the "Previous Question", somewhat as Sir John did in the Session of 1886 when he split the Opposition over the Riel issue. I suggested a friendly French Canadian being put up to move a straight condemnation of the Gov't. for not having disallowed the Ontario Statute. Then let another friend move the Previous Question and compel the Grits to vote aye or nay on the motion. If they vote yea it will kill them in Ontario, if nay, how can they attack the Gov't. in Quebec for not doing what they refuse to condemn them for not doing. The scheme is a good one, and ought to work out.'

It is a far cry from Ontario to Mesopotamia. Yet among Sir Joseph Pope's letters is one from his old friend General Maude,

who on the 24th of August 1916 took over the command of the
army in that theatre of operations from that distinguished soldier,
Sir Percy Lake. The letter bears the date upon which General
Maude assumed this highly responsible command. It is doubtful if
there exist many such documents in which a general officer command-
ing-in-chief writes in such an intimate and simple manner of past
and projected operations of no little importance. To students of
history it is a tremendous advantage to obtain a definite impression
of the commander's attitude of mind during the time he was
preparing that brilliantly executed series of operations which led to
the capture of Baghdad, and which, in consequence, exerted
considerable influence on the course of the Great War as a whole.

24th August, 1916.

My dear Pope,

*. . . I forget when I last wrote you, and whether I have done so
since the fall of Kut. We had a good try to get through but the problem
was too stiff a one, and I should say well-nigh impossible. Four factors
militated against us. First there was the shortage of river transport on
these long lines of communications, which limited the sending up of
men, supplies and stores. Secondly, there was the limited time in
which we were expected to carry out a lengthy operation. Thirdly,
there was the increased difficulties caused by the vile weather and by
the floods. And fourthly, there was the shortage of men at the front to
replace casualties, for when you have casualties daily men are not
machines, and quite apart from the depleted ranks which require
filling, there is also the necessity of stiffening the spirits of the troops
by fresh blood, and officers particularly are required as leaders.
However, my division did splendidly and during the few days that we
were attempting the relief lost 75% of its officers and 45% of other
ranks. The loss in officers was especially serious as in fighting such as
we have here the leadership of officers is more than half the battle.
Whether the relief could have been carried out by other methods is now
an interesting point for academic discussion, but one which can never
be satisfactorily proved. Personally I appreciated the situation from
time to time and would have suggested less frontal attacks, which would
have meant perhaps slightly more risk but a quicker and possibly a
decisive result. But on the whole looking at it dispassionately I am
inclined to think that the problem was really insoluble.*

Since then we have been more or less quiescent. The heat has been intense and movement by day has been quite out of the question. The sick rate has been high, and you will understand that this has been so when I tell you that during the latter part of June and most of July the thermometer has been 120° to 126° under cover most days. Now things are getting a bit cooler, especially in the early mornings, late evenings, and at night, though it is still pretty hot during the daytime.

At the beginning of July I was ordered, much to my surprise, to take over command of the Tigris Corps from Gorringe. It was a big step for me, meaning as it did the command of four divisions and a cavalry brigade, and an interesting one too, as it comprised Indian as well as British troops. Following on this ten days ago I received orders to take over command of the Army from Sir Percy Lake, and I am now on my way to do this. It will be a most interesting experience, for not only have I command of the whole army in Mesopotamia, but there are numberless political questions connected with Persia, Arabistan and Afghanistan. The conduct of any expedition is a big matter, but this one has exceptional difficulties. The long line of communications, the shortage of river transport, the lack of railways and roads, the intense heat, and later the floods and rains, the total absence of local supplies, and the time which it takes to get our main supplies and war stores here all make it an exceedingly complex problem. Still it is none the less interesting, and if tackled resolutely and with determination it should be possible to drive the matter through to a successful issue. Organisation is what we require most, for nearly everything hangs on supplies and transport. I hope to spend about three weeks at Basrah, get things together, and see how we can make improvements here and there, and speed up matters generally. Then I hope to get to the front to take over command in the field, for I feel that if I keep my headquarters at Basrah, I shall be quite out of touch with all that is going on. Time is short now before the rains come in December, and therefore every day is of value, so we must get a move on, and with one strong pull altogether overthrow the opposition which bars our way.

Hope you, your family and all my old friends are very flourishing. Give them all my love when you see them, and if you have time write me a line as to how it fares with you all in Canada.

Things look brighter almost in every direction now. We have got at last some of the right men at all events controlling military opera-

tions, and it looks as if we might before long bring this lengthy
business to a really satisfactory conclusion.

Yours ever,

F. S. MAUDE

Sir Joseph Pope, K.C.V.O., C.M.G., I.S.O.,
  Under-Secretary of State for External Affairs,
    Ottawa, Canada.

During the summer of 1916 Sir Joseph Pope spent several weeks
near Portland on the Atlantic coast in an endeavour to obtain some
respite from the heat in Ottawa. But his leave suffered several
interruptions. On the 31st of July he was required to journey to
Toronto to greet the Marquis Inouye, the Japanese Ambassador to
Great Britain, who was proceeding to Japan via New York, Toronto,
and Vancouver. Marquis Inouye spent some two days in Toronto,
and appeared to be much pleased with his reception and the entertainments given in his honour on his arrival in Canada.

A little more than a fortnight after his return to Portland from
Toronto Sir Joseph was instructed by the Prime Minister to proceed
post-haste to Washington to protest against the reintroduction of a
bill in Congress designed to prohibit the entry of Canadian-caught
halibut and salmon on the Pacific coast into the United States. It
would seem that such a bill had previously failed to be adopted by
Congress, but that it had been revived by being tacked on to the
Revenue Bill.

Sir Joseph arrived in Washington on Saturday the 26th of August,
and immediately got in touch with the staff at the Embassy, the
Ambassador being away for the weekend. A meeting was arranged
with Mr. Lansing, the Secretary of State, for the following Monday,
at which Sir Joseph, who was accompanied by Mr. W. A. Found
of the Department of Marine and Fisheries, presented the Canadian
case. Further meetings were held during the next two or three days,
at the last of which Mr. Lansing, who had received Sir Joseph with
all kindness, stated that he could not undertake to act for the
withdrawal of the bill to which Canada had taken objection. He said
that the case was simply one of Ketchikan versus Prince Rupert,
and that the western senators were of the opinion that this legislation was called for in the interests of Ketchikan. The Secretary of

State's reply was not altogether unexpected by Sir Joseph, who, while he returned to Ottawa satisfied that he had done his best for Canadian interests, was somewhat disappointed by his apparent lack of success. He had not been back in Ottawa for a week, however, when he was able on September 8 to record his satisfaction at the successful outcome of his mission: 'The good news reached us today that the objectionable measure in the u.s. Revenue Bill has been struck out by the Senate. The Western Senators are very angry and accuse me of lobbying in Washington which is amusing.'

On the 11th of October the Duke of Connaught relinquished his appointment as Governor-General, and returned to England to the unfeigned regret of the entire population, who would have considered it a great honour had His Royal Highness found it possible to prolong his stay in Canada.

To students of Canada's political history, the period of the Great War was one of accelerated development. Indeed, it is possibly not too much to suggest that during those four or five critical years the country progressed as far towards independence as she would have done in a generation of peace. It seems reasonable to suppose that at this time Sir Robert Borden felt that Canada was taking the final steps leading, as he himself was to put it later, 'to the portal of nationhood' and that of necessity the old order must give way to the new. But change need not be unaccompanied by consideration, and there is reason to believe that at times His Royal Highness felt hurt in that even the outward forms of respect towards his high office were not always observed. In referring to this the diary sadly records: 'It is such a mistake and so unnecessary. And the pity of it is that nothing is intentional. It all comes from a neglect of Sir John's view that *forms are things*.'

Later, on the 12th of October 1916, the day following the Governor-General's departure from Ottawa, the diary reads: 'I am told positively, and the fact is well known to certain members of the Cabinet, that the Duke intended and desired to remain as G.-G. until the war was over, and that he asked for his recall only because he could no longer stand the way military matters were being administered. He left a saddened and disappointed man. This is true.'

The Duke of Connaught was succeeded as Governor-General by
the Duke of Devonshire, who, together with the Duchess of
Devonshire and his staff, arrived in Ottawa on the 13th of November.
It is evident that Sir Joseph had for long been considered a permanent official on whom implicit reliance could at all times be
placed, and the diary for the 14th of November, the day following
the new Governor-General's arrival at his seat of government, makes
this abundantly clear:

'The G.-G. sent for me this morning and we discoursed for half
an hour. He seems to be a pleasant, outspoken, sincere sort of man.
He asked me a number of question on various subjects, among others
the French-Canadian School question, upon which I expressed my
oft-repeated views that I considered the Ontario Government had
behaved in a harsh manner, and that the true policy in regard to
language was to give the conquered peoples full liberty in respect
of its use.'

The above entry makes it, perhaps, not inappropriate at this
point to recall the quite remarkable role played by Sir Joseph Pope
as unofficial counsellor, either directly or indirectly, to a long
succession of Governors-General beginning with Lord Minto, and
perhaps even with Lord Aberdeen. The diaries make frequent
mention of his having been summoned to Government House to
advise the Governor-General of the day, or to receive members of
the household staff having a similar object in view. Oftener than
not he found his position to be one of considerable delicacy and
was obliged to say that his views were those of the Prime Minister
'whose deputy he was'.

On other occasions he was able, in all propriety, to speak freely
lest His Excellency dash his foot against a stone, for well-intentioned
persons are sometimes moved to proffer unsound advice. Thus the
diary of the 13th of December 1915 reads:

'I heard from Sladen that somebody (he did not give the name)
has been stuffing the G.-G. with the idea that because the B.N.A.
Act says the G.-G. shall appoint Senators, that therefore he can
make these appts. off his own bat. I told Sladen emphatically that
whenever the G.-G. is mentioned in the B.N.A. Act as doing something it means the G.-G. act'g on the advice of responsible ministers,

and that any other interpretation would produce a revolution here in a fortnight.'

On another occasion it appears that some months previously a Governor-General had declined to approve a minute of Privy Council until he had seen some correspondence relating thereto. These papers had been promised him by the responsible minister but had not yet been produced, and Sir Joseph's visitor doubted if they were in existence. The Governor-General had been pressing the Prime Minister in this connection, but it appeared that even the latter's efforts had been in vain. In these circumstances it was said that the Governor-General was thinking of attending a Cabinet meeting in person, of bringing up the subject, and of arraigning the recalcitrant minister. What did he think of this?

Sir Joseph's reply was to the point. He began by saying that the question was a delicate one to have put to him, but as it had been put, he would reply that he most strongly advised against any such course of action. The Crown had not attended a Cabinet meeting with a view to influencing its policy for two hundred years. The Governor-General would thereby precipitate a crisis in which he would infallibly be worsted. That the proper course would be for him to speak freely and unreservedly to his First Minister who, he had no doubt, would find a way of meeting the Governor-General's wishes; that any other procedure was madness.

Another instance arose during the early summer of 1920, when the political situation was somewhat confused by the fact that Sir Robert Borden was about to retire from public life and that there was much doubt as to his possible successor. The diary for the 2nd of July reads as follows:

'The G.-G. sent for me this morning and we had a long talk over the situation. He understands that a majority of the ministers want White, and entirely agrees with me that an alliance between Sir L. Gouin and White would be the best solution of present difficulties. I endeavoured to let him see that in supporting his ministers who enjoyed the support of the House of Commons he was acting most constitutionally, and I quoted, and afterwards sent to him, Ld. Dufferin's speech at the time of the Pacific Scandal in 1873, to the effect that he had regard only to the voice of Parliament.'

The year 1917 saw no diminution in the number of trips Sir Joseph was required to make to New York and Washington. While the object of these visits was usually some matter of public business of pressing urgency, they were, as a rule, carried out with due regard to the ease and comfort of the traveller. But every rule has its exception. At one o'clock on Saturday, the 10th of February, Sir Robert Borden, who was to leave for England on the following Monday, sent for Sir Joseph, and suggested that he proceed to New York at half-past three that afternoon to meet Sir Cecil Spring-Rice or someone deputed by him in order to ascertain if the Ambassador desired to communicate anything to His Majesty's Government in London which he did not care to put on paper or even to send in cipher. Sir Joseph duly left Ottawa on Saturday afternoon during a violent snowstorm. On his arrival at Montreal he was informed that traffic over the Rutland Railroad was completely disorganized, so he continued his journey by the Delaware and Hudson train which left Montreal at approximately midnight. The storm continued in its fury during the night, and at 5.30 next morning Sir Joseph found himself at St. John's, some twenty-seven miles from Montreal. The train was not equipped with a diner so that he was obliged to go on short rations until he arrived at Saratoga, where he obtained a sandwich and a cup of tea. There were many delays; the storm had gripped the entire Atlantic seaboard; and to cap all, several hot-boxes developed, so that the train only arrived in New York at 6.40 p.m., just twelve hours late. On his arrival Sir Joseph found a note awaiting him from Sir W. Wiseman, an intelligence officer attached to the British Embassy, asking him to call at a certain address. This he did, and having received the message the British Ambassador desired to communicate to Sir Robert Borden, Sir Joseph caught the 7.45 p.m. train for Ottawa, having spent but one hour in New York. The train arrived in Ottawa somewhat late, but nevertheless in sufficient time to enable Sir Joseph to see the Prime Minister as he was leaving for England, and thus, in spite of considerable difficulty, he had the satisfaction of accomplishing that which he had set out to do.

On the 21st of April Sir Joseph again visited Washington. On this occasion he accompanied Sir George Foster, who on behalf of the

Canadian Government went down to meet the Balfour Mission to the United States. There arrived in Washington at the same time a French Mission headed by Marshal Joffre and M. Viviani. Then followed a series of dinners and receptions with regard to which the diary makes the following comment:

23 APRIL   'Called this morning on Mr. Balfour and party to whom have been assigned the MacVeagh House, 2829 16th Street. Dined at the White House. The President was most gracious. Spoke to me for some minutes, explaining in apologetic language why they had not come in sooner, but assuring me that now they were in, they were in for good. He gave me to understand that any earlier entrance would not have met with the support of the whole people who had to be educated up to it.'

29 APRIL   'At 1 p.m. went to Mount Vernon the guests of the Secretary of War, Mr. Daniels. In the course of a most impressive ceremony Messrs. Balfour and Viviani, in the name of England and France respectively, laid wreaths on Washington's tomb. In my heart of hearts, while recognizing the necessities of the occasion, I could not feel enthusiastic for I could not help feeling that whatever Washington's claims to distinction may be, they rest upon the humiliation of England.'

5 MAY   'At noon went to the House of Representatives to hear Mr. Balfour address Congress which he did very well. The ceremony was impressive, though Mr. Balfour gave the impression of speaking with restraint, so much so that a prominent Irish-American Congressman was afterwards heard to observe his gratitude that he (Balfour) "took no advantage of the occasion to embarrass them" which I thought significant. In the afternoon, having some business at the Mission, I met Mr. Balfour at tea. I told him this, whereupon he laughed and said: "Did he expect me to make a violent anti-home-rule speech?" '

8 MAY: 'To the Senate this morning to hear Mr. Balfour's address which was excellent. He let himself out more than in the Lower House.'

And on the 10th of May, the day before he returned to Ottawa: 'The spirit here is all that could be desired, but they are in a woeful state of unpreparedness and lack co-ordination and system. I fear it will take them some time to co-operate effectively as regards *men*. No doubt they can help a lot with food, money, munitions, etc., and their desire to do so is all that could be wished. The Government find themselves dreadfully embarrassed and hampered by Congress which is inordinately jealous of its powers, chary of giving the President *carte blanche* to act.'

Towards the end of May Mr. Balfour addressed the Canadian Houses of Parliament in joint session, a circumstance which gave rise to the following characteristic entry in the diary:

28 MAY 'Heard Mr. Balfour address the Senate and House of Commons in Joint Session today. Sir Robert and Sir Wilfrid spoke afterwards. All three very fine. Mr. Balfour particularly so, though I could not help wondering how a *Cecil* really enjoyed the office of eulogizing democracy.'

By the autumn of 1917 the appointment of a Canadian Minister to Washington had been accepted in principle by His Majesty's Government in England. With regard to this development in Canada's progress to the national status which she has now attained, Sir Joseph Pope's views are not without interest:

22 OCTOBER 'Colonel Henderson wanted my views on the proposal to appoint a Canadian representative at Washington who should be independent of the Embassy, but I said that now the policy of the Government had been declared I had nothing to say. That my views were those of the Prime Minister whose deputy I was.'

23 OCTOBER 'Spoke amongst other things of this new position at Washington, but now that the Government has decided to do it I can say nothing and I said nothing further than that the war justifies almost any departure from established usage. "Who", said I, "would have expected five years ago to see the Lord Chief Justice of England financing in Wall Street?"[1]'

31 OCTOBER 'Sir Cecil Spring-Rice called at my office this morning and we had a long talk on different subjects. His Excellency, while evidently not relishing the appointment of a Canadian Commissioner at Washington who shall be independent of the Embassy,

[1] Lord Reading was President of the Anglo-French Loan Mission to the U.S.A. in 1915.

takes the correct attitude that his duty is not to oppose but rather to facilitate the wishes of the Canadian Government. I was very glad to hear this, for while the proposal is a shock to me, I hope it will, like the Reading and Northcliffe appointments, be only for the war, and I feel quite sure that no member of the present Government has any desire to weaken the tie which binds us to the Mother Country. My chief apprehension is that this office might be a weapon in the future in the hands of men not so loyal to England as I am convinced Sir Robert Borden is. On that, however, we must take chances.'

Sir Joseph Pope, constitutionally, was averse to change, and this characteristic became stronger as he got on in years. But while he did not like to break with tradition, he realized that change is inevitable. Later, in 1918, when recording a conversation he had had with Colonel Henderson regarding a proposal that communication with the Imperial Government should in future be between Prime Ministers instead of between the Governor-General and the Secretary of State for the Colonies, he observes, 'The system of government under which I have grown up is passing away, and we may as well realize the fact.'

Several months later the subject appears still to have been a matter of discussion, for amongst Sir Joseph's papers is to be found a letter from Sir Cecil Spring-Rice in which he describes the method which hitherto had been employed in the conduct of Canada's diplomatic relation with the United States and in which he refers in a most flattering manner to the part played by Sir Joseph in his frequent missions to Washington during the period of the war.

GOVERNMENT HOUSE
OTTAWA

Jan. 31, 1918.

My dear Sir Joseph,

I have given the memo. with the suggested alterations to H.E. *You have a copy of it I presume.*

I have explained to him that the operation of the system described—that is of the peculiar method in which the relations of Canada and the U.S. *are conducted, very much to our advantage—turns upon yourself personally. Without your excellent relations with the* u.s. *Government and officials, and the invariable tact with which you have carried on business with the Embassy . . . I don't see how the system could have worked . . . certainly it could not have worked so well. You won the esteem and confidence of the State Dept. and of all the* u.s. *officials with whom you were in contact, and as you must be aware, you were regarded with real affection and respect by all the members of the British Embassy; it was in this way that you were able to conduct such complicated relations, of a three-sided character, without any friction whatever.*

I hope that in the future you may continue to visit the u.s., *on occasions, as before; and that your department, if necessary, may be strengthened in order to enable you to go to Washington from time to time without hindrance to business. I don't think the present system could be improved, except* perhaps *by the appointment of a more or less permanent* business *representative of Canadian interests, who could serve as a point of call, and also of a means of communication, always at hand, with corresponding* u.s. *interests.*

Diplomatically speaking the present arrangement acts very well and this is mainly due to your personal characteristics.

Yours sincerely,

CECIL SPRING-RICE

To this reply was made as follows:

Ottawa, 1st February, 1918.

Dear Sir Cecil Spring-Rice,

Let me thank Your Excellency for your kind, though too flattering letter. I fear you have over-estimated the extent and value of my services at Washington, but whatever measure of success may have attended them, is due entirely to Your Excellency and the Staff of the Embassy, without whose benevolent and skilful guidance I could not have accomplished anything.

I fancy that my term of usefulness at Washington is drawing to a close, and as far as my personal inclinations are concerned, in view of impending changes there, I am not altogether sorry, as I am getting old to begin and build up friendship anew.

Would you have the kindness to send me a memo of the changes you made in the paper you dictated in my office, in order that I may possess a complete copy thereof?

Thanking you once more for your uniform kindness and consideration

*towards me, and with feelings of deepest gratitude and regard,
coupled with every good wish for Your Excellencies' future, I am,*
Yours sincerely,
JOSEPH POPE

His Excellency, The Rt. Hon.
Sir Cecil Spring-Rice, G.C.M.G., G.C.V.O.,
Government House,
Ottawa.

Slowly the year 1918 wore on to the never-to-be-forgotten day
of the Armistice. In so far as his duties were concerned, Sir Joseph
had long since begun to take war conditions as a matter of course,
but the diary indicates only too clearly that the strain due to private
reasons became more wearing as the months passed by. From the
official point of view the late winter and summer seem to have been
devoid of general interest.

Towards the end of August Sir Robert Borden asked Sir Joseph
Pope to go out to Victoria with Colonel Henderson in the following
October to meet Prince Higashi Fushimi, who was to travel across
Canada on his way to England. During this tour Sir Joseph was to
act as the Government's representative. His Imperial Highness was
duly met at Victoria on the 8th of October, and there followed the
usual journey across the country with stops here and there, where
entertainments and visits to places of interest were arranged in
honour of Canada's distinguished visitor. It is not proposed to
describe this tour, which Sir Joseph, as he took leave of the Prince
at Halifax on the 19th of October, sums up in these words: 'So
concludes what on the whole I regard as my most successful tour.
Not a hitch of any kind from beginning to end.'

On this occasion His Imperial Highness presented Sir Joseph with
the insignia of the Grand Cross of the Order of the Rising Sun of
Japan, a high distinction of which he was very proud.

A few weeks later came the glad tidings that an armistice had been
signed, and that the awful conflict which had endured for over four
years had at last come to an end. The diary indicates very clearly
the powerful emotions which overcame Sir Joseph Pope on this, one
of the great days in the history of the world. It is not the intention
here to break through what Mr. Stanley Baldwin somewhere refers

to as 'our English reserve', but as the object of biography is to portray the man, as well as to describe the events of his time, it may be said that on that dark morning when the whistles and the bells of Ottawa made known to him that the Armistice had been signed, his first act was humbly to thank his Maker for His mercies and goodness to him during the period of the war. And on the following Sunday at the conclusion of High Mass when the choir aloft sang the *Te Deum*, that great hymn of praise and thanksgiving, deep emotions surged within him and from a full heart and with streaming eyes he poured forth his gratitude that those dear to him had been spared and that his country had been sustained.

1919 — 1925

The Prince of Wales's Visit to Canada /
Revision of the Arms of Canada / British
and Canadian / Inability to Progress with the
Times / Breakdown in Health / Otium cum
dignitate */ Appreciation by the Press / The End /*
The Product of his Generation

THE Armistice found Sir Joseph Pope in his sixty-fifth year. It was
not a particularly advanced age. The long strain of the war, however,
had demanded its toll, and it is doubtful if the veteran official was
now able to apply himself to the solution of the manifold problems
which arose with the cessation of hostilities with the same strength
and energy that had characterized him in former times. On the
other hand, his long experience in matters of state enabled him in
various ways to render valuable advice and aid to the Governments
he served to a greater extent perhaps than is disclosed in these
pages. Another instance of this appears in the diary for the 5th of
November 1919:

'The House of Commons passed the Grand Trunk Bill last night
with a comfortable majority. It went to the Senate this morning.
This afternoon Sladen came to see me—no doubt from the G.-G.
He put a hypothetical case. Suppose, said he, the Gov't. were to
submit to His Excy. the names of certain appointees to the vacancies
in the Senate, would the G.-G. have the right to protest, knowing

that these appts. were made with a view to carrying the Grand Trunk Bill? I replied shortly that the Gov't. were not seeking to enlarge the number of Senators, but merely to fill up the authorized number. That they had every right to do this at any time, but particularly so just now when their object was to give effect to the will of the people as expressed by the House of Commons. That this matter was purely a Canadian one involving no Imperial interest, and I thought one to which the Crown could not object. Sladen said that Sir G. Foster had seen the G.-G. this mg. upon other matters and that in the course of conversation alluded to the possibility of the Senatorial appts. saying that he viewed such appts. with repugnance. The G.-G. also expressed himself to the same effect. I told Sladen that the G.-G. could say anything he liked, but he must say yes, and I strongly advised him to put nothing in writing, as he had no case. The Gov't. were clearly within their absolute right.'

As in the past he continued to make the necessary arrangements in connection with the visits of Royalty and of distinguished strangers to Canada. In February 1919 he proceeded to Victoria to meet General Pau and his mission, and as the Government's representative he attended the French General during the latter's journey across Canada. While this tour to some extent taxed his strength, he enjoyed it to the full. General Pau's charm of manner amply repaid him for the work the tour entailed, while the intellectual attainments of Dr. Siegfried and M. Leclerc-Motte, who were of the General's staff, made their society more than a pleasure.

During the months of June and July Sir Joseph, in association with Col. Henderson, found himself quite busy arranging for the Prince of Wales's forthcoming visit to Canada. While the work was familiar, it was none the less arduous. Visits had to be paid to all the cities in eastern Canada which were to be included in the Prince's tour, and the local officials, in many instances, required considerable assistance and advice with regard to the programmes which were drawn up for the entertainment of His Royal Highness.

The Prince of Wales landed at Saint John on the 15th of August. The initial reception was an unqualified success, which augured well for the veritable triumph which was to attend the Royal visitor as he travelled throughout the length and breadth of the Dominion. The itinerary was from Saint John to Halifax, thence to Charlottetown and Quebec, and in each city the Prince of Wales by his charming and gracious manner won the hearts of all. Sir Joseph's memories were stirred by the visit to Charlottetown, for he writes: 'My first recollection was seeing Edward, Prince of Wales, there 59 years ago, and this visit of his grandson, another Prince of Wales, is probably my last.' From Quebec the Royal party proceeded to Toronto and from thence to Ottawa. Sir Joseph was unable to accompany the tour beyond the capital, but if the flesh was weak, the spirit was all that could be desired, and from his office he followed the Prince's triumphant progress from one Canadian city to another. Later, as His Royal Highness was leaving Canadian shores, he proceeded to Halifax to arrange the dinner tendered the Prince by the Canadian Government, and the closing references to the tour in the diary read: 'The success of the Prince of Wales's visit to Canada was wonderful in its completeness, and coming when it did when something of the kind was needed cannot fail to produce beneficial and lasting results. For myself I am willing to sacrifice myself a dozen times to see such results so fraught with advantage to the Monarchy achieved. God save the King and bless the Prince of Wales.'

During the spring of 1919 Sir Joseph was appointed to a committee set up by the Government to consider the revision of the Arms of Canada. It will be remembered that formerly the Canadian Arms consisted of an aggregation of some of the provincial Arms. Several provinces had been created subsequent to the adoption of the original Arms, and these newer provinces were not happy with the existing design. The work of this committee was of a nature which particularly appealed to Sir Joseph. He described its first meeting in the following words:

3 APRIL   'Today I attended the first meeting of a Committee appointed by the Governor-General-in-Council to consider the question of the revision of the Arms of Canada. The members of the Committee are Mulvey, Doughty, Gwatkin and myself. Gwatkin was not present. Doughty and I elected Mulvey, President. I find my colleagues in entire agreement with myself as to the absurdity of the prevalent idea that the Arms of Canada must necessarily

consist of an aggregation of the Arms of the Provinces. We consider that in the question of Arms Canada should be looked upon as an entity distinct from the Provinces of which it is composed; that the Arms of the Dominion should be simple and distinctive containing some recognition of (1) The Monarchical principle, (2) The French Régime, and (3) Something Canadian such as the maple leaf. I am writing Ambrose Lee the York Herald on the subject and on receipt of his letter the Committee will meet again.'

The committee sat from time to time, and laboured diligently, with the result that a year later its design was submitted to and received the approval of the cabinet on the 29th of April 1921. The particulars of the design were cabled to the Secretary of State for the Colonies in order that the grant of the Arms might be expedited. His Majesty's approval was duly received, but it would appear that the Heralds' College expressed some opposition to the design which gave rise to the following characteristic entry in the diary for the 29th of September:

'Had a meeting of the Arms Committee today at which we definitely decided to proceed with the adoption of the new Canadian Arms despite the opposition of the Heralds' College. This attitude— a most unusual one for me—is justified by the fact that the King had approved our draft, and that this approval was officially communicated to us by His Majesty's responsible Minister, the Secretary of State for the Colonies. This is enough for me. The Heralds raise all sorts of objections, some puerile as I think, so supported by H.M.'s sanction we are going ahead. Our Arms are very handsome, loyal, British, Monarchical with due recognition of Canada, in fact everything that can be desired. The motto ''A Mari usque ad Mare'', which is an original suggestion of my own, I regard as very appropriate.'

The use of the word British in the foregoing extract makes it appropriate here to state that, while Sir Joseph Pope naturally referred to himself as a Canadian, he disliked thereby the distinction now frequently implied that he was not also British, and that this appellation applied only to those resident in the United Kingdom.

On the 18th of May 1921 the following note appears in the diary: 'The Governor-General sent for me today and showed me what he proposed to say at the ceremony of the presentation of the chair.[1] I thought it all very appropriate, but ventured to suggest that instead of saying that he had been a member of the British House of Commons, simply to say that he had been a member of the House of Commons, as the emphasis put on "British" might imply that *we in Canada* are not British. I am constantly objecting to this sort of thing. As I said years ago, how much do we want an adjective which shall bear the same relation to the United Kingdom as *British* does to the whole Empire.'

Towards the end of June the Duke of Devonshire, whose term of office as Governor-General was drawing to its close, left Ottawa for Quebec, whence he sailed for home on the 18th of July. 'They have done very well, and I am sorry to see them go,' writes Sir Joseph the day he bade their Excellencies farewell. A few weeks later the Duke of Devonshire addressed to him this very kind letter:

July 24, 1921
Empress of France

My dear Sir Joseph,

I hope you and Lady Pope will accept my most grateful thanks for the very kind telegram which you sent me on the departure. We were both very sorry to say good-bye to Canada, but we shall always have the happiest memories of our stay here.

I hope you will soon be coming over to England and that we shall have the pleasure of seeing Lady Pope and yourself there.

I should like to take the opportunity of again thanking you for all the kindness you have shown to me during my term of office and the great help which you have been to me. I often think of our conversations in my room and the number of interesting things you told me.

I know how busy you are but if you could every now and again drop me a line to tell me how things are going on. Mind you write a book and call it 'Governors-General I remember'. No one but you could do it and it would be most useful, entertaining and interesting.

With best wishes,
Yours v. sincerely,
DEVONSHIRE

[1] The Speaker's Chair, presented to the Canadian House of Commons by Rt. Hon. James Lowther (afterwards Lord Ullswater) on behalf of the United Kingdom Branch of the Empire Parliamentary Association.

Shortly after Lord Byng's arrival as the new Governor-General, Sir Joseph had occasion to reflect on the length of his service to the State:

7 SEPTEMBER   'Walked out to Government House this afternoon and entered our names in the Visitor's Book. I could not help reflecting, as I walked up the Avenue, how many régimes I had lived through. When I entered the Government service of Prince Edward Island, Lord Lisgar was Governor-General of Canada, and as a Dominion officer I have served Lorne, Lansdowne, Stanley of Preston, Aberdeen, Minto, Grey, Connaught, Devonshire and now Byng—9 in all.'

Lord Byng appears to have continued in the habit of his predecessors, for a fortnight later the diary reads: 'The Gov.-General sent for me today and we had a long talk over things in general.

'This is my first interview with Lord Byng. His Ex. is very desirous to do the right thing, and asked me to speak to him at all times upon any subject that I considered it would be desirable to offer advice or opinion. He said he knew that I had been here from the beginning, and that he wished to profit by my experience. All of which was very gratifying to me, but I remember the Bishop in Gil Blas.'

As these pages have clearly shown, Sir Joseph Pope was nothing less than a thrice-dipped Tory and one to whom the very idea of political independence or, indeed, any change in our relations with the United Kingdom, were quite repugnant, yet he found some aspects of the Chanak crisis of September 1922 more than he could accept. Thus the diary for the period:

16 SEPTEMBER   'Tonight the astounding announcement is made that H.M. Gov't. has called upon the Dominions to send troops to fight the Turks in Asia Minor. A regular bolt from the blue, and one calculated horribly to embarrass the Dominion Gov't.'

18 SEPTEMBER   ' No fresh war news. The fact that Lloyd George should have sent out such an amazing call for assistance to the Dominions is more of a mystery than ever. No doubt that there has been a leak, but why he should have ever considered it necessary to send such a message remains inexplicable and indicates very little consideration for the various Dominion Gov'ts. No doubt it was

intended as a big bluff for Turkey, but why could not the same result have been attained in more general and contingent terms?'

His conception of the role of the Governor-General, however, appears to have undergone little change.

3 OCTOBER   'The Near East crisis seems to be quietening down. An extraordinary feature of this event is that during the past fortnight, when the destinies of peace or war were terribly in the balance, our Governor-General was absent from his Capital, attending bazaars and tea parties in the Northwest. His attitude is all the harder to understand when it is considered that he is a military man, and that as such his advice and counsel would have been of great value to his Ministry at the present juncture. One would have thought, too, that at a time when the influence of the Crown is on the wane, the King's representative in this country would have thought it in the interests of his high office to be "on the job". His prolonged absence from Ottawa of more than three months cannot but further diminish the prestige of the office, already fallen almost to zero.

'All this while affording further ground for declaiming against what the Rads. style the uselessness of the office of G.-G. cannot but make the judicious grieve.'

The extent of Sir Joseph Pope's career is perhaps most strikingly disclosed when it is remembered that, when he commenced work as junior to the Assistant Treasurer at Charlottetown in 1870, his native land was yet a separate colony, that not a full year had elapsed since Rupert's Land and the North-West Territories had been formally united to Canada, and that within a few months of his retirement, the Dominion of Canada together with the other self-governing Dominions had been proclaimed to the world by the Imperial Conference of 1926 as equal in status and in no way subordinate to the United Kingdom.

In view of his long service, it was inevitable that Sir Joseph became somewhat set in his ideas, and that he preferred the conventions under which he had been trained as a young man to those of more modern times. A case in point is found in the diary under date of 7 July 1920, at the time that Sir Robert Borden was about to resign the Premiership:

'Great excitement today when it was announced that Sir Thomas White had arrived in town this morning and had seen the Governor-General and Sir Robert Borden. The upshot being that he absolutely declines to accept the Premiership on the grounds of ill-health. In this I think he is quite sincere. It now appears certain that Meighen will be summoned. In fact I was consulted as to the form of an announcement which should be given to the Press tonight. I myself did not see the necessity for such an announcement, at any rate until the resignation had actually taken place, and the new man sent for, but the Government House people thought otherwise and published an absurd statement to the effect that Sir Robert's resignation would take effect on Saturday next, and that *the G.-G. would accept it on that day with regret*. This official announcement that the G.-G. on an occasion still in the future would experience certain emotions struck me as very comical. However, everything is wrong nowadays, so I suppose it is right that this should be in keeping with the rest.'

And nearly a year later:

5 MAY 1921   'Parliament passed a law last year doing away with various church holidays, among them Ascension Day. Then it was promised in the House that no Catholic Civil Servant would thereby be debarred from attending to his religious duties. This, naturally, gave rise to other enquiries in the course of which the Government has haggled ridiculously ending up yesterday with instructions that everyone was to have the holiday, so we are where we started. What a wise man was Ld. Melbourne when he said, "Why can't you leave things alone?" '

While with regard to the wider sphere of world affairs, he could not bring himself to believe that the Covenant of the League of Nations gave the Powers an assurance of permanent peace. When this subject was discussed in his presence it was his habit to quote, with evident approval, Lord Morley's opinion: 'I have not read it [the Covenant] and I don't intend to read it. It's not worth the paper it is written on. To the end of time it will always be a case of "thy head or my head"; I have no faith in such schemes.'[2]

In May 1923 Sir Joseph was called to give his views with regard

2 J. H. Morgan, *John, Viscount Morley* (London, 1924), p. 91.

to the administration of the Civil Service before a special committee
of the House of Commons appointed to enquire into the operation
of the Civil Service Act of 1918. On this occasion he expressed
himself without reserve, as may be judged by the following statement, which formed the major part of his evidence:

Ottawa, 7th July, 1922.

Dear Mr. Cory,

*In reply to your letter of the 3rd instant, asking for my experience
of the workings of the Civil Service Commission, I desire to say that I
regard the whole system upon which the Commission rests as funda-
mentally wrong, and I believe that until the responsibility of the
Government for administration, and its control over the Service is
resumed, it is hopeless to look for any satisfactory result from the
operation of the present system.*

*Apart from this paramount consideration, the principle upon which
the Commission works is faulty in several leading respects, among
which I may mention the system under which a clerk's salary is determined exclusively by the position he holds—that is, of ignoring the
personal qualities of the clerk, of failing to recognize that one, let us
say, shorthand writer and typist may be many times better than
another, and should be rewarded according to the value of his services
—not necessarily in direct ratio thereto, but that his natural abilities,
usefulness, aptitudes, quality of suggestiveness, age, experience and
other personal factors should be taken into account in determining
his remuneration. Until that is done, you will never have a satisfactory
Service. The present inflexible, rigid, mechanical, iron-bound system
destroys initiative, kills individual effort, is subversive of discipline,
and tends to the creation of a Service the members of which rely more
upon combination, intrigue and cabal among themselves to advance
their interests, than upon honest hard work. Until a radical change is
effected in this and other respects, there is no use talking about a
satisfactory Service. I object, moreover, to the present complicated
classification in force, which besides being a positive hindrance to
effective administration, requires a special education to understand.*

*One reads nowadays the most appalling trash in the newspapers
about the 'evils of patronage', as though patronage was necessarily
an evil to be shunned. I wonder if these sapient journalists ever reflect
for a moment who is best fitted to exercise the patronage of the Government—the Ministers, for the most part men trained in public affairs,*

responsible to the Crown and to Parliament for their every action, or an inexperienced unrepresentative and irresponsible body such as the Civil Service Commission.

The present unconstitutional, cumbrous and hugely expensive system should be done away with as soon as circumstances permit. The power to classify and promote and also to regulate salaries should be resumed by the Government. To the Commission might be left the application of entrance tests, and also of ascertaining the qualifications of those whom the Government proposes to promote, though as a matter of fact, I believe the Deputy Heads are much better judges of such fitness than any Civil Service Commission.

The Civil Service Act of 1908 was far from perfect, but in view of what we have suffered since those days, I would be glad to see the Government go back to that Statute as furnishing the best practical solution of the present intolerable situation.

In conclusion I would say that my observations are not in any sense directed against the individual members of the Commission, but relate only to the system under which they operate. Personally, I have found Messrs. Roche, Larochelle and Jamieson, together with their Secretary, Mr. Foran, courteous and as obliging as it is possible for them to be consistently with exercising the powers with which they are invested by Parliament and are called upon to administer.

In all this I am of course only giving expression to my personal views.

Yours sincerely,

JOSEPH POPE [3]

W. W. Cory, Esquire, C.M.G.,
    The Deputy Minister of the Interior,
        Ottawa.

Sir Joseph's interest in astronomy did not wane with advancing years. He continued as an active member of the Royal Astronomical Society and occasionally he prepared and delivered lectures before this body in Ottawa. In December 1920 he was informed that he had been elected President of that body, which drew from him the remark that 'This choice can only be justified by Dr. Johnson's maxim, "To drive fat oxen one need not be fat".'

As late as January 1925, when in his seventy-first year, accompanied by his secretary, he journeyed to Young's Corners near

---

[3] Journals, House of Commons, 1923, Appendix 5.

Hamilton to witness the total eclipse of the sun that occurred on the 24th of that month. But, as in Labrador in 1905, the weather proved unkindly, and from a scientific viewpoint the eclipse was a failure. Sir Joseph's disappointment was intense, and for almost the first time a touch of bitterness is discernible in the diary. 'From about 6 a.m. it was more or less cloudy until after the critical hour had passed. It was a great disappointment for us all. I was much impressed by the darkness which I thought was more pronounced than in Labrador at the total eclipse of the 30th August 1905. I met Chant there on that date and also at the Young's Corners today and on both occasions he bore himself like a hero. One has to be a philosopher to stand much of this sort of thing. I have always been an astronomical votary and feel that I don't deserve this sort of treatment from the powers that be, but probably I do not know what is best for me and must be content to bow in submission to the great Ruler and Disposer of all.'

Towards the end of October 1921 Sir Joseph experienced a breakdown in health from which he never fully recovered. He relates this occurrence in his own words, under date of 29 October: 'Remained in bed today. Saw Dr. Lyman who says I must take a prolonged rest of several weeks in bed. Am suffering from an overstrained heart. I feel that this time the doctor is right, and that I have been overdoing it when I consider that I have had 43 years of continuous public service, and that in all that time have never had a leave of absence on account of illness, and only one leave of absence from any cause whatever, I feel the time for a let-up has arrived.'

While a complete rest for some six weeks enabled him more or less to regain strength, he gradually failed from this time. It was nature's warning signal that the machine had begun to run down.

The remaining years of his service do not require much comment. He continued the administration of his department, ably assisted by Mr. Walker, the Assistant Under-Secretary of State for External Affairs, and Mr. F. Baker, his faithful secretary, on whose services he relied more and more as time went on.

Early in 1924 he discussed his eventual retirement with the Prime Minister. On this occasion Sir Joseph stated that he realized that his service must some time come to an end, and that his desire was that the fiscal year 1924–5 should be his last year of active service, to be followed by a year's leave of absence, which would give him three years' service in his present salary, and so enable him to qualify for full superannuation. The diary records that during this interview, as indeed at all times, Mr. King showed him great kindness and consideration. Sir Joseph states that Mr. King 'could not have been nicer. He said that he hoped that I would remain long yet, and that when the time did come he would be glad to assist me in any way that he could.'

Gratitude has somewhere been defined as being a lively sense of future favours but in this instance Sir Joseph Pope's recognition of Mr. King's delicate consideration remained with him to the end. His interest in current political affairs underwent no abatement and he continued to make an occasional entry in his diary. Thus, on the 2nd of September 1925, he wrote: 'Things seem to indicate the probability of a General Election in the near future. I do not propose to take any part in this contest but to continue the neutrality I have always observed in politics. Mr. King has been very kind to me and I am not ungrateful to him. And anyway, he is just as much a Conservative as Meighen or Borden. Tories of that type are not to my taste.'

And again three days later: 'The Prime Minister at a meeting at [a word is missing in the diary] announced the dissolution of the House of Commons and the holding of a General Election fixing the polling for the 29th October next. I renew my resolution not to take any steps to the prejudice of Mr. King and his Gov't. who have been so kind to me. People talk of a wave setting in against the Gov't. It *may* be, though I don't see where the Opposition are to get their majority. As far as I am concerned one thing is certain that Borden and Meighen are no more Conservative than King. Tories seem to have perished from the face of the earth, and we hear nothing nowadays in regard to the Colonial relation, nothing but equality of status and suchlike nonsense.'

Sir Joseph duly retired from active service, as he had planned, on the 1st of April 1925. Of his last days in office he writes as follows:

30 MARCH   'This afternoon I was presented by the Prime

Minister in the name of the whole staff of the Department of External Affairs with a farewell address, accompanied by a handsome travelling-bag on the occasion of my retirement from office as Under-Secretary of State for External Affairs. There was a large assemblage. Mr. Walker read the address. I made a suitable reply and everything passed off well. It was quite an effort for me, but I bore it very well, and all passed off as it should. The Prime Minister has been most kind throughout, and I am very grateful to him for everything.'

31 MARCH 'Went to my old office for the last time. Met Dr. Skelton. Introduced him to Mr. Walker and Baker, and put him in possession of the Department.'

Thus closed Sir Joseph Pope's official life, after more than forty-six years in the service of his country.

The wrench caused by his retirement was solaced to some extent by many kindly references made in the press of the country at large, one of which is appended. This notice, which appeared in the *Montreal Gazette* of the 2nd of April 1925, he ascribed to the pen of his old friend, Mr. R. S. White.

SIR JOSEPH POPE

In the retirement of Sir Joseph Pope the Civil Service of Canada loses its most distinguished member. It is nearly half a century since he entered the service, and no contemporary, as few predecessors, has had so varied an experience nor gained greater reputation. Many of his years were passed as private secretary to Sir John Macdonald, in which capacity he had unusual intimacy with that great man whose biographer he became. Sir Joseph Pope's activities were subsequently of a more public nature. To him was given position after position of high importance relating to the foreign affairs of Canada, and in all of these his duties were discharged with exceptional ability and signal success. His industry has been remarkable. Whatever his hand found to do he did with all his might, and always with a single eye to the welfare of his country, for above all Sir Joseph is an ardent Canadian. His mental equipoise is unusual, his outlook never that of a partisan but always unbiased. He would hear the other side. The esteem by which he is held in the Service had expression on Monday in the presentation made him by the Premier on behalf of Sir Joseph's colleagues, and the regard in which he is held is the result of merit. In some ways reticent and retiring, he is a delightful companion, frank, warm-hearted, friendly and considerate to those who have had the privilege of intercourse with him. The public service of Canada is poorer for the retirement of Sir Joseph Pope, and the earnest good wishes for health and happiness from a host of friends will go with him in his well-earned retirement. He withdraws from the heat and burden of laborious office with honours thick upon him.

And so, comforted by the good wishes of his friends, he passed into private life. But it was not to be for long. He was worn out. He had never learned to play, and he had no hobby. Throughout his whole life his sole interest had been the public service of his country, and when that had passed there was nothing to sustain him. Slowly his strength ebbed from him and gradually he descended the slope until on that early morning of the 2nd of December 1926 when he came to the end of his days.

Just as it is held that the fall of the First Empire marks the close of the eighteenth century, so may it be said that the succeeding chapter of the world's history ends with the Great War of 1914–18. On this computation Sir Joseph Pope was of the nineteenth century.

He had been born and brought up in Prince Edward Island when that delectable province was but a small Crown Colony. In early manhood his mind had been moulded by his intimate association with Sir John Macdonald, that chief artisan of Confederation, whose main preoccupation had been the consolidation of that momentous legislative act. Man's capacity for continual development has its limits, and Sir Joseph Pope was the product of his generation. That nothing that lives remains unchanged, that constant change is a rule of nature, he readily admitted, but the important developments of Canada's place in the Empire which marked the Great War and the years which succeeded it he found impossible to accept. That the country's important sacrifices in its own defence, as well as in that of the Empire, had made it inevitable that she should increase her influence in the British Commonwealth of Nations he would not admit. His compass had been set in earlier times; in his old age he was unable to adjust its orientation. The maintenance of the ties which bind us to the Crown and to the Mother Country was the course he had set himself, and he felt, erroneously perhaps, that the independence of the Dominion might weaken the connection which was so dear to his heart.

But his views were not based entirely upon sentiment. To his mind Europe still was and would continue to be, for yet some generations to come, the centre of western civilization of which we form a part. He felt that Canada was still a young country, comparatively lacking in tradition, and that its entire population was completely occupied in its material development. In this he saw a danger. He feared that, immersed as we were in the study of the important economic problems that confront us, we incurred the danger of developing a too materialistic point of view. Such a possibility he deplored. He felt that more and more as our material interests prospered, so it became increasingly important for us to continue to draw upon the cultural resources of Western civilization as expressed by English tradition, just as his French compatriots had never ceased from the time this country passed under the British flag to be inspired by the culture of old France. In every sense of the word a Canadian, he could not see why the development of a Canadian spirit in any way should be antagonistic to that broader and more comprehensive spirit of Empire which he felt should be characteristic of all its members of Anglo-Saxon origin.

During the summer of 1925 one of his sons who was undergoing a course of instruction in England sent him a paper he had written on the development of intra-Imperial relations. The thesis set was, as the Empire is a brotherhood of free nations, what type of organization is required efficiently to control the Imperial forces in the event of another World War. The paper expressed the view that as, so far as Canada was concerned, the development of the British Empire from the earliest times had been based on the principle of decentralization, no organization or machinery of control was either desirable or possible, and that the full Imperial effort would result only by reason of that intangible yet immensely powerful tie that springs from our allegiance to the one Crown.

In what was probably the last letter he ever penned Sir Joseph replied as follows:

Ottawa, 16th September 1925

My dear Son,

I have carefully read your paper on Imperial Defence, and congratulate you thereon. I think you have made a good attempt towards finding a solution of the problems which beset the students of the subject. My great difficulty in recent years has been how to view the Imperial relation in its modern aspect. How are we readily to conceive of Colonies which shall at once form part of an Empire and yet each part at the same time insist on being considered of equal status with the rest? I can understand the Empires of that past where predominant powers were vested in a central authority which exercised dominion over the whole group. But how are we going to get on when every member claims an equal status with the rest; where each Dominion shall have an army and navy, and not only an army and navy, but also a diplomacy of its own? To my way of thinking such an Empire is an impossibility. I must leave the solution of the problem to younger and more vigorous minds than mine. I do not want any change in the present relations between the Dominion and the Mother Country, and hope I may never see one. The present suits me very well. As Ruth said, 'Where thou diest, will I die, and there will I be buried: the Lord do so to me, and more also, if aught but death part thee and me.' These are my sentiments towards the Mother-land.

We have all the liberty that is good for us, and some people think a good deal more.

Your affectionate father,

JOSEPH POPE

And with these words fitly closes the record of the life of Sir Joseph Pope.

Appendix

THE following extracts from the diary record Sir Joseph's private account of his conversation with Lord Alverstone on the 13th of September 1903, and his subsequent comments on the conduct of the Lord Chief Justice. They are provided here as a supplement to the restrained account given on page 151.

'I wrote down this account of my conversation with Lord Alverstone on my return to London on the afternoon of the 14th Sept. It will be found that although substantially the same as my more extended memo of the 10th Oct.[1] among my Alaska papers, this version represents Lord A. as being less definite in his statements than the record of the 10th October shows him to have been. The reason for this is that on the 14th Sept. I believed I was noting down an absolutely secret and confidential conversation, and I did not consider myself justified in putting in writing, no matter how secretly, confidences which I felt should not have been imparted to anyone in advance of the case. On the 10th Oct. however I knew he had not

[1] Not found among Sir Joseph Pope's papers.

only violated my confidence but perverted it, and therefore in self defence I felt it necessary to record his indiscretions without any veil.'

JOSEPH POPE

1 2 SEPTEMBER 1903 'I went down to Ld. Alverstone's country place to spend Sunday.'

13 SEPTEMBER '. . . I had a long private talk with Ld. A. about Alaska matters. His Lordship spoke very confidentially. He told me he thought we had a convincing case on the Portland Channel and also for a mountain boundary. Adding that he feared our case for the heads of inlets was correspondingly weak. All this agreed quite with my own opinion. He added that of course this last opinion might be modified on hearing the arguments of our Counsel. He asked me if he (*sic*) thought Canada would be satisfied if we could get Wales and Pearse Islands and a mountain line. I said that I feared not. He asked which would they prefer—that or an absolute draw—3 and 3 all round. I said I thought the latter. Personally I would greatly prefer the former, which I thought was all we could expect, but I added people were as unreasonable in Canada as elsewhere and that the inlets were the question. He told me I could let Sir W. L. know that he was most indignant at recent press reports, that he was influenced by nothing but a desire to render a just decision and that nobody had remotely suggested conciliating the u.s. at the expense of Canada. Altogether, he intimated he was going for Portland Channel and a mountain line and against our claim to the heads of inlets, but this was absolutely confidential between us. I was greatly relieved at this for I feared from the opening day that he was going to be dead against us all through.'

8 OCTOBER 'Dickinson concluded his argument today and the Tribunal adjourned. The impression prevails that Ld. Alverstone has entirely gone back on us. Something occurred today which disturbed me a good deal. Mr. Sifton told me that Alverstone had announced his resolve to give judgement against us, and had urged as a reason that I had told him Canada wd. be content to give up heads of inlets and take instead Portland Channel and a mountain line. Also that I told him Sir W. Laurier did not expect a favourable decision. He thus not

merely violated our confidential conversation in his house on the
13th Sept. but he also distorted & misrepresented it. I explained the
circumstances to Mr. Sifton who said I was not to blame, but
severely reflected on the L.C.J. who he thought had behaved badly as
indeed he has.'

13 OCTOBER   'To the Tribunal. Lunched with them. Rec'd letter
from Sir W. Laurier this afternoon expressing himself re the Alaska
decision exactly in harmony with my own ideas. He wrote that he
wd. be satisfied to get Wales and Pearse islands, but if they went
against us in that he wd. feel we were badly sold. He evidently does
not expect a favourable decision on inlets.'

17 OCTOBER   'Mr. Sifton had an interview with the L.C.J. this
mg.—after which Ld. Alverstone said in my ear—"Mr. Sifton tells
me you misunderstood him in telling me that Canada wd. accept a
reasonable compromise if she couldn't get anything better. I told
him you originally told me yr. Govt. wd. not accept anything short
of the heads of inlets, and that they wd. prefer a deadlock, but that
after seeing him you had modified yr. tune. I want to tell you that he
has just told me exactly what you led me to infer were his views.
Exactly the same." '

19 OCTOBER   'Mr. Sifton told me this evening that Lord A. had
told him that I had said nothing to him more than (he) Sifton had
said. "He said differently to Aylesworth & Jetté however," added Mr.
Sifton. We did not go to the Goldsmith's Dinner tonight which was
awkward but I quite sympathized with Mr. Sifton's feelings and if he
wouldn't go none of us would.

'Dined and spent evg. quietly at hotel. Got a note from Lord
Lansdowne asking me to call and see him tomorrow.'

20 OCTOBER   'Called at Lansdowne House this mg., and had a chat
with Ld. L., a memo of which will be found in my Alaska papers.
Thence to the Tribunal where, after keeping us waiting two hours,
the award was finally signed at 2.15 p.m. and delivered to the two
Agents in the presence of the Secretaries of the Tribunal. The ceremony was not open to the public and consisted merely of the President handing a signed copy of the award to each Agent.'

24 OCTOBER (*at sea*)   'This evg. in the smoke room Senator
Turner said to me: "Don't you think that Aylesworth and Jetté

made a mistake in publishing their protest?'' I answered: ''I don't know about that.'' ''It seemed to me like an arraignment of Lord Alverstone.'' I made no reply to this, and turned the subject.'

30 OCTOBER 'Landed from *Cedric* at 8.30 this mg. . . . Interviewed by newspaper men, but wouldn't talk.'

31 OCTOBER 'Arrived at 11.40. . . . Great excitement over the Alaska decision. My idea is that all this talk is very undignified. Having consented to the reference, Canada must abide by the result, and play the game. At the same time I think Alverstone has behaved badly. No one blames him for finding against us on the heads of inlets. Personally I don't see how he could have done anything else, but he told me himself that our case for the Portland Channel and a mountain line was unanswerable—overwhelming in its strength. Why at the last minute he should have robbed us of much of the advantage of Portland Channel by giving Sitklan and Kannaghunut Islands to the u.s. I do not know, unless it was a compromise. The u.s. never claimed those islands. Nobody ever suggested their division, and the very day the award was signed Lord A.'s Secretary told me he didn't know where the l.c.j. got the idea, which he (Robertson) had never heard of till a few hours before.'

Index